Circuits in the Sea

CIRCUITS IN THE SEA

THE MEN, THE SHIPS, AND THE ATLANTIC CABLE

CHESTER G. HEARN

PRAEGER

Westport, Connecticut
London

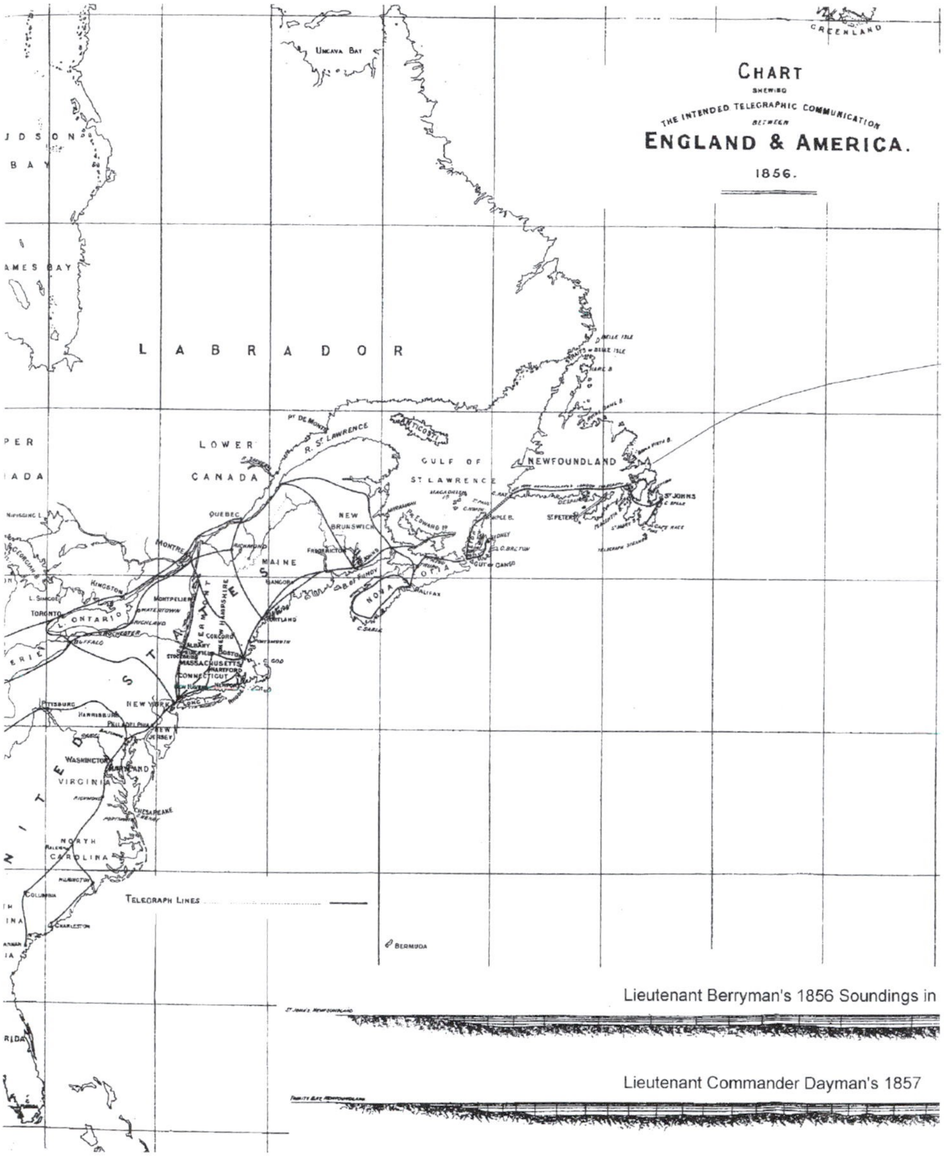

Lieutenant Berryman's 1856 Soundings in

Lieutenant Commander Dayman's 1857

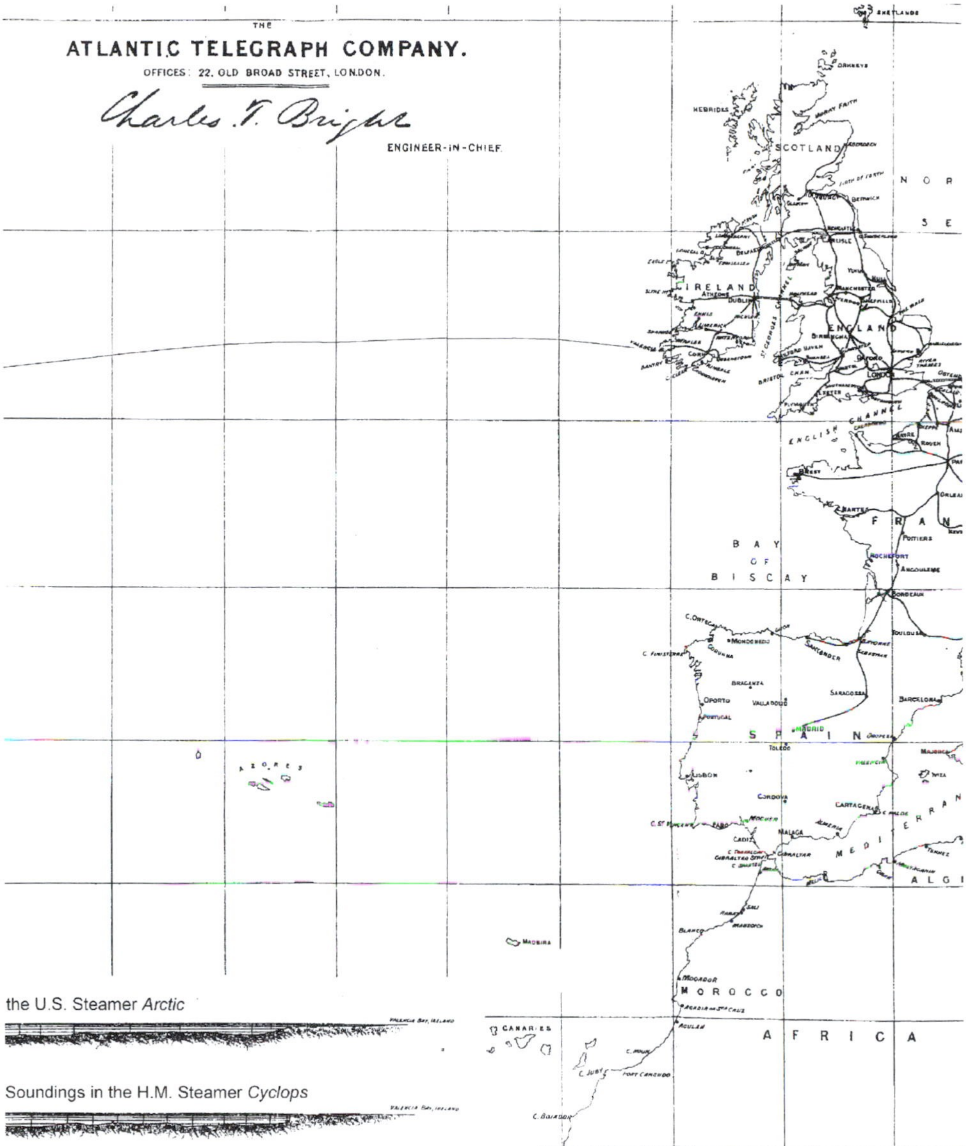

Original map drawn by Charles Bright showing the general path taken by the cable crews in laying the first successful Atlantic cable. (From Edward Brailsford Bright, *The Life Story of the Late Sir Charles Tilston Bright*. Digitized and modified by Debra Peffer.)

Library of Congress Cataloging-in-Publication Data

Hearn, Chester G.
Circuits in the sea : the men, the ships, and the Atlantic cable / Chester G. Hearn.
p. cm.
Includes bibliographical references and index.
ISBN 0-275-98231-9
1. Cables, Submarine—Atlantic—History. 2. Field, Cyrus W. (Cyrus West), 1819–1892. 3. Great Eastern (Steamship) 4. Brunel, Isambard Kingdom, 1806–1859. I. Title.
TK5611.H43 2004
384.1'5—dc22 2004049561

British Library Cataloguing in Publication Data is available.

Library of Congress Catalog Card Number: 2004049561
ISBN: 0-275-98231-9

First published in 2004

Praeger Publishers, 88 Post Road West, Westport, CT 06881
An imprint of Greenwood Publishing Group, Inc.
www.praeger.com

Printed in the United States of America

The paper used in this book complies with the Permanent Paper Standard issued by the National Information Standards Organization (Z39.48–1984).

10 9 8 7 6 5 4 3 2 1

To Ann, Chet, Dana, and Sarah

CONTENTS

Preface and Acknowledgments

The idea for writing this book emanated from writing another, one called *Tracks in the Sea: Matthew Fontaine Maury and the Mapping of the Oceans*. During the late 1840s Lieutenant Maury of the U.S. Navy began an investigation of the ocean's winds and currents that led in 1850 to organizing sailing tracks for ships to follow that guided them to their destinations by the fastest and truest route. He also began a study of the ocean's bottom across the North Atlantic, where he found a shallow stretch of seabed between Ireland and Newfoundland that he instinctively named the telegraphic plateau.

Having discovered the connection between Maury and the Atlantic cable—and since I had already collected a segment of the research—I could not resist the temptation to investigate the cable's history. What I found was a fascinating collage of scientific and human effort that created a bridge between the discovery of electricity and fiber optics.

Most of us, having grown up during the latter half of the 20th century, never stop to consider that the use of electricity, the mechanization of industry, the evolution of iron ships, the science of the seas, and the development of telegraphic communication are all recent innovations. Together they bloomed into practical uses during the mid-19th century. Nowhere in the world did this sudden burst of technical energy merge into a vast, spreading industrial revolution faster than in Great Britain. Without each stage of these remarkable advances coalescing together, an Atlantic cable could not have been laid, and it took eleven years to make it a commercially viable reality.

What began in 1855 as an idea by a wealthy American visionary named Cyrus West Field, who knew nothing about telegraphy, eventually evolved into a project that engaged some of the most brilliant minds in England, Scotland, and America. The scheme attracted men of science, men of wealth, men of curiosity, and international governments. Four presidents of the United States became involved with the project—Franklin Pierce, James Buchanan, Abraham Lincoln, and Andrew Johnson—drawing in congress, the state department, the U.S. Navy, the attorney general, and the post office.

Field, the tenacious promoter, invested his wealth in the project, but men of Great Britain like John Brett, Charles Bright, William Thomson, Samuel Canning, Richard Glass, and dozens of others, many of whom would become knighted for their work, made the cable a reality. Nor could a cable be dispensed across a body of water as broad and stormy as the North Atlantic without the massive ship designed by Isambard Kingdom Brunel, Britain's foremost engineer, or the financial backing of Thomas Brassey, the era's greatest builder of railroads.

No company in the United States could have manufactured the cable. S. C. Bishop of New York was the only insulation manufacturer in America. The firm produced the first submarine cable, used iron wire covered with three coatings of gutta-percha insulation, sank it in shallow water using lead weights, and it failed. For many decades reliable deepwater submarine cables could only be manufactured in England.

Despite hostilities that developed between the United States and Great Britain during America's Civil War, Cyrus Field never stopped urging his British associates to perfect a cable that could pass clear signals through water two-and-a-half miles deep. Without the unified effort of this small cadre of determined engineers, decades may have passed before submarine cables became reliable. Some called the Atlantic cable the greatest feat of the nineteenth century for good reason. It perfected transoceanic communications and connected the world with circuits in the sea.

The primary sources used in this book came from the records of mechanical and electrical engineers, correspondents, and observers who lived during the development of the Atlantic cable. But to complete the project required the help of many.

The main collection of Cyrus Field's papers is in the New York Public Library. I owe Jim Moske a debt of gratitude for guiding me to their location, and to Ann King, as independent researcher, for supplying me with the content I needed. With help from Mary Goodrich, I also found a smaller collection of Field papers in the Library of Congress, along with the papers of Salmon P. Chase, James Buchanan, and others. I also want to thank Alyssa S. Morein and Marybeth Kavanaugh at The New-York Historical Society for locating another treasure trove of Field documents and photographs.

Mary Goodrich had previously supplied me with the collection of Matthew Fontaine Maury in the Library of Congress and his correspondence in the Navy Records, Naval Observatory Letters, in the National Archives and Records Administration. She continued to be most helpful, pruning the archives at the Smithsonian Institution to locate documents of interest pertaining to Joseph Henry, and the Library of Congress for Samuel F. B. Morse's papers. Christine Weideman at the Sterling Memorial Library assisted me in locating more of Morse's correspondence at Yale University.

Carol Salomon provided Peter Cooper's papers from Cooper Union, and those pertaining to the Atlantic cable, which were sifted for information by my New York research assistant, Ann King.

In the United Kingdom, Mary Godwin, Director, Cable and Wireless Trust and Museum of Submarine Telegraph, at Porthcurno, in Cornwall, led me to many sources that included art and manuscripts in the trust and the papers of Charles Bright. Rachel MacGregor and Sophia Popham at the Birmingham City Archives located the diaries and correspondence of Sir Daniel Gooch. Richard Asplin and Sally Trussler led me to the documents on Isambard Kingdom Brunel at Brunel University.

I also want to thank Debra Peffer of Gannon University for digitally preparing the photographic work that forms an important part of this book, and a word of grateful appreciation to my daughter-in-law, Dana Hearn, who computer enhanced a number of images contained in this book.

The National Maritime Museum in Greenwich, London, contained an enormous amount of maritime art, newspaper clippings, logbooks of *Agamemnon* and *Great Eastern*, and collections of documents pertaining to the ships and men who participated in laying the Atlantic cable. For much of the research assistance in the United Kingdom I depended upon Robert Smith, who was referred to me by the Public Records Office in London, and was kind enough to integrate some of his research time into an academic project of his own for which I am reciprocating assistance from this side of the ocean. He has pulled many British newspaper accounts and left me with a number of people to thank whose names I do not know.

Once again I must thank Evelyn Wesman and the staff at the Erie Public Library for collecting some forty books and microfilm from around the country to help in my research.

And for those who I have forgotten, please accept my apologies, for this has been a joint effort with many participants.

— Chapter 1 —

Harnessing the Knowledge

Hezekiah, King of Judah 4,000 years ago, said: "It is the glory of God to conceal a thing: But the glory of [wise men] to search out a matter."[1]

Electricity was the "matter" that fascinated men of curiosity since they witnessed the first bolt of lightning arc from the skies to elicit a response from the god of thunder. In the mid-sixteenth century Otto von Guericke found electricity in his globe of sulfur. In 1729 Stephen Gray found it in a glass tube with silken cords. In 1748 Benjamin Franklin sent a spark of electricity across the Schuykill River, near Philadelphia, but nobody knew what to make of it. A year later, during the summer of 1749, he foolishly tried to capture a giant bolt with a kite, and volts from the sky traveled at great speed down his wet kite string and registered on a key. In 1753 a Russian named Richmann repeated the experiment in St. Petersburg and died of electrocution. Nobody invented electricity, but credit belongs to those scientists who gave new ideas—and sometimes their lives—to the search, and to successors who converted those ideas into practical applications. Such was the way of the Atlantic cable.[2]

None of the early experimenters understood enough about electricity to consider it a vehicle for telegraphy. They contended with imperfect knowledge. Their labors stimulated curiosity, forming footsteps for others to follow, turning imagination into reality. Who gets the credit often becomes subverted in the history of the telling. As London *Times* correspondent William H. Russell observed while chronicling the bridging of the Atlantic, "there have been many [Amerigo] Vespuccis in the world who have given names to places they never found, and taken or received credit for what they never did."[3]

Most discoveries begin with need. The earliest modes of telegraphic communication consisted of a train of signal fires, which, by preestablished arrangements, warned of the approach of the enemy and summoned the inhabitants for defense. American Indians used smoke. Until the early nineteenth century, runners, pigeons, men on horseback, or ships carried messages between two points. In 1801 the British built a chain of towers with semaphore arms to link London with Deal. A test of the seventy-two mile system demonstrated that a visible signal could be sent and returned in eight minutes. Civilization existed without efficient communications.

Centuries before the Christian era, Greeks used a primitive telegraph system during military campaigns. The tools consisted of two earthen jars, each with a small hole of exactly the same size plugged in the bottom. Each jar carried an identical float with an upright arm projecting above the jar and a duplicate list of twenty or more messages, one above the other with separations in between. The general on the hill kept one jar and the spy sent to infiltrate the enemy's camp carried the other. When the spy discovered the enemy's intentions, he hoisted a flag by day or lit a signal fire by night, giving notice when the plugs were to be simultaneously removed from the jars. As the water trickled from the spy's jar and the arm of the flag dropped to the desired message, he signaled the general to re-plug the jar. The general, however, had no recourse to intelligence not on the list.[4]

Over great distances sailing vessels provided the fastest means of communication. During the early nineteenth century and before steamships, the average time to get a message from the United States to Europe averaged forty days in good sailing weather. To get a response required extra time because of contrary trade winds. When Queen Victoria came to the throne in 1837, the system of communication with her far-flung empire was no better than the one used by Julius Caesar in 60 B.C.

A few men began to pioneer the development of electrical knowledge and gave their names to the new science—James Watt (1736–1819) of Great Britain, Alessandro Volta (1745–1854) of Italy, Georg Ohm (1787–1854) of Germany, and André-Marie Ampère (1775–1836) of France. They studied electrical current and began to define its character. To honor their names, scientists created a new vocabulary with terms such as watts, volts, ohms, and amperes.

Noticing that electricity traveled like a swift "electric fluid" through conducting wires tempted scientists to investigate its uses. In 1796 Dr. M. de F. Salvá constructed the first telegraph line, a twenty-six-mile "electric spark telegraph" that ran from Madrid to Aranjuez and kept Spanish authorities current with the latest news. Salvá lacked the knowledge to make the line a viable proposition for sending coherent messages, and no person other than Salvá understood how his "electric spark" device actually worked.

Two years later Alessandro Volta published a paper in the *Transactions of the Royal Society* describing his voltaic pile, thereby introducing an important new discovery for measuring electricity. Experimenters on both sides of the Atlantic eagerly grasped this new instrument—they called such devices galvanometers—that could measure constant-flow electricity. Volta gave the world the first battery and placed in the hands of scientists an electricity of dynamics, which made the telegraph possible.[5]

In Munich in 1809 a German scientist named Samuel T. Sömmering designed a "chemical telegraph." For each letter of the alphabet he provided a separate wire and immersed them in the bottom of a water-filled glass container. When passing a current through a wire of choice, a bubble formed at its end. By recording the letter represented by the wire with the bubble, an observer could laboriously string together the transmitted characters into words. Though the method failed as a practical device, Sömmering's invention attracted enough attention to put greater minds to work.

In 1816 Sir Francis Ronalds developed an elaborate system designed around the principles of static electricity. Above his garden at Hammersmith, London, he strung eight miles of wire, using it to receive messages passed through the line by the movement of light pithballs arranged over letters. As a sender sent impulses across the line, an electrical repulsion swung the pithballs aside and exposed the letters being transmitted. Had Sir Francis lived another 150 years, he would have seen his experiments adapted to the development of the electric typewriter. Sir Francis offered his invention to the Admiralty, who replied that they were perfectly content using the Royal Navy's current "telegraph"—a system dependent upon clear weather and a string of semaphore towers between Portsmouth and London. On foggy days, and there were many, messages delivered by horseback reached their destination faster. "Telegraphs of any kind were then wholly unnecessary," said the Admiralty, "and . . . no other than the one in use (meaning the semaphores) would be adopted."[6]

Systems like those developed by Sömmering and Sir Francis proved impractical because they lacked a simple method for detecting and directing the flow of electricity. By 1820 experimenters had developed an electric arc that created a brilliant flash. They separated water into oxygen and hydrogen, and demonstrated the use of positive and negative currents in electroplating. But in that year the most important discovery came from Hans Christian Oersted, a Danish physicist and chemist who noticed that a magnet placed near an electric current deflected. If so, Oersted surmised, then electricity must exert a force. He concluded that a magnetic field surrounded a wire carrying electric current and linked together electricity and magnetism. Oersted's work led to the discovery of the electromagnet and hundreds of other devices such as motors, generators, telephones, electric streetcars, and power plants.[7]

In 1834 Baron von Schilling proposed an aerial telegraph line to Nicholas I, one that would run from St. Petersburg to Peterhoff, near Kronstadt. Muscovites laughed at him, but the baron built his aerial line, hung it from poles, and transmitted the emperor's messages using a code similar to one adopted by Samuel F. B. Morse. Schilling devised a magnetic telegraph, using the movement of a needle over black or white segments on a card. In Schilling's alphabet, the letter A became "black-white"; the letter B, "black-black-black"; and the letter C, "black-white-black," and so on through the alphabet. Schilling's code, combined with Oersted's discovery of electro-magnetic force fields, opened the way for the world's first practical telegraph.

In 1835 two essentials for making a recording telegraph possible began to emerge: a reliable battery with unvarying voltage and the means of transmitting over long distances. Batteries developed under the voltaic plan quickly weakened, giving off unequal force. In 1836 John Frederic Daniell solved the problem by creating a battery with cells that overcame cross-contamination. He used a zinc pole in a solution of zinc sulfate and dilute sulfuric acid and a copper pole in a solution of copper sulfate, separating the two solutions with a porous pot. No aspiring telegrapher could have done anything of commercial value without Daniell batteries, which solved the problem of reliability by providing steady power to transmit over long distances.[8]

After batteries became available, Charles Wheatstone, Professor of Physics at King's College, conceived the idea of sending telegraphic messages under water. After associating his name with a number of basic patents on electricity, he teamed up in 1836 with William Fothergill Cooke. Cooke abandoned his medical studies at Heidelberg to become a practical scientist, providing he could find an electrical expert who could put his ideas into practice.

Wheatstone took an interest in Cooke's concepts and in 1837 produced their first telegraph patent—an instrument having a vertical needle that pointed to the right or left. To prove the viability of their patent they built a mile-and-a-quarter line connecting two London railway stations. The early messages moved at a snail's pace, but they could be sent or read by semiskilled operators. The Wheatstone-Cooke patent made both men rich as the new technology expanded across Europe. Remote British railway stations still used the equipment well into the twentieth century. Wheatstone and Cooke eventually separated, driven apart by an argument over which of them invented the telegraph when in actuality neither of them did.

In 1832, while sailing back to the United States from a visit to Europe, the concept of a national telegraph attracted the curiosity of Samuel Morse—a modestly talented portrait painter—much as it had induced Cooke to terminate his medical studies. Morse and Cooke shared one characteristic in common: both were amateur scientists who needed to consult a professional to get anything done. Where Cooke collaborated with

Wheatstone, Morse went to Joseph Henry, America's great pioneer of electromagnetism.

While professor of natural philosophy at the College of New Jersey (Princeton University), Henry developed in 1836 what may have been the first telegraph line using the earth as a conductor. He extended a wire across the front grounds of the campus from the upper story of the library to Philosophical Hall, where he had his laboratory, and connected the line to his house. Ever since Oersted's discovery of the relationship between electricity and magnetism, Henry had been quietly experimenting. His reticence to announce his own discoveries allowed such notables as Michael Faraday to steal his thunder on the principles of magnetoelectricity—a disappointment that Henry lamented for the remainder of his life. When Morse knocked on his door asking for assistance, Henry became most helpful, enabling the artist-turned-scientist to produce in 1836 his first working telegraph instrument. Morse and Henry would eventually become involved in the same squabble over priority that separated Wheatstone and Cooke.[9]

Many years later Henry wrote, "The electro-magnetic telegraph was invented by me, in Albany, in 1830. Professor Morse, according to his statement, conceived the idea of an electro-magnetic telegraph in his voyage across the ocean in 1832 but did not until several years afterward (1837) attempt to carry his ideas into practice; and when he did so, he found himself so little acquainted with the subject of electricity that he could not make his simple machine operate through the distance of a few yards." If Henry actually invented the electromagnetic telegraph, as he claimed, he failed to apply for a patent, giving as a reason that he "did not then consider it compatible with the dignity of science to confine the benefits which might be derived from it to the exclusive use of any individual. In this perhaps I was too fastidious."[10]

Morse, or perhaps Henry, created a marvelously simple gadget when compared with all the cumbersome devices produced abroad. Instead of many wires, Morse's mechanism depended upon just one because he incorporated Henry's idea of using the earth to provide the return (negative) charge. His transmitter was a single key to make and break the connection. Using dots and dashes, a trained operator could send any combination of characters, branching them into words and sentences. Morse could not have perfected his transmitter without assistance from Joseph Henry or from Dr. Leonard D. Gale, who gave him a short course at no charge on the subject of batteries and magnets. While learning under Gale, Morse said, "If I can succeed in working a magnet [meaning a magnetic wire] ten miles, I can go around the globe."[11]

Morse's first receiver contained a magnet-operated pen that inscribed dots and dashes on paper that resembled a ticker tape. This provided a permanent record, but Morse later developed a buzzer that the human ear

Samuel F. B. Morse at the time he began experimenting with telegraphy. (Courtesy of the Library of Congress. Digitized by Debra Peffer.)

could interpret as short and long impulses. Well into the twentieth century these beeps were still in use and could be picked up by shortwave radios.

To transmit messages over great distances, Morse needed a relay utility. Henry probably invented the relay Morse adopted. Because a telegraph line depended upon batteries, which eventually weakened, Morse needed a device to pick up the feeble signals received at the end of a transmission line to feed a second Morse key and start a new current from another set of batteries operating at a relay station. Morse's relay evolved into a "repeater," which automatically resent the message and eventually replaced the relay. But in 1841 Morse still had nothing to show for his efforts but a patent. In writing to his friend, Alfred Vail, Morse lamented, "I have not a cent in the world."[12]

The Wheatstone-Cooke telegraph system spread across Great Britain and Europe but stopped at the sea. In 1840 Wheatstone appeared before the House of Commons and proposed a submarine cable across the English

Channel. While a committee studied the proposal, Wheatstone laid a short cable in Swansea Bay, Wales, where he successfully communicated between a boat anchored offshore and the lighthouse. Morse had been in Great Britain trying to sell his invention where the Wheatstone-Cooke patent enjoyed a temporary monopoly. Wheatstone wanted no competition, so Morse returned to New York financially crippled but convinced that a telegraph could operate under water.[13]

With financial help, Morse emulated Wheatstone's experiments in New York Harbor and during October 1842, stretched a submarine cable from Castle Garden to Governor's Island, successfully sending signals through a rubber-coated wire encased in lead pipe. Three years later Ezra Cornell put a cable under the Hudson River, connecting New York City with Fort Lee, New Jersey. Cornell soon pulled out of the growing cable competition, paving the way for Morse to proudly proclaim, "The first submarine telegraph cable was laid by me on one moonlight night in the harbor of this city, which proved experimentally the practicability of submarine telegraphy."

Late in 1842 he sent a current across the canal at Washington, D.C., and with his enthusiasm reinvigorated, he tackled Congress for funding. One senator approached Morse and said, "There is no use in your staying here. The Senate is not in sympathy with your project. I advise you to give it up, return home, and think no more of it." Dejected, Morse went to his hotel, paid the bill, and tried to sleep on his final night in Washington. With his last thirty-seven and a half cents in his pocket, he bought breakfast. Miss Annie G. Ellsworth, daughter of the commissioner of patents, rushed into the dining hall, her faced flushed with excitement, and briskly walked to Morse's table. "Professor," she said, "I have come to congratulate you."

Morse asked, "For what?"

"On the passage of your bill," she replied, "The Senate, last night, voted your money, $30,000," to construct a line between Washington and Baltimore.[14]

Arthur C. Clarke observed: "The debate over the allocation does not reflect much credit on the elected representatives of the American people; several of them were quite unable to appreciate the difference between magnetism and mesmerism."[15]

Two years later Morse strung his first operating line from the railroad depot on Pratt Street, Baltimore, to the Supreme Court in Washington, and gave the United States its first telegraph. On May 25, 1844, during a ceremony to open the line, Morse sat by his telegraph key in the judicial chamber, and before a group of distinguished observers, tapped out: "Dot, dash—dash—space—dot, dot, dot, dot—space—dot, dash." The message sped along forty miles of wire that separated him from Alfred Vail in Baltimore. When an observer asked what the message said, Morse replied, "What hath God wrought."[16]

On April 1, 1845, the Washington-Baltimore telegraph line opened for commercial business. After nine days, revenues totaled only three dollars and nine and a half cents. Morse, always desperate for money, offered the line and his rights to the government for $100,000. The postmaster general did Morse, and the country, an unintended favor by rejecting the offer, declaring that telegraph revenues "could never be made equal to its expenditures." Determined to make something out of his invention, Morse pooled a few partners and formed the Magnetic Telegraph Company.[17]

Without the telegraph, the expanding nation may never have become a united country, but the postal service wanted to tax the wire to replace anticipated lost revenues from people deserting the mails. Two years before, when serving as a Tennessee congressman, Cave Johnson, the incoming postmaster general, had openly ridiculed the telegraph. Now he proposed a one-cent tax on every four characters. After three years of battling for a tax, Johnson lost his argument, and another century passed before taxation of communication lines became a reality.[18]

Though Wheatstone and Morse gave their respective countries a functioning telegraph, neither man could claim credit for establishing the first underwater transmission. In 1839 Dr. O'Shaughnessy Brooke, Superintendent of Electric Telegraphs in India, hauled a wire insulated with split rattan and tarred yarn across the Hooghly at Calcutta and produced an electrical phenomenon on the opposite shore. Barely anyone noticed.

Men with money, smelling an opportunity for making more, leaped into the new technology. In 1846 Samuel Colt, the American patentee of the revolver, and George Robinson of New York laid a submarine wire from Manhattan to Brooklyn, and another from Long Island to Coney Island.

Four years later John Watkins Brett, a wealthy and retired forty-five-year-old British antique dealer, decided to link England with France. With his younger brother Jacob, an engineer interested in submarine telegraphy, the Bretts formed the General Oceanic and Subterranean Electric Printing Telegraph Company. In 1845 the brothers registered the company to lay the first Atlantic cable, but it remained a paper corporation. No one had yet taken a step to span the English Channel. Brett decided to try and obtained a ten-year concession from France to bring the line from Dover to Calais. During the negotiations he oversold the alacrity with which the project could be completed. The agreement contained a fatal deadline. If Brett failed to establish communication by September 1, 1850, his concession would lapse. The press derided the project as a gigantic swindle, which may have influenced the French to assassinate it quickly if it failed.

Brett's exuberance to expedite the manufacture of the cable proved to be its undoing. To the company's credit, it used solid copper wire and covered it with a quarter inch of gutta-percha, a recently discovered substance having elastic insulating properties far superior to rubber and a few troublesome deficiencies. A serious delay occurred after tests revealed that the gutta-percha surrounding the wire contained air holes that allowed water to reach the conductor and leak current into the testing tank. The Gutta Percha Company repaired the faults, coiled the cable on a drum, and shipped it by steamtug to Dover. The Bretts assumed that once the cable rested on the seabed nothing could harm it, so they spent no money to have the insulation armored. Only the shore ends received protection, being strung through lead tubing.

Those who viewed the cable as a swindle were rewarded when one gentleman, upon seeing it paid out at Dover, told his listeners that the Bretts were fools. Nobody could drag a cable that long across the bed of the English Channel. Many of those within earshot agreed, but he lost part of his audience when he said that signals were to be transmitted by jerking the cable. The suggestion was not altogether outlandish. Victorian homes were strung with hand-operated systems of ropes and pulleys connected to bells, using sound as a medium of communication.[19]

When the Bretts loaded their twenty-five nautical miles of cable on the steamtug *Goliath*, they had only three days to make the connection at Cap Gris-Nez, France, and pass the messages required to secure their ten-year concession. The cable had been coiled on a huge seven-foot reel and fitted to the afterdeck of the tug. As *Goliath* paid out the line, the great drum turned slowly, yielding cable grudgingly, at times stressing the protective insulation as the ship lurched up and down the rollers. Because the cable did not sink properly, *Goliath* paused every hundred yards so the crew could attach a lead weight.

On September 28, despite the difficult crossing, *Goliath* eased into Cap Gris-Nez. Brett's technicians rushed ashore and connected the printer to the cable. Everyone waited for the first message to come through—a greeting from John Brett in the station at Dover to Prince Louis Napoleon Bonaparte. When the automatic printer produced a string of undecipherable squiggles, technicians disconnected the device and replaced it with one of Wheatstone's needle machines. This time enough words flowed though the line for Brett to claim his contractual rights, but signals from both directions remained muddled. The Bretts discovered that a thinly insulated cable that worked so well when buried on land would not work when surrounded by the conductive medium of water. Signals no longer passed through the wire at the same speed. Impulses backed up and dots caught up with dashes, scrambling messages and rendering them unreadable.

Hours after the first electrical impulses made their submarine voyage across the channel, the line suddenly went dead. No amount of effort could restore it. The Bretts had enough electrical savvy to know that something had happened to the wire near the French coast. The cause of the problem would haunt all cable operators for decades to come. A fisherman, trolling near shore, snagged onto something he had never seen before—a new species of seaweed with a metal core. He cut through the insulation and found, much to his glee, bright metal he thought might be gold. Taking a length of his remarkable discovery ashore at Boulogne, he showed it to his friends. How often fishermen returned to the same spot to gather more samples cannot be known, but it is certain they destroyed the cable.

The Bretts proved that a cable could be laid under the channel, and the effort provided a side benefit, elevating awareness among interested scientists to the hazards beneath the sea. Thomas R. Crampton, a railway engineer, took the lead and raised £30,000, half of it being his own money. With help from others, Crampton designed his own cable. Instead of a single wire, he used a conductor of four gutta-percha insulated copper wires wrapped tightly in tarred Russian hemp. Küper & Company, a manufacturer of wire ropes, spun a spiral layer of ten galvanized iron-armoring wires around the core to protect it during the paying-out process and from vagaries of the deep such as rocks, anchors, and fishing lines.

Crampton's cable began to shape the design for the first transatlantic cable. It weighed thirty times as much as Brett's cable and sank without weights. The sheer weight of the cable—seven tons to the mile—almost proved its undoing. When laid on September 25, 1851, the cable paid out so rapidly that the brake could not slow it. During the crossing from Dover to Calais, wind and tide carried the ship off course, wasting more of the cable. One mile off the coast of France the cable reached its end. Crampton held the boats offshore and returned to England to buy a few more miles of cable. He fused the two lengths together, sealed the joint with gutta-percha and hemp wrappings, and sent the land end ashore. After several weeks of testing he opened the cable to the public and brought England no more than a few seconds away from every telegraph station in Europe.[20]

Crampton's successful cross-channel effort created a great impression, even among the skeptics, and launched what became the submarine cable boom of the nineteenth century. Gutta-percha became the sole substance that made the cable work underwater. It was neither rubber nor plastic, but its properties behaved more like the latter than the former.

Captain S. A. Garnham and Robert L. Hadfield, who coauthored *The Submarine Cable*, opened their story with an attention-getting statement: "The submarine telegraph was brought into being at the crack of a whip in the hands of a Malay." In 1822, while serving with the East India Company in Singapore, Dr. William Montgomerie (also Montgomery) noticed that Malays used whips made of material neither rubber nor leather, but of a substance known by the inhabitants, and translated phonetically from their language, as gutta-percha. Like rubber, the product's milky juice oozed from certain sapotaceous *Isonandra* gutta trees on the Malayan peninsula. Unlike India rubber, it was not elastic, and though it softened in warm water and could be formed into hats, basins, piping, tool handles, and many other things, it hardened in cold water. Insulating wires used in land telegraphy are comparatively simple, but laying wires on the seabed in the highly conductive environment of water is not. Michael Faraday, Britain's foremost authority on electricity, suggested using gutta-percha as an insulating material. Until the discovery of plastics a hundred years later, gutta-percha remained the only durable insulating material for submarine cables.[21]

During the two years following Crampton's success, the Gutta Percha Company, which monopolized the supply of the material, shipped more than 1,500 miles of covered conductor core to manufacturers who provided the outer armoring. Europe laid twelve lines of submarine cable before the United States took a serious interest in the technology. Some firms like England's Electric and International Telegraph Company ignored the lessons taught by Crampton. To save costs they rejected the heavy cable and laid four underwater lines to Europe using light wire. After paying staggering repair bills, they picked up the wire and replaced it with armored cable.

Interest in submarine cables came to America through the front door of Canada, the sparsely inhabited province of Newfoundland where seafarers often stopped during transatlantic voyages. In Newfoundland's foggy and rugged interior there were neither towns nor roads. The province drew its entire wealth from the sea, the chief industry being fishing, and the only places of importance were a few villages on the eastern shore that had grown up around the island's provincial capital of St. John's. To visit his diocese annually, Bishop John I. Mullock sailed about Newfoundland's indented coast in his private yacht. No trails had been cut through the forest to enable travel on horseback.

One day in 1850 the bishop's yacht lay becalmed off Cape Ray on the southwestern tip of the island. From the middle of Cabot Strait in the Gulf of St. Lawrence he could almost see Cape North, the closest point between Nova Scotia and Newfoundland. While mulling over the condition of his poor neglected island, he wondered whether Newfoundland might benefit by being taken into the track of communication between Europe and America. When the bishop returned to St. John's, he submitted his thoughts in a November 8, 1850, editorial to the public. Mullock may have received news of John Brett's cable to Calais (September 28, 1850) because he recommended that a telegraph station be established at St. John's, an aerial line passed between the sliver of land separating Trinity Bay from Placentia Bay, and continued overland to another station located four hundred miles away at Cape Ray. Then, the bishop added, if a submarine cable could be laid across Cabot Strait to Nova Scotia, "news could be communicated to the whole American continent forty-eight hours, *at least*, sooner than by any other route." Bishop Mullock also wanted to establish a link with all the isolated fishing villages that lay along coastal areas and could only communicate by sea.[22]

The bishop proposed that England, Canada, or the United States adopt his scheme: he did not care which. Long fingers of cable lines already stretched from New York into Maine, and from Maine eastward into sections of New Brunswick and Nova Scotia.

While credit for the idea often goes to the bishop, during the winter of 1849–1850 an Englishman named Frederick Newton Gisborne proposed a similar link. He had immigrated to Quebec some years before to establish a farm. The long winters induced him to find other employment, and he eventually became chief operator for the Montreal Telegraph Company. Convinced that Canada would someday be connected to the entire continent, he joined the Nova Scotia Telegraph Company with the intention of connecting the maritime provinces with Quebec. He soon became a competent, self-taught engineer, spreading lines across Nova Scotia from Halifax to towns bordering New Brunswick. Like Bishop Mullock, he had studied a map of the North Atlantic and observed that New York lay about 1,200 miles farther from Ireland than from St. John's.

In the spring of 1851, while chief officer for the Nova Scotia Telegraph Company, he booked passage on a Halifax steamer and sailed to St. John's to discuss the Newfoundland telegraph. Gisborne had been in England when the Brett's laid the English Channel cable and knew it failed. He spoke before the Newfoundland legislature, whose members had already heard from the bishop. Gisborne looked like the right man with the right credentials to implement the bishop's proposal. He appeared to be a practical man, one willing to string an overland cable to Cape Ray but not so foolish as to want money for running a cable under Cabot Strait, at least not yet. Gisborne offered a more acceptable solution. If a telegraph could be built across Newfoundland to Cape Ray, small steamers or pigeons could carry the messages across the strait to a station on Cape Breton, speeding them from there by telegraph to New York.

Much to the chagrin of his family and friends, Gisborne resigned his position with the Nova Scotia Telegraph Company and in 1852 formed the Newfoundland Electric Telegraph Company. The legislature granted him £500 to make an exploratory survey for a line to Cape Ray and passed a law authorizing its construction. For his efforts, Gisborne also received a handsome tract of land, though in the mid-1800s Newfoundland remained an uninviting 42,734-square-mile island consisting of rocky shores, deep fjords, and vast unexplored forests.

Gisborne tried to do too much. He put one gang to work building a telegraph line from St. John's to Conception Bay and another gang on a sixty-mile stretch into the wilderness. With construction underway, Gisborne set out on a 400-mile trek with a small survey party consisting of himself, two white men, and four Indians. While the construction crews tried to cut a swath through the forest, Gisborne disappeared for three months into the island's formidable interior. His six-man survey team entered an almost impenetrable and resourceless wilderness. Two of the party deserted, one died, and the other three, including Gisborne, nearly starved to death. The idea, however, still held great merit.

Gisborne, acting as superintendent and company engineer, drastically underestimated the work involved. When he returned to St. John's he learned that his crew had failed to cut the first leg of the telegraphic trail into the wilderness. After chopping their way through a few miles of forest, they stopped. Nonetheless, Gisborne spoke in favorable terms to the legislature, urging them to increase the scope of his work to include a submarine cable connecting Newfoundland with Nova Scotia. Since the legislature would not have to do the work or provide more funds, they granted Gisborne an exclusive right to erect telegraphs in Newfoundland for thirty years and made generous land concessions.

Armed with a pocketful of incentives to be granted upon the completion of an aerial line from St. John's to Cape Ray, Gisborne went to New York to obtain financial partners. After two men, Horace B. Tebbets and Darius B. Holbrook, agreed to finance the company, Gisborne said good-bye and departed for England to buy a submarine cable. After witnessing the success of Crampton's underwater line to Calais, he returned to the provinces in the fall of 1852, hired a small steamer, and laid the first submarine cable in America: an eleven-mile affair under Northumberland Strait, connecting New Brunswick to Prince Edward Island. The cable soon broke and years passed before anyone replaced it.[23]

In the spring of 1853 Gisborne returned to St. John's, hired a crew of 350 men, and supervised the work on the ground. Instead of cutting through the forest, he decided to bury the cable in shallow trenches, so the digging began in earnest. After penetrating a few miles into the forest, he found the soil only inches deep and resorted to poles supported by rock piles. Forty miles into the interior Gisborne ran out of money, and Tebbets and Holbrook stopped paying the bills. The company went bankrupt, leaving debts of $50,000. Creditors sued Gisborne, and after he failed to find another source of capital, local authorities threw him in jail. Gisborne relinquished his remaining resources to buy his freedom. The experience would shatter the nerves of most promoters, but Gisborne had a vision he could not shake.[24]

The success of Crampton's Dover-to-Calais cable induced Gisborne to abandon his carrier pigeon and steamer shuttle system. He now wanted to lay a submarine cable beneath Cabot Strait to tie the two provinces together, but he had no money and no prospects of raising any. He still needed to find capital to stretch the abandoned section of line another 360 miles across Newfoundland's wild interior.

Fired with new enthusiasm, Gisborne boarded a steamer to New York where he hoped to find someone willing to back his now defunct company. His prospects were not good. Probably no one in the United States still remembered Samuel Morse's prediction in 1843 when the artist-turned-telegrapher wrote Secretary of Treasury John C. Spencer and declared "The practical inference from this law [of telegraphy] is that a telegraphic communication on the electric-magnetic plan, may with certainty be established across the Atlantic Ocean. Startling as this may seem now, I am confident the time will come when this project will be realized."[25]

Gisborne never heard Morse's prediction, nor had he given any thought to spanning the Atlantic, but in January 1854, he had the good fortune to be in the lobby of Broadway's Astor Hotel at precisely the right moment. Quite by accident he met Matthew Field, a civil engineer who had been building railroads and suspension bridges in the rapidly expanding West. Intrigued by Gisborne's plans and experiences, Matthew arranged a meeting between the bankrupt Newfoundlander and his wealthy younger brother, Cyrus West Field, who seemed to be settling without much success into early retirement. Having been a partner in one of Cyrus' mills, Matthew understood the nervous energy that flowed through his brother's body, and he knew that Cyrus needed a challenge to stay motivated.[26]

From such rare accidents of coincidence are great schemes hatched.

— Chapter 2 —

A Man without a Mission

At the age of thirty-four, Cyrus Field became a wealthy man of leisure, but Matthew noticed that his brother needed something to do. "I never saw Cyrus so uneasy as when he was trying to keep still." Gisborne needed financial advice and Cyrus could provide it. Beyond that, Matthew never expected his brother to take an interest in the Englishman's problems. But Matthew underestimated the zeal with which Cyrus could attach himself to an idea. He should have known better.[1]

When Cyrus left the family home in Stockbridge, Massachusetts, at the age of fifteen with only eight dollars in his pocket, he headed for Manhattan to make his fortune. A product of Puritan ancestry, he descended from Zachariah Field, who had immigrated to America in 1631. His grandfather, Timothy Field, had served as a captain in George Washington's army, and his father, David Dudley Field, graduated from Yale and became a distinguished minister. Being the youngest of seven sons, Cyrus chose to find his own niche in the city of opportunities. After three frustrating years in Manhattan, and unearthing no wealth serving as a clerk for two dollars a week in a dry goods store, he returned to Massachusetts to work as an assistant to his brother Matthew, who at the time was a papermaker.

In 1839, at the age of twenty and having learned something about making paper, Cyrus went into business for himself. A year later he married his childhood sweetheart, Mary Bryan Stone of Guilford, Connecticut, and eventually moved back to New York, where he became a partner in a large wholesale paper consortium. Six months later the firm failed, and Cyrus settled the company's debts at thirty cents on the dollar in exchange for equity. Out of the wreckage of the firm he built Cyrus W. Field & Company and began manufacturing quality bond papers for printing high-class documents such as stock, bond, and bank certificates. He avoided the competitive newsprint business, but he understood the importance of getting the first news from around the world into print. By the age of thirty-three he had repaid all his debts and retired with $250,000 in the bank—all of which he made in nine health-shattering years—and became one of the thirty richest men in the city. He moved into a large house facing Gramercy Park on 84 (later 123) East 21st Street. His brother, forty-seven-year-old David Dudley Field, Jr., built beside him, and both men would live there for the rest of their lives.

Under doctor's orders to relax, Field took his wife to Europe and spent five months in a tumultuous tour through Great Britain, France, Germany, Austria, Italy, innumerable smaller countries, and back to England again. Field rested little during the constant travel. The experience opened his eyes to Europe's massive industrialization. Electrified by the genius of Michael Faraday, Great Britain operated railroads, telegraphs, mills, and foundries far in advance of anything in America. Novel toys and products molded from a curious substance called gutta-percha fascinated Field. He wondered why people carried tubes made from the material in their hats until he spied an advertisement for railway conversation tubes that read "With these marvelous tubes passengers can converse in so soft a whisper as not to be overheard even by a fellow traveler. They are portable and will coil up so as to be placed inside a hat." His Grace the Duke of Devonshire liked the tube so well that he installed one in his church, connecting it from the pulpit to his pew.[2]

Field found England fascinating. With Faraday's urging, miles of underground telegraph lines coated with gutta-percha networked England. John and Jacob Brett, along with a young engineer named Willoughby Smith, were about to lay a cable insulated with gutta-percha beneath the English Channel. Field thought of introducing the material to the United States, but the British controlled the patent and the raw material. Instead, he looked for technological advancements in papermaking of use to Field & Company.

While Field toured Europe, the company enjoyed record profits. In 1852 Field & Company became one of the most successful businesses in New York, making Cyrus even wealthier. In addition to his personal portfolio, the company showed a capital surplus of more than $300,000. Field believed the money should be invested, but an old friend and landscape artist from Hartford, Connecticut, Frederick E. Church, talked him into a tour of South America. Field agreed and turned the management of the firm over to his brother-in-law, Joseph Stone. Together Field and Church crossed the Andes—a rigorous feat for a man who had spent most of his life in an office—and returned on October 29, 1853, with souvenirs: a live jaguar on a leash, a flock of parakeets, and a knife-belted Indian boy named Marcos. The jaguar soon proved unfit to be among the Field's five children, and Marcos, who proved to be equally troublesome, returned to Colombia and became a bullfighter.[3]

Two years away from the office restored Field's health. He no longer looked thin, drawn, and pale, but his narrow face, sharp nose, receding red hair, and milky blue eyes gave him no conspicuous marks of distinction. All his energy, endurance, and quick intellect came from within. Field could have settled into a busy social life, perhaps one of philanthropy or even one of obscurity, but he unknowingly launched a new and even more tumultuous career when three months after his return from South America he invited Frederick Gisborne to his home.

Field spent a pleasant evening listening to Gisborne's misadventures in Newfoundland. He knew absolutely nothing about the island. Gisborne's experiences sounded like a Homerian saga without a future. He made no commitments to Gisborne, nor did he promise financial help.

During the meeting Gisborne mentioned nothing of his plans to cable Newfoundland to Nova Scotia. He concentrated exclusively on finishing the line to Cape Ray, which did not sound like a productive way for anyone to spend his money. Gisborne, however, had much to gain if he could retain his telegraphic rights to the island.

After Gisborne departed, Field returned to his library to mull over the Englishman's visit. He understood the importance of speeding news across the Atlantic, but fitting Newfoundland into the equation made no sense to him. He approached a large globe in the library and discovered, to his surprise, that Newfoundland lay much farther to the east than New York.

Gisborne had mentioned that Halifax was already connected to Maine, and Field now began to understand why Gisborne wanted to run a telegraph line across Newfoundland. He vaguely remembered that the Bretts had run a cable across the English Channel. He looked again at the globe and concluded that if the Bretts could span the Channel, someone ought to be able to span the Gulf of St. Lawrence and tie Newfoundland to Nova Scotia. Connecting Newfoundland to Manhattan made even more sense if a steamer shuttle service could be established between Ireland and St. John's. And until a cable could be laid beneath Cabot Strait, another pair of steamers could shuttle the news between Cape Ray and Cape Breton. News would reach New York four or five days sooner. With telegraphic rights, a new company would be in position to make millions.

But why be shortsighted? he asked, as his brain began to work. As he ran his finger from St. John's to the southwestern tip of Ireland he felt a tingling sensation, suddenly realizing that Newfoundland's telegraph merely provided a link for a far more important project. Why wait in a wilderness telegraph shack for news from Europe when a cable beneath the North Atlantic could do the same in seconds? Henry Field recalled: "It was while thus studying the globe that the idea first occurred to him, that the telegraph might be carried further still, and be made to span the Atlantic

Cyrus West Field never understood the science that went into perfecting the Atlantic cable, but without his promotional skills, the first oceanic cable may not have been laid for decades. (Courtesy of the Library of Congress. Digitized by Debra Peffer.)

Ocean." Field hooked himself so hard he could not sleep. Questions tormented his thoughts. Could the Atlantic actually be spanned? Was it possible to lay a cable in such great depths and transmit intelligible messages? He knew nothing about the Atlantic or what hazards lay on the bottom. Nor did he know the distance between the continents. What he needed was an opinion from a trustworthy engineer. When morning came he dispatched a servant with a message for Matthew, who soon joined him in the library.[4]

Field had much to learn about submarine cables, and Matthew gave him guarded encouragement. Ten years had passed since Samuel Morse predicted it could be done. Many years later Matthew's grandson, Wells Field, summed it up when his teacher asked him to tell the class about his uncle's laying of the cable. "My pa told Uncle Cyrus he could do it," Wells replied, "so he done it."[5]

Before holding another conversation with Gisborne, Field wrote letters of inquiry to two men of knowledge: Samuel Morse, the leading authority on the electric telegraph in America, and forty-eight-year-old Lieutenant Matthew Fontaine Maury, Superintendent of the U.S. Naval Observatory and the world's foremost authority on oceanography. Morse merely repeated what he had said in 1843—that in his opinion a magnetic underwater current could be passed across the Atlantic. Maury, however, ignited Field's interest in becoming the person to do it.

Maury happened to be one of the few men in America who agreed with Morse. His topsy-turvy life in the navy, shattered by an accident that lamed him and threatened to end his career, led to his assignment as Superintendent of the U. S. Naval Observatory. Using hundreds of old ships' logbooks he began tracking the winds and currents of the seas, observing consistencies and seasonal shifts, and in 1847 produced the first chart of the North Atlantic. By 1854 he had developed dozens of "Wind and Current Charts," written several editions of his *Sailing Directions* to accompany the charts, and given to the world such knowledge of the sea that a sailing shipmaster could travel between two ports using the fairest winds, much like today's motorists plot their routes using roadmaps.

Field knew about Maury's work on the surface of the seas, but he did not know that Maury had people working on soundings across the North Atlantic. The lieutenant had included a chapter on the Atlantic seabed in his latest edition of *Sailing Directions*, which would later reappear almost verbatim in the first edition of his *Physical Geography of the Sea*.

In 1840 Maury began urging the navy to study the bottom of the North Atlantic using deep-sea sounding equipment. Nine years passed before Congress appropriated enough money to develop the mechanisms Maury needed. By then, England, France, and the Netherlands had sounded to 10,000 feet. Beyond that depth no one could accurately measure.[6]

Maury experimented with many devices in an effort to find a way to reach greater depths. He discovered that accurate measurements could not be taken from a drifting ship because the sounding line bowed and dragged. He also discovered that a sounding ball slowed as it descended, a phenomenon that eventually became part of the equation of calculating accurate depths. Sounding became a mathematical problem, on the one hand knowing the sounding line's rate of descent and on the other hand tracking the ship's rate of drift, thereby enabling a sounding team to calculate the true perpendicular axis after the ball struck bottom.

> We could tell very nearly when the ball ceased to carry the line out, and when . . . it began to go out in obedience to the current and drift alone; for currents would

sweep the line out at a uniform rate while the cannon ball would drag it out at a decreasing rate.[7]

In October 1849 Lieutenant J. C. Walsh went to sea in the schooner *Taney* to make soundings every 200 miles across the Atlantic. Walsh lost a good share of his surveying equipment during a storm, but he brought back enough data to encourage further efforts.

In 1852 Maury attempted to create the first orographic (vertical profile) map of the ocean's bottom along the 39° north latitude. The Navy turned the brig USS *Dolphin* over to Lieutenant Otway H. Berryman to gather Maury's data. Berryman returned in 1853 with a wealth of new information, but Maury's inquisitive nature only led him to the next question: "What is the use of knowing how deep [the Atlantic] is unless we know what is at the bottom . . . be it ooze or mud, or rock, or sand." No one in the world had designed apparatus for bringing up samples from a seabed two miles deep.[8]

After Maury's contraption to retrieve samples from the seabed failed in deep water, John M. Brooke, a young passed midshipman who worked with instruments in the observatory, took an interest in Maury's problem and solved it. Brooke used a sixty-pound ball and drilled a hole through its center. Through the hole he closely fitted a metal rod, allowing both ends to protrude a few inches from the top and bottom. He hollowed out the lower end of the rod and filled it with soft tallow, enabling whatever lay on the seabed to stick to the substance. The upper rod end contained a hinged arm with two notches, which held the ball during its descent. When the rod protruding from the bottom of the ball struck the seabed, inertia carried the ball down the rod, releasing the fingers that held it. Samples from the ocean's floor stuck to the tallowed rod, which the sounding team reeled, less the ball, back to the surface. On July 7, 1853, men of the *Dolphin* gave Brooke's sounding mechanism a trial in 12,000 feet of water. It worked. Maury now had his samples, but not the analysis.[9]

At the time of Brooke's experiments, 14,000 miles of telegraph line had already been strung in the United States. For the use of lines leading to New York in 1852, the Associated Press alone paid more than $70,000. At the time, Maury never suspected that his work would directly influence anyone's decision to promote the Atlantic cable.

The substance brought up from the deep resembled clay. Berryman preserved the samples in jars and in November 1853 delivered them to the observatory. Maury turned the specimens over to microscopists for evaluation and soon learned, to everyone's surprise, that the ocean bed consisted of tiny shells showing no signs of abrasion. Not a speck of sand or gravel turned up in the samples. The evidence suggested that the bottom of the ocean contained a soft cushion for a cable to rest upon: a virtual millpond without waves or currents.

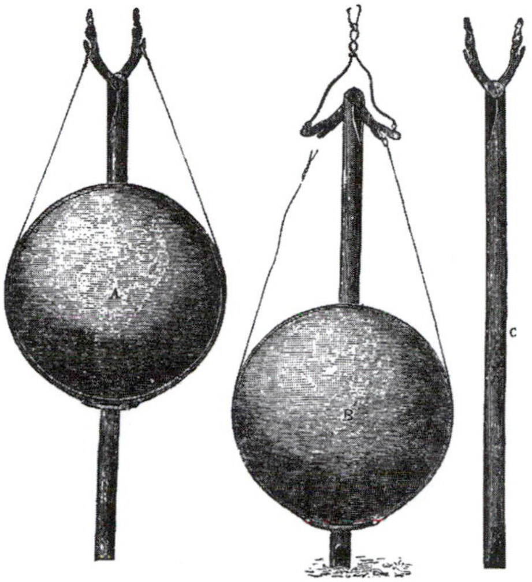

Passed Midshipman John M. Brooke, who became one of the U.S. Navy's outstanding ordnance engineers, designed deep-sea sounding equipment capable of picking up specimens from an ocean bed two and a half miles deep. (From Charles Bright, *The Story of the Atlantic Cable*. Digitized by Debra Peffer.)

Maury also used Berryman's soundings to draw the first bathymetrical map of the North Atlantic. He found no trenches or any steep underwater mountains: rather a gradual slope into the deeper sections of the ocean. His deductive talents quickly grasped the significance of Berryman's expedition, and on February 22, 1854, he wrote Secretary of the Navy James C. Dobbin:

> From Newfoundland to Ireland, the distance between the nearest points is about 1600 [nautical] miles and the bottom of the sea between the two places is a plateau which seems to have been placed there especially for the purpose of holding the wires of a submarine telegraph, and of keeping them out of harm's way. It is neither too deep nor too shallow, yet it is so deep that the wires being once landed will remain forever beyond the reach of vessels' anchors, icebergs, and drifts of any kind, and so shallow that the wires may be readily lodged upon the bottom.
>
> The depth of the plateau is quite regular, gradually increasing from the shores of Newfoundland to the depth of from 1500 to 2000 fathoms as you approach the other side.[10]

Field's letter of inquiry reached the observatory on the same day that Maury completed his survey report. "Singularly enough," Maury replied,

Lieutenant Matthew Fontaine Maury became the Superintendent of the U.S. Naval Observatory and through his offices discovered the telegraphic plateau. (Courtesy of the U.S. Naval Historical Center.)

"just as I received your letter, I was closing one to the Secretary of the Navy on the same subject." He fueled Field's enthusiasm by adding that he believed the transatlantic telegraph to be so important that he recommended "the government should offer a prize for the first message across, a slice of the public lands." He sent a full copy of his report to Field and enclosed another to Morse, who appeared to be pursuing the same objective but without resources.[11]

The correspondence gave birth to Maury's so-called "telegraph plateau," which years later would be identified as an apron without crevasses or sharp peaks along the northern foothills of the Mid-Atlantic Range. Had Berryman sounded the Atlantic a few hundred miles to the south, he would have discovered slopes and currents in depths running to 7,000 fathoms.[12]

Maury understood the hazards on the surface of the ocean and reminded Field of the difficulty of finding "a time calm enough, the sea smooth enough, a wire long enough, a ship big enough, to lay a coil of wire sixteen hundred [nautical] miles in length." Had Field taken these simple warnings into consideration, he may have proceeded with less impetuosity.[13]

After reading Maury's report, Field received a reply from Morse, who agreed to come down from Poughkeepsie and discuss the project in more detail. When he arrived, those who observed the pair in conference soon noticed a sharp contrast. Field effused vigor and enthusiasm. The older Morse, now gaunt and gray, wore features marked by years of adversity. For ten years he had waited patiently for someone to grasp the significance of the Atlantic telegraph, and the man who stepped forward to promote the idea was a person who knew absolutely nothing about electricity. Nevertheless the two men, both hardheaded in their own way, soon warmed to each other. Morse understood telegraphy and Field understood money, but neither man understood the host of technical problems confronting them.

For Field to proceed he needed access to Morse's patents at reasonable cost. The efficiency and effectiveness of an Atlantic cable depended upon having control of the land links. Seeing a role for himself in the enterprise, Morse responded with interest, providing Field raised the capital to finance the scheme.

Morse had good reason to jump on Field's bandwagon. He complained constantly to his attorney, Amos Kendall, of being swindled out of royalties and dividends. "This is the only source on which I can calculate for the means of subsistence from day to day with any degree of certainty," he grumbled.

> Out of 40,000 miles of telegraph, all of which should pay me something, only 225 miles is all that I can depend upon with a certainty; and the case is a little aggravated when I think that throughout all Europe . . . not a mile contributes to my support or has paid me a farthing.[14]

So in the closing weeks of 1854, Morse and Field needed each other but for different reasons.

Armed with Morse's credentials and Maury's endorsement, Field brought other men into his growing circle of confidants. For legal advice he consulted his oldest brother, David Dudley Field, Jr., a distinguished New York lawyer. David agreed to handle all legal matters, and if necessary, to shed clients. He realized that his name and reputation, added to that of his brother, would induce others to invest. For both men the arrangement had aspects of convenience. Living side by side, they could communicate daily. Field could only guess at how much money might be needed, so he set out to raise a million dollars by enlisting ten men of wealth.[15]

His search for financial backing began next door where wealthy industrialist Peter Cooper lived. Now sixty-three years old, Cooper had made his fortune as an inventor and an industrialist. He had grown up with little formal education but with an enormous talent for contriving mechanical devices. He saved money and invested $2,000—all he had—in a shabby glue factory. He resurrected the business using his own engineering talents and was soon clearing $100,000 profit a year.

In 1830 he became involved in the iron business, and in the face of public ridicule designed and manufactured America's first locomotive, the Tom Thumb. Almost single-handedly Cooper put the Baltimore and Ohio railroad on the tracks. In the process he amassed an enormous fortune in iron, coal, and glue.

Cooper enjoyed the publicity of having his name attached to great accomplishments, and by the 1850s he ranked as one of the wealthiest men in America. He believed that his money should be used to benefit the public. After leading the effort to establish a public school system in New York, Cooper became deeply involved in making one of his dreams come true: the building of Cooper Union, an enormous technical college—situated at Astor Place in Manhattan—designed to provide tuition-free education for the working classes. Cooper had many reasons to not invest in Field's venture—he had just spent $650,000 on Cooper Union, a free gift to the city. But as he chatted with his persuasive neighbor, he began to realize that a transoceanic cable would indeed greatly benefit the public, and be immensely profitable for the stockholders.[16]

At first, Cooper made his participation contingent upon Field's success in attracting other investors. He did not need any more financial entanglements in his already full and complicated life. In addition to building Cooper Union, he still managed the glue factory, controlled Cooper & Hewitt ironworks, and served on several New York committees. But when the banks refused to finance Field's enterprise, Cooper committed large sums,[17] admitting:

> It was an enterprise that struck me forcibly the moment [Field] mentioned it. I thought I saw in it . . . a means by which we would communicate between two continents, and send knowledge broadcast all over the world. It seemed to strike me as though it were the consummation of that great prophecy, that "knowledge shall cover the earth, as the waters shall cover the deep," and with that feeling I joined him . . . in what then appeared to most men a wild and visionary scheme; a scheme that fitted those who engage in it for an asylum where they could be taken care of as little short of lunatics.[18]

Cooper's reputation for making profitable investments became the catalyst for drawing other wealthy Americans into the enterprise. Moses Taylor, a New York importer and future president of City Bank (precursor of today's Citibank), listened to Field's proposal with understandable skepticism. The two men had never met before, and the first meeting took place at Taylor's home. "I shall never forget how Mr. Taylor received me," Field recalled. "He fixed on me his keen eye, as if he would look through me; and then, sitting down, he listened to me for nearly an hour without saying a word." Taylor, not one to throw money away, agreed to participate, providing others joined the venture.[19]

Taylor made arrangements for Field to meet Marshall Owen Roberts, who ran the U.S. Mail Steamship Company. Field and Roberts had met before, but five years had elapsed since their last conversation. Roberts' rise from poverty read like a Horatio Alger story. Orphaned at eight without a friend in the world, he rose to wealth by gambling on ventures that became great successes: floating palaces on the Hudson River, the Erie Railroad, and the massive growth in maritime commerce precipitated by the California gold rush. Getting a commitment from Roberts proved to be easy. Roberts liked to invest in worthy long shots, and Field's proposal looked like the perfect place to throw some money.[20]

Chandler White did not live in New York, but he became prospect number four on Field's short list. Like Field, White had made his money in the papermaking industry and retired to a lovely home near Fort Hamilton. He lost a few dollars when Field, several years before, involved him in a mineral-seeking expedition up the Amazon River. The excursion turned into a near disaster for White, who temporarily disappeared as if swallowed up by the jungle in an area roamed by alleged cannibals. After the South American debacle, White might judiciously have steered clear of his friend's scheme. But Field, whose salesmanship continued to sharpen with every new contact, persuaded White to join the venture and dragged him into the enterprise by his coattails.[21]

Field now had five investors, and during a gathering at the Clarendon Hotel on Broadway one evening, he announced his plans to secure five more. Cooper looked at the wealthy group assembled and asked, "Why will five not do as well as ten?" To this all members agreed and suggested bringing Gisborne into the discussion. They needed to examine the charter of the defunct company to learn more about what Gisborne had done, what he proposed to do, what property the company held, what debts it owed, and decide whether the enterprise offered sufficient inducements to invest more than a million dollars in a new company.[22]

For four nights in succession, ending on March 10, 1854, the investors met with Gisborne in Field's large dining room. They poured over a spread of maps and sketched a route to lay a land wire. With Gisborne they estimated the cost of the work, and after he departed for the evening, they worked the numbers and projected a tidy return on their investment. Armed with facts and figures inferred from Gisborne's statements, coupled with a generous dependency on rose-colored glasses, five men of wealth unanimously agreed to form the New York, Newfoundland, and London Telegraph Company, but only if the legislature of Newfoundland agreed to grant a new charter with additional concessions. The group named Peter Cooper, president; Moses Taylor, treasurer; Field, White, and Roberts, directors; and David Dudley Field, Jr., counsel. If everything worked according to plan, Gisborne stood to receive $40,000 for surrendering all the rights of the bankrupt Newfoundland Electric Telegraph Company, and Field's consortium agreed to assume $50,000 of Gisborne's debts.[23]

On March 15 Field, accompanied by White, Gisborne, and brother David, departed from Boston on a steamer for Halifax. Three days later they booked passage on a tiny steamer running ferry service to St. John's. The voyage left an indelible mark on David Field's memory.[24]

> Three more disagreeable days, voyagers scarcely ever passed. . . . It seemed as if all the storms of winter had been reserved for the first month of spring. A frost-bound coast, an icy sea, rain, hail, snow and tempest, were the greetings of the telegraph adventurers in their first movement towards Europe. In the darkest night, through which no man could see the ship's length, with snow filling the air and flying into the eyes of sailors, with ice in the water, and a heavy sea rolling and moaning about us, the captain felt his way around Cape Race with his lead, as the blind man feels his way with his staff, but as confidently and as safely as if the sky had been clear and the sea calm . . . the light of morning dawned upon deck and mast and spar, coated with glittering ice, but [we floated] securely between the mountains which form the gates of the harbor of St. John's.[25]

The delegation from New York met with Newfoundland's attorney general, Edward M. Archibald, and the governor, Kerr Bailey Hamilton, who urged the executive council and legislature to hear Field's proposal. Field sold his plan in three days. He received a guarantee of 5 percent interest on $250,000 in bonds (a hefty sum for Newfoundlanders) for twenty years, an immediate grant of fifty square miles of land, an additional grant of the same on completion of the telegraph across the ocean, a payment of $25,000 toward construction of a bridle path to carry telegraph lines across the island, and a remission of duties on the importation of wires and material needed for the work. He also bargained and received the exclusive right for fifty years to land cables on Newfoundland and Labrador. Such an agreement automatically embraced every province from Nova Scotia to Quebec and connected them with Maine lines that fed down the eastern seaboard and into the South. The governor assured Field that the conditions would be met. Elated by this assertion, Field departed for Halifax to buy a steamer. He left his associates behind to settle the details. Field purchased the steamer *Victoria*, and the company now had a flagship.[26]

David Field remained at St. John's to repeal the charter creating Gisborne's company and clear the way for the New York, Newfoundland, and London Telegraph Company. The new charter contained two phases, the first being an "Inter-Continental Telegraph" connecting Newfoundland to New York. Like Gisborne's original concept, fast steamers would bring messages to St. John's. The company's steamer would intercept the messages off St. John's and carry them to the telegraph station on shore where clerks would relay them, via Cabot Strait, to their continental destinations. Although the charter called for "a line of the swiftest steamships ever built" to operate between St. John's and Ireland, no party was designated to provide them.[27]

The second phase involved connecting Ireland with St. John's by transatlantic cable. This section of the charter remained poorly articulated because neither Field nor his associates understood the requirements. Nobody had been to England to discuss the enterprise, nobody had investigated the technical ramifications, and the only assurance motivating such optimism came from Samuel Morse, Matthew Maury, and the self-imposed enthusiasm emanating from the five investors in the New York, Newfoundland, and London Telegraph Company. Another inducement may have been the pro forma profit projections inked on March 10 during the late night meeting in Cyrus Field's dining room, but those records have since disappeared in the pothole of posterity.

As with all grand events, and there were so few to celebrate in Newfoundland, the promulgation of the new charter called for a banquet. The new company commissioners dipped into the till and feted the members of the legislature and the city's notables to a feast they would not forget for years to come. Even the town's commoners found reason to celebrate. Chandler White drew $50,000 on New York banks and paid off Gisborne's debts. The lucky Englishman received his $40,000 fee and had the good sense not to reinvest it in any more cable schemes.[28]

As a bonus, the legislature of Prince Edward's Island extended to the company exclusive cable rights for fifty years, a free grant of a thousand acres of land, and an additional grant of $1,500 per annum for ten years. Canada eventually passed an act enabling the company to build telegraphic lines throughout the provinces and remitted all duties on the importation of wire and materials.

Cyrus Field returned to New York, conscious of how acutely he needed help. He wrote Maury on April 15 and offered him a financial interest in the company. Maury politely declined, pointing to the impropriety of using "any official influence which I might possess with the government, in order to further a scheme in which I am privately interested." He promised to help where he "rightfully" could, but what Field sought from the U.S. Navy was a pair of vessels to lay the cable. One might wonder what Field was thinking by asking a mere lieutenant for the use of two naval vessels, and Maury, concerned by the outbreak of war in the Crimea, gave him no encouragement.[29]

Maury, however, did plan to send the survey ship *Dolphin* into the Atlantic to recheck Berryman's soundings. As he suspected, the Crimean War put the navy's participation on hold. Maury received no more soundings until 1856, and neither did the New York, Newfoundland, and London Telegraph Company.

On May 6 David Field and Chandler White returned to New York to report mission accomplished. Cyrus asked everyone to meet at 6:00 A.M. the following morning at his brother's home to finalize the company's formation. As the first rays of morning sun streamed through the windows of Field's library, the five principals accepted the charter, subscribed the stock, and elected officers. Cooper remained president; Taylor, treasurer; Chandler White became the vice president and secretary; and Roberts and Cyrus Field remained directors. During those few minutes five men subscribed a million and a half dollars—a huge sum in the mid-1850s—to put the company in business. Into the coffer went most of Cyrus Field's life savings—$200,000.[30]

Had these men truly understood the enormity of the task, they would not have been so quickly beguiled by the persuasiveness of Cyrus Field, but as a group they represented some of the sharpest minds in America. As Henry Field observed, "There is nothing in the world easier than to build a . . . railroad, or . . . telegraph, *on paper.*" But if the five partners succeeded, enormous profits would fill their pockets. They all believed in the enterprise, so much so that when Peter Cooper said, "Why will five not do as well as ten," they all agreed because they wanted to monopolize the profits. The full task of implementation fell to Cyrus Field. He became the company's chief operating officer, and so he should. After all, the telegraph was his idea.[31]

—— Chapter 3 ——

The Learning Curve Begins

While launching the cable company, Cyrus Field encountered an unexpected setback in May 1854 when Joseph Stone died, leaving Field & Company without a chief executive. He considered selling the firm, but he had committed most of his net worth to the project and needed to maintain a source of income. He reorganized the company under new managers, but in doing so created a dual responsibility for himself. On the heels of becoming the cable enterprise's chief operating officer, he also became Field & Company's chief executive officer, though mostly in absentia. That this arrangement would continue until 1863 never occurred to him.

Field recognized that he needed a great deal of help. After Maury politely refused to participate, Field turned to Morse, who was enamored of the project and expected a vice presidency. After a series of negotiations mingled with heavy doses of flattery, Morse signed on as honorary electrician. For an investment of $10,000 he acquired a tenth interest in the cable company. In exchange, Morse granted the company use of his patent telegraph lines from the Canadian border to New York at half rates once the connection with Europe was made, but he also gave the company exclusive rights to build parallel lines. Morse created a problem by granting telegraphic rights he did not have in Canada or in Britain's Canadian territorial waters. Though his patents were used in Canada, he never bothered to protect them by act of Parliament.[1]

Amos Kendall, Morse's attorney, warned his client that he had given Field's enterprise rights he did not have and compounded the problem by being overly generous with rights he did have. Kendall knew that Morse had been flimflammed into yielding too much, but for the moment, Morse seemed content with the arrangement. He would eventually discover the wisdom of Kendall's advice.[2]

Field's implementation plan called for speed on both sides of the Atlantic. Though he eventually hoped to network the country, his immediate task was to connect St. John's with New York. His ambitious program would give the company control of all the lines along North America's eastern seaboard. For the Newfoundland leg, he organized a three-prong attack. While one team of workers ran a 400-mile landline from St. John's to Cape Ray, another team would build the 140-mile landline from Halifax to Aspy Bay on the tip of Cape Breton. He sent Chandler White to St. John's to act as general agent and put his brother, Matthew, in charge of construction. Frederick Gisborne, who had not completely disconnected himself from the company, served as consulting engineer. For his own role, Field sailed to England to arrange for two cables: the first to span Cabot Strait (Gisborne's carrier pigeon flyway over the Gulf of St. Lawrence) and the second to cross the Atlantic.[3]

Matthew Field departed at once for St. John's. He had never seen the island and wanted to study the topography. What he discovered stunned him. Gisborne took him along the forty-mile trail, following the original wire through mostly level country before being stopped by the forest. Beyond that point a rider on horseback could disappear into the wilderness and never return. The company's charter specified a bridle road with bridges eight-feet wide to facilitate regular inspections of the wire. Matthew could not even find an old Indian trail to follow. Gisborne never mentioned the difficulties in crossing the island. When Matthew studied the survey he discovered mountains to hurdle, granite ridges to blast, marshes to fill, and rivers to bridge. The company's timetable called for the work to be done by late summer. Matthew chucked the survey and chose to follow the long, irregular coastline on the premise that the interior could not be reached with supplies.

To organize the project Matthew hired 600 laborers, divided them into battalions, and set them to work on separate sections of the line. He directed the effort by compass, using inaccurate maps to guide him. To keep the men and animals provisioned, he shipped supplies by sea. The steamer *Victoria* constantly plied the coast delivering barrels of pork and potatoes, kegs of powder, pickaxes, and implements of labor to predetermined delivery points inside dozens of fog-smothered fjords ringed by 2,000-foot cliffs. The men who unloaded the ship transported supplies to camp on their backs. Because poles could not be driven into the rocky landscape, laborers banked them with stones. Cooper & Hewitt ironworks made a little money on the venture by supplying wire for the landline, but no firm in America knew how to manufacture submarine cable.

Henry Field became the chronicler of the Atlantic telegraph, writing:

In many respects, it had the features of a military expedition. It moved in a great camp. The men were sheltered in tents, when sheltered at all, or in small huts they built along the road. But more often they slept on the ground. It was a wild and picturesque sight to come upon their camp in the woods, to see their fires blazing at night while hundreds of sleepers lay stretched on the ground. Sometimes, when encamped on the hills, [their fires] could be seen afar off to sea.

Often the rain fell in torrents. . . . But as the season advanced, all these difficulties increased. For nearly half the year the island is buried in snow. Blinding drifts sweep over the moors and choke up the paths of the forest. At such times the expedition lay floundering in the woods; what hardships and sufferings the men endured . . . can never be fully told.[4]

Cyrus Field did not get away to England for several months. The loss of his four-year-old son, Arthur Stone Field, left him depressed and delayed his departure. Matthew's difficulties stringing the Newfoundland wire gave him no cheer, as his timetable called for the overland line to be finished during the summer of 1855. The projection looked doable on paper, but there it ended. Matthew did not finish the work until the summer of 1856, performing a Herculean effort while simultaneously draining much of the company's cash. Mindful of Gisborne's experience, directors meeting nightly at Gramercy Park never questioned the drafts drawn by White on New York banks, but after expenditures reached $500,000 they became concerned.

At the close of 1854 Field sailed for England. Had he known the cable business would take him across the ocean more than fifty times, he may have stayed at home. On his first trip he knew no one in London, but Gisborne gave him a letter of introduction to John Brett. For most of the voyage Field suffered seasickness, an inescapable malady for any landlubber crossing the stormy North Atlantic in midwinter.[5]

Without Brett, Field could have muddled about England for weeks talking to the wrong people. As head of the Magnetic Telegraph Company, Brett understood cable technology and knew the reputable manufacturers. For openers, Field wanted a cable eighty-five miles long for the link across Cabot Strait. Brett suggested "a strand of three copper wires individually insulated with gutta-percha, wound with rope yarn, and covered with another sheath of gutta-percha, the whole thing being protected with a covering of iron wire."[6]

Field followed Brett's advice. He ordered the cable from Küper & Company, a young firm soon to become part of Glass, Elliot & Company of London. From Küper he also borrowed one of the firm's young engineers, Samuel Canning, who had laid cables in the Mediterranean. Canning agreed to come to Newfoundland and meet the 500-ton bark *Sarah L. Bryant*, which Field chartered to deliver the cable to Port aux Basques, a tiny hamlet near Cape Ray designated by the company as the eventual terminus for the Newfoundland line.

Field returned to the United States without clearly understanding, though Brett informed him, that eighty-five miles of cable could not be laid without paying-out machinery. Every move Field made turned into a new learning experience, and every misstep became enormously expensive for the company. Field had no reason to hurry because Matthew informed him that the landline would not reach Port aux Basques before the summer of 1856. Though rankled by the delay, Field insisted on laying the cable to Cape Breton during the summer of 1855 and sent a letter to Brett urging him to provide paying-out machinery. Field eventually got everything he needed to lay the cable but the right kind of vessel.

Anticipating *Sarah L. Bryant*'s arrival at St. John's, Field proudly and generously chartered at $750 a day the swift *James Adger*, a luxury side-wheel steamer of the Charleston Line. He invited the directors, their families, many friends, and three members of the clergy—perhaps as a divine hedge against misfortune—to join in a grand excursion to the Gulf of St. Lawrence to witness the laying of the company's first cable. Scientists and journalists accepted invitations, for such a cable had never been laid in the western hemisphere. Morse brought a telegraphic instrument to instruct the passengers in the mystic art of sending messages over electric lines. Frederick Gisborne joined the cruise to witness his old dream come true. Henry Field made the trip to continue his chronicle. John Brett received no invitation, though he had bought a few shares of stock in the company when Field was in England. Matthew Maury accepted an invitation and arrived at the dock with his wife and two oldest sons. When he learned the festivities might continue for many weeks, he grumbled that "he should not be out of the country so long" and returned to the observatory.[7]

When *James Adger* arrived off Port aux Basques, *Bryant* and her cargo of cable were nowhere in sight. Samuel Canning, who had been waiting onshore to take charge of laying the cable, rowed out in a boat and reported *Bryant* missing. The news rattled Field. He waited offshore for a few days and then ordered *Adger* to St. John's. After hiring a band and spending a few pleasant days ashore, Field took the steamer and his guests back to Port aux Basques and found the bark sheltered inside a cove. The sightseers spent the next two days watching as Canning's crew took the end of the cable ashore at Cape Ray, where a sandy bottom offered a quiet nesting place.

Having no facilities at Cape Ray to house the telegraph or the operators, Field sent *Victoria* back to Port aux Basques for lumber to build a shack. The steamer returned but could not get the materials to shore through the shallows; so the expedition lost another day while workmen built rafts to float the lumber ashore. Breakers smashed the rafts, upset the poling crews, and scattered planks all over the cove. Once again Gisborne proved his value. A number of passengers had purchased Newfoundland retrievers at St. John's, and Gisborne turned the large black web-footed animals loose.

The dogs dove into the water, clamped their jaws on the planks, and paddled the boards ashore, right down to the last shingle.

If Field thought his bad luck had finally changed, he still had much to learn about sailing ships and laying cable. In late August, after a fresh breeze cleared a dense two-day fog from Cape Ray, Captain Turner of *Adger* attempted to pass a hawser to *Bryant* to take her in tow. The brig had all the cable coiled beneath her deck with a single strand leading through the drums of the paying-out machinery. As *Adger* drifted toward *Bryant*, their captains began hollering at each other to back. Neither did. *Bryant*'s crew could not raise her anchor, so they slipped it, but not in time. According to Peter Cooper, the captain of *Adger* "ran his steamer into the [*Bryant*], carried away her shrouds and quarter-rail, and almost ruined our enterprise the first thing, dragging the cable over the stern of the vessel with such force as to break the connection; and we were obliged to cut the cable and splice it again."

Hours later, Turner passed a 200-foot, four-inch-diameter towing cable to *Bryant*, but in the process entangled it in *Adger*'s wheel. Turner hollered at the *Bryant* to cut the cable. While he fussed with the tangled hawser, a strong breeze carried *Bryant* across the bay and toward shore. "We had to expostulate with the captain of the steamer," said Cooper, "until the [*Bryant*] was within two or three hundred feet of the rocks, before he would consent to attempt her rescue; and by the merest good luck, we got out a rope to her and saved her from going on the rocks." The accident ended the cable-laying effort for the day and put the two skippers at odds with each other.[8]

The following morning a bright sun and calm sea came as a divine blessing to the harried shipmasters. The telegraph team on *Bryant* spliced the cable, dropped it into the shallows, and passed a hawser over the bow to *Adger*. The brig had little steerage, and paying out the cable depended upon *Adger* steaming in a straight line to the connecting point on Cape Breton.

To assist Captain Turner in maintaining the correct position, Canning hoisted a flag on the telegraph shack. He took Turner aside and told him to keep *Adger* aligned with the flag and a large white rock on the mountain behind it. Turner grunted, and Canning returned to *Bryant*. Turner ordered all ahead, and the two vessels moved slowly into Cabot Strait. Though the paying-out machinery on *Bryant* required constant attention, the cable slithered rapidly into the strait, jerking in spasms as the brig bounced gently up and down on yesterday's swells.

A mile or two later Peter Cooper noticed that *Adger* had wandered off course. He went to the bridge to alert the captain, but Turner stiffly replied, "I know how to steer by my compass." Cooper detected a little surliness in Turner's reply and said, "Your instructions were to steer by the flag and the rock on the mountain." Turner was in no mood to take instructions from a landsman. He stared straight ahead and said, "I steer by my compass."[9]

When Turner showed no inclination to follow Canning's instructions, Cooper

> then got a lawyer who was on board to draw up a paper warning the captain that if he did not change his course we should hold him responsible for the loss of the cable. He then turned his course and went as far out of the way in the other direction.[10]

The pleasant morning breeze intensified and soon whipped into a freshening gale. Canning shouted from *Bryant* that twenty-four miles of cable had been paid out, but Turner's meandering course had taken the two vessels little more than nine miles from shore. The constantly changing speed of *Adger* made it impossible for *Bryant*'s crew to control the paying-out machinery, and great lengths of cable flopped into the water in kinks. The captain of the brig could no longer control her, and he asked Canning what to do. Canning already knew that too little cable remained in the hold to reach the opposite shore, so he told the captain to run up the signal flag to abort the effort and cut the cable.

Turner set a course for Sydney, Nova Scotia, with the bark in tow. Through white-crested waves a detail from *Bryant* rowed Canning over to *Adger* for a conference. The directors praised Canning for his effort, but they had lost $350,000 on the expedition and wanted answers on what went wrong. Though Turner could be condemned for ignoring instructions and overreacting to criticism, the root cause emanated from using a towed sailing vessel to lay the cable. In the future, only a single steamer would be used.

Some forty miles of cable lay at the bottom of Cabot Strait; the other forty-odd miles went into storage at Sydney. Cyrus Field, after such high expectations, felt personally devastated. He was somewhere on the learning curve but knew not where. He felt personally responsible for the company's losses, but Cooper consoled his partner, blaming the debacle on Captain Turner. Guests on *Adger* expressed a proper amount of sympathy and after doing so prepared a costume party. In this bizarre atmosphere the *Adger* returned to New York, and Field recovered from another bout of disappointment. A few days later he encouraged the directors to replace the lost cable and give the strait another try.

Peter Cooper blamed the company's disastrous losses on Captain Turner, writing some years later, "We had spent so much money, and lost so much time, that it was very vexatious to us to have our enterprise defeated in the way it was, by the stupidity and obstinacy on one man. This man was one of the rebels that fired the first guns on Fort Sumter. The poor fellow is now dead."[11]

The company still had a few dollars in the bank, and any member who felt financially stressed had ample reason to cut his losses and fold. Ahead of Matthew Field's telegraph-building team still lay about two hundred miles of wilderness. Finishing the line would cost a thousand dollars a mile. The directors expected the replacement of the cable and the landline to Halifax would cost $300,000 more. Having spent more than $800,000, the question the directors confronted was how to raise capital for financing the Atlantic cable. During August, Cyrus Field squandered $30,000 on chartering *James Adger*, which proved to be a $350,000 liability rather than an asset because the captain could not steer his ship.[12]

Before any members of the company lost faith in the venture, Field sailed for England to purchase more cable. Using a combination of newly acquired wisdom combined with sharp negotiating skills, he signed an agreement with Küper & Company to make and lay the cable at their own risk, using their own ship, the steamer *Propontis*, and their own engineer, the now familiar Samuel Canning. Field relieved his mind of such details as paying-out machinery by leaving matters in the hands of experts. He returned to the United States with a signed agreement and held the company together. Some years later Peter Cooper admitted, "It was in great measure due to the indomitable courage and zeal of Mr. Field inspiring us that we went on and on until we got another cable across the gulf."[13]

Matthew Field finished the line to Cape Ray and the line from Cape Breton to Halifax weeks before *Propontis* arrived. Canning took charge of the operation and laid the cable across the strait. To form the telegraphic core, the new cable contained stranded conductor wires instead of a solid wire. For nine years the cable performed its duties to the satisfaction of the public and the stockholders, transmitting messages over one thousand miles of wire from St. John's, Newfoundland, to New York and beyond.

After two weary years, the company now had something to generate dividends. The first successful enterprise cost the five stockholders more than a million dollars and consumed much of the firm's capital. The most difficult task still lay ahead. Cyrus Field, invigorated by success, told the directors he was ready to tackle the North Atlantic.

During the company's two years of labor on the Newfoundland line, competition and technology changed. Lines radiating from New York spread across the frontier. Different companies staked their claims in the growing West using patents Morse contested. In 1854 Morse finally established priority for his patents when the U.S. Supreme Court decided in his favor, but for a continental telegraph to work, the nation needed a single uniform system linking major cities to the same network. On the heels of Morse winning his years-old patent case, Field discovered that improved transmitters and receivers were superseding Morse's patents. New lines strung by ruthless competitors like Taliaferro P. Shaffner forced Field to devote time and energy to domestic issues affecting the future profits of the company. Shaffner, who was building the New Orleans & Ohio line, warned Morse that his men were well armed and would do their duty if anyone meddled with their work. Morse lashed back, threatening to use legal recourse instead of bloodshed, but he privately hoped that Field would intercede.[14]

Field paid no attention to Morse or Shaffner. Instead, he and Peter Cooper formed the American Telegraph Company, and with eight partners invested $100,000 in a patented printing device that transcribed electrical impulses into letters. Royal E. House had invented the printer and established a telegraph line from New York to Boston. He then sold the printer patent to David Hughes, a Kentucky professor of music, but retained the telegraph line. Cooper and Field bought the printer patent rights from Hughes and the line from House. The American Telegraph Company intended to use the printer on every line they controlled. Experts touted the printer as "so superior to existing telegraphs that it would supersede them all." With a total capital of $200,000, the new company incorporated on November 1, 1855, with Peter Cooper as its president.[15]

The American Telegraph Company's goal to monopolize all lines on the eastern seaboard began to gather momentum. Cooper no longer needed Morse's patents. He planned to expand into the South and West by buying or leasing lines erected by small, independent operators. This conflicted with the plans of Hiram Sibley, the president of the Western Union Telegraph Company, who had engaged Shaffner to build the lines contested by Morse.

The new company's business strategy also conflicted with Morse's interests, and he rebelled. He still insisted that his patent covered any form of message transmitted over telegraph wires anywhere in the United States and Canada. He became especially indignant when he heard that the American Telegraph Company, of which he was no part, intended to replace his system with Hughes printers.[16]

Feeling betrayed by Cooper and Field, Morse asked for an explanation. Field, vice president of both companies, somewhat disingenuously told him that his rates were too high. Attorney Amos Kendall, who represented Morse's patent rights, analyzed the trouble accurately and informed his client: "Field & Co. are shrewd business men not unfriendly to you or me but more friendly to themselves. It was not friendship to us that induced them to buy the Hughes instrument; but it was in fact, say what you will, to hold in *terroreur* [*sic*] over our heads and the heads of our Companies to induce us to let them have our lines at a reduced rate."[17]

The remark put Morse on guard and made him more circumspect, especially of Field and Cooper. Three months later he received a warning from his cousin, who wrote: "Keep your eye on this excellent friend of yours—Mr. Cyrus Field."[18]

For several years the New York, Newfoundland, and London Telegraph Company and the American Telegraph Company would operate out of the same office. Despite Morse's grumbling, he continued to serve the former company as honorary electrician while jabbing condemnations at the other. Chandler White died after witnessing the debacle in the Gulf of St. Lawrence, and Robert Lowber, an attorney on the *Adger* that day, filled White's seat on the board. Peter Cooper added a friend to the board, Wilson Hunt, who had recently lost in his bid to become mayor of New York. Hunt neither understood his role nor expressed much interest in the company, but he had wealthy connections and the New York, Newfoundland, and London company needed money.

Field planned to return to London to make arrangements for the Atlantic cable. His two-year effort to lay a cable across the Gulf of St. Lawrence taught him a lesson, though he still had many more to learn. When the company's coffers bulged with cash, a few small errors of judgment could be tolerated. But there had been no small errors, just large costly ones caused by a combination of haste and ignorance. With this in mind, it occurred to Field that Berryman's 1853 soundings of the Atlantic had occurred before any serious commitment had been made to actually laying a cable. Three years had passed and new devices had been invented for probing the great depths of the oceans: so Field asked Maury for another survey.

In 1855 the directors had gratuitously offered Maury "the use of the wires of the New York, Newfoundland, and London Telegraph Company . . . free of charge for the purpose of determining longitude and to use them first."[19] Such generosity deserved reciprocity, but Field asked for nothing until the Crimean War ended in 1856 and the Newfoundland line had been laid in the gulf. Then he approached Maury with a battery of questions, some of which the lieutenant had no business answering. Maury's advice on cable design was bad, but Field had so much confidence in the lieutenant that he believed that the cable should be quite light because Maury said, "There is no running water [current] at the bottom of the deep sea along the telegraph's plateau and nothing to try the strength of any electric cord, however slender when once lodged there."[20]

On the matter of new soundings, Maury considered them "still important and very desirable," but he was personally losing control of the work to Alexander Dallas Bache, superintendent of the Treasury Department's Coast Survey. The two men, both egotistical scientists, feuded constantly over issues involving scientific propriety, and on the soundings Field requested, Maury replied, "[Bache] hopes to get a vessel for deep sea soundings. It would be unfortunate if the Coast Survey were to be mixed up in it for that's my thunder."[21]

Maury had reason to be concerned. On May 5, 1856, he had asked Secretary of the Navy James C. Dobbin for three vessels to further explore

Alexander Dallas Bache, Superintendent of the U.S. Coast Survey, vied frequently with Lieutenant Maury over who produced the better science. (Courtesy of the U.S. Naval Historical Center.)

"the bottom of the ocean with Brooke's sounding apparatus," but received no reply.[22]

While Maury left Washington for several days, Dobbin recalled Lieutenant Berryman and Midshipman John S. Barnes from the Coast Survey and restored them to the navy. He assigned them to the steamer *Arctic* to perform the soundings requested by Cooper and Field. He made the mission responsible to himself, thereby removing Bache and Maury from direct involvement. When Maury returned from his travels he became outraged by the secretary's assumption of the legitimate work of the observatory's Hydrographic Office. Dobbin listened to Maury's complaints but made no change in command responsibility. Knowing nothing about the techniques used in deep-sea soundings, Dobbin left the choice of devices up to Berryman. Bache recommended the new Massey Indicators that the Coast Survey used in coastal waters. Dobbin voiced no objections when Berryman chucked Brooke's Deep Sea Sounding Apparatus and fitted *Arctic* with Massey Indicators. Berryman also doubled the size of the balls normally used, adding another variable to interpolating the data.

Field unknowingly became entangled in the growing feud between

Maury and Bache, and more recently between Maury and Dobbin. Field enjoyed friendly relations with all three men and did not want to alienate any of them. Maury, however, wanted to see a copy of Berryman's orders and asked Field to visit *Arctic* in New York. Unaware that Field was performing a mission for Maury, Berryman gave him a copy of Dobbin's orders. Field forwarded them to the observatory, equally unaware that he was setting the stage for a future dispute between Maury and everyone else over the validity of Berryman's soundings.

On July 31, 1856, *Arctic* began sounding the telegraphic plateau. Arriving at Queenstown, Ireland, on August 23, Berryman turned around and made additional soundings on the way back. In accordance with Dobbin's instructions, he turned his findings over to the Naval Observatory. Maury compared them with the bathymetrical map made in 1854 and noticed that Berryman's soundings disagreed with those made three years before. Maury quizzed Berryman on the differences, and the latter made a new chart, also with fatal flaws. After waiting impatiently for Maury's report, Field received a letter that read: "[Berryman's] official records are utterly at variance and irreconcilable with each other. In short, his work in the *Arctic* does not add one iota to the information we already possessed concerning the depth of the Atlantic." Maury went on to say that in his opinion the Massey Indicator, which the Coast Survey persuaded Berryman to use, caused the errors, and that Berryman exacerbated the problem by failing to perform tests to verify the instrument's accuracy.[23]

The dispute over Berryman's soundings carried into the next administration. President James Buchanan named Isaac Toucey secretary of the navy, and the latter had barely settled into office when Maury paid him a visit. To resolve the months-old dispute over Berryman's soundings, Maury recommended that a staff of "competent officers not connected with the Observatory" review all of Berryman's charts and records to determine their value. Instead of following Maury's recommendation, Toucey chose three men *from* the observatory because they were the most competent deep-sea experts in the navy. Unfortunately, their unbiased report agreed completely with Maury's conclusions, and Berryman's friends in the Coast Survey refused to accept it. The dispute over Berryman's report forced Field to add soundings to his list of unfinished business.[24]

Before departing for London he renewed an old request, asking Maury for two favors: help in securing two or three vessels from the navy to assist in laying the cable, and a map of the best route to follow when laying the cable during the summer of 1857. On the matter of securing naval vessels, Maury agreed to help, though he promised nothing. Regarding sea routes, he suggested that the cable be connected between two steamers in the middle of the ocean, one going east and the other west, on or about the 20th of July. "I think that between that time and the 10th of August, the state of both sea and air is usually in the most favorable condition possible." As usual, Maury was right on the weather, which he understood better than anyone in the world.[25]

During the summer of 1857 the British Admiralty, aware of the American dispute over Berryman's soundings, decided to make their own survey. Scientists and shippers in England held Maury in the highest regard: his charting of the seas had reduced their voyages and their insurance rates, saving them millions. When he spoke, they listened, and when he said that Berryman's soundings were defective, they believed him. The Admiralty acknowledged another reason for sounding from Ireland to Newfoundland. In 1853 John Bright's cable spanned the Irish Sea and connected the Magnetic Telegraph Company to Ireland, and in 1856 Field's company connected Newfoundland to New York. The only strand missing was one connecting the two continents.

Early in the summer of 1857, Lieutenant Joseph Dayman of the Royal Navy put a modified version of Brooke's deep-sea sounding apparatus on board the HMS *Cyclops* and surveyed the ocean bottom from Ireland to Newfoundland. The new device included a spring-loaded scoop at the end of the rod protruding from the bottom of the ball. After being driven into the ooze, the scoop closed and brought a much larger sample to the surface.

Dayman followed Maury's guidelines for measuring depth and sounded a route slightly to the north of Berryman's track. He increased the number of soundings near the coast, decreasing the number to every twenty or thirty miles as he steamed farther from shore. Dayman corroborated Berryman's 1853 findings and validated Maury's claim that the soundings taken by Berryman in 1856 were faulty. Dayman also blamed Berryman's errors on the Massey Indicator. He verified the existence of a plateau free of currents with a featherbed of microscopic shells composed of carbonate of lime. Many years later, other sounding teams discovered high mountains and deep trenches with strong currents on both sides of the plateau, making Berryman's early discovery fortuitous indeed. Maury had been quite right in 1854 when he informed the secretary of the navy of "a plateau which seems to have been placed there especially for the purpose of holding the wires of a submarine telegraph, and of keeping them out of harm's way."[26]

Dayman summed up his survey, saying:

> This space has been named by Maury the telegraphic plateau, and although by multiplying the soundings on it, we have depths ranging from fourteen hundred and fifty to twenty four hundred fathoms, these are comparatively small inequalities in its surface, and present no new difficulty to the project of laying the cable across the ocean.[27]

The sharpest change of depth occurred about 300 miles off the coast of Ireland where the sea bottom dropped from 550 to 1,750 fathoms in a space of a dozen miles. Dayman found rock at 550 fathoms and ooze at

1,750 fathoms, and "this," he said, "is the greatest dip in the whole ocean." Dayman should have red-flagged this information to the cable layers of the future. The importance of knowing the composition and configuration of the ocean bottom every step of the way determined the amount of slack needed for the cable to reach the bottom. Too much cable paid out in the shallows tended to kink; too little cable paid out in great depths tended to stretch, strain, or hang suspended above the seabed. Rocks caused problems at any depth, especially where currents flowed. Cyrus Field would find scientists in England who understood these problems, but even they made mistakes.[28]

After four years of trial and error, the New York, Newfoundland, and London Telegraph Company now had some answers but not much capital. They needed fresh funds and turned to the man who had lured them into this cash-consuming business. Who better to raise subscriptions in England than Cyrus Field? Lieutenant Dayman was still at sea sounding the North Atlantic when the directors sent their chief operating officer to London to solicit the participation of the British government.

Field had learned something about the cost of mistakes. He would not repeat many of the same errors, but his ascent on the learning curve had only begun. The lessons of the future would be as brutal as those of the past.

CHAPTER 4

THE BRITISH ALLIANCE

In July 1856 Cyrus Field sailed for London with his wife and sister Mary on the steamer *Baltic*. Never had he seen such calm seas and pristine weather. He remembered it as one of his rare pleasant crossings among the many he took during the cable-laying years. Morse agreed to follow later. Having reconciled his differences with Cooper, Morse grasped the significance of having his name, influence, and patents associated with the project. He also felt needed. Field wanted to have his own electrical expert in England, but he also needed Morse's reputation if he hoped to get a farthing out of the British.

"Our little company," Field reflected some years later, "raised and expended over a quarter million pounds sterling ($1,250,000) before an Englishman paid a single pound." His lamentation ignored the intention of the five original partners to monopolize revenues and profits, but having spent their initial investment, were now willing to solicit capital from England, which had become home for the world's most advanced cable technology.[1]

Field's warm relations with John Brett, who headed the Magnetic Telegraph Company, and Edward Bright, who managed the firm, opened many doors. The three men corresponded often, and Brett clearly understood his American friend's purpose in returning to England. Field took rooms near Hanover Square where Brett lived and began his campaign the following day.

The New York, Newfoundland, and London Telegraph Company already enjoyed something of a reputation in England, having laid the second longest submarine cable in the world in the deepest water (2,160 feet). Only the cable laid in 1854 from Italy to Corsica (110 miles) was longer, and the Magnetic Telegraph Company laid both.

Through Brett, Field began to meet men of wealth and vision who had dreamed of oceanic cables long before his small group of neighborhood investors grasped the significance of connecting two continents. One of them, twenty-four-year-old Charles T. Bright, worked as Brett's chief engineer. Before the age of twenty, Bright had already obtained twenty-four patents for electrical inventions. Soon after joining the Magnetic Telegraph Company he began stringing England with telegraph lines. He became the first to wrap underground wires with gutta-percha, and on a single night in 1852 he laid a complete telegraphic system under the streets of Manchester. A year later, at the age of twenty-one, he laid the first successful deepwater telegraph cable between England and Ireland. Bright replaced the single solid wire conductor with small stranded wires, thereby avoiding a loss of conductivity if the single wire arrangement broke. When Samuel Canning laid the Gulf of St. Lawrence cable, he used Bright's stranded copper conductor.[2]

In 1853 the notion of laying an Atlantic cable infected Field and Bright at the same time. Two years later, while Field was making the final arrangements for laying the gulf cable, Bright was independently surveying the west coast of Ireland to find a suitable site for landing an Atlantic cable. The two men would become great friends.

On September 26, 1856, Field signed a document of intent with Brett and Bright to form a new company. Field now became entangled in a fourth company, three in the United States and one in England. The document read:

> Mutually, and on equal terms, we engage to exert ourselves for the purpose of forming a Company for establishing and working of electric telegraphic communication between Newfoundland and Ireland, such company to be called the Atlantic Telegraph Company, or by such other name as parties hereto shall jointly agree upon.[3]

Solidifying the new company required a number of experiments before Field could launch his campaign to raise capital from a growing number of British scientists who voiced no faith in the project. Such notables as Sir George B. Airy, Astronomer Royal, announced that "it was a mathematical impossibility to submerge a cable in safety at so great a depth," and "if it were possible, no signals could be transmitted through so great a length."[4]

Dr. Edward O. W. Whitehouse, a physician turned electrician, worked with Bright to prove that signals could be transmitted through a length of insulated line thousands of miles long. Whitehouse's first middle initial stood for Orange, but Obstinate better fit his personality. He preferred to be called by his second middle name, Wildman, which better described him. Being a self-trained telegrapher, and often doubtful of his own assertions, he learned by experimentation. So when Morse and Field arrived in London, Whitehouse intended to prove that "retardation of movement [of an electrical impulse], in consequence of distance, did not occur at a rate which could seriously affect a cable across the Atlantic." He also planned to demonstrate that large-diameter wire in insulated marine conductors slowed the speed of transmission, but even with heavier wire, the velocity of the transmission would still "satisfy [most] commercial and financial requirements in a line crossing the Atlantic."[5]

To make his point, Whitehouse borrowed the 5,000-mile underground telegraph system operated by the English and Irish Magnetic Company. On the night of October 9, 1856, he used a section 2,000 miles long and during three trials transmitted clear signals at the rate of 210, 241, and 270 impulses a minute. Morse witnessed the experiment and wrote:

> The admirable arrangements made at the Magnetic Telegraph Office in Old Broad Street, for connecting ten subterranean gutta-percha insulated conductors, of over two hundred miles each, so as to give one continuous length of more than two thousand miles during the hours of the night, when the telegraph is not commercially employed, furnished us the means of conclusively settling, by actual experiment, the question of practicability as well as practicality of telegraphing through our proposed Atlantic cable. The doubts are resolved . . . and the great feat of the century must shortly be accomplished.[6]

Morse often hedged his opinions around the words practicable and practical, which to him meant entirely different things while others accepted them as synonymous. To Morse, practicable meant that which has not yet been worked out but seems feasible; practical meant success in meeting defined demands made by actual use. When Morse used both terms together, it was an expression of unbridled confidence. People meeting him for the first time found his phraseology puzzling, and his persistent combination of "practicable" with "practical" became an annoying eccentricity.

Morse became excited when Whitehouse and Bright modified the induction coils and receiving magnets on the London lines to activate one of his recording instruments. Michael Faraday, the British inventor of electromagnetism, had predicted a delay when sending signals through so lengthy a wire. He also cautioned that electric currents could leak over long distances, thereby slowing the signal or rendering them indecipherable. When the tests using Morse's device proved Faraday wrong, Morse rejoiced again.

Field already knew what to expect because he had spoken to Faraday, but he still wanted tests made. "You just won't get [an] instantaneous message," Faraday declared. "How long will it take?" Field asked. "Possibly one second," Faraday replied. The tests corroborated Faraday's remarks, but those tests were not performed on submerged cables.[7]

Armed with Whitehouse's results, and having received favorable information from the Admiralty's survey of the telegraphic plateau, Field felt emboldened enough to enlist financial help from the British.

When Field launched his fund-raiser, "wild and undeveloped criticisms" came from pseudoscientists and schemers who wished to reap a personal benefit by injecting themselves into cable discussions. Because pressure increases on an object as it descends in water, a small number of scientists believed the cable would be destroyed by compression as it sank and recommended that buoys be laid across the Atlantic to hold the wire close to the surface, thereby enabling ships at sea to stop at midocean toll stations to send messages. One authority that evidently knew nothing of North Atlantic weather recommended using a transoceanic string of balloons to hold the cable near the surface without explaining how to keep them airborne. Bright knew the cable would merely increase in specific gravity as it descended, while the equal bulk of water surrounding it would continue to have very nearly the same specific gravity as at the surface; hence, the cable could not be damaged by pressure.[8]

One gentleman gave a demonstration with a one-inch specimen of cable, remarking most seriously. "Now I understand how you stow [the cable] away on board. You cut it up into bits beforehand, and then join up the pieces as you lay." Another gentleman, this one a naval expert, assured the company that "no other machinery for paying out was necessary [other] than a handspike to stop the egress of the cable." Prince Albert suggested that the entire transatlantic line be encased in a glass tube. The most grandiose idea came from a group who took out patents for "converting the laying vessel into a huge factory, with a view to making the cable on board in one continuous length, and submerging it during the process."[9]

Meanwhile, Bright hired a fishing smack and began exploring the harbors and beaches between Dingle and Bantry Bay on the southwest promontory of Ireland. He located a sheltered landing site among the soft, sandy beaches at Valentia in County Kerry. For many decades, Valentia Island would become the cable site of choice.[10]

When Field learned that Berryman had arrived at Queenstown, he left the scientific work to Morse, Bright, and Whitehouse and took a steamer to Ireland. The lieutenant had just completed his survey using Massey Indicators; results that Maury in the coming weeks would challenge. Field knew nothing about Berryman's sounding techniques. When the lieutenant confirmed the existence of a telegraphic plateau, Field stuffed a copy of the findings into his carrying case to take back to London.

On the return trip he shared a compartment with a short man in a tall beaver hat who he immediately recognized as Isambard Kingdom Brunel. Field introduced himself, noticing that Brunel kept his filing cabinet in his beaver. The chance meeting between the greatest British engineer of the nineteenth century and the cable neophyte from America would in future years combine the works of the former with the tenacity of the latter to accomplish what so many learned minds deemed to be the impossible.

Brunel inherited his engineering talents from his father, who in 1825 began building a pedestrian tunnel under the Thames, using his son as resident engineer. From this early experience, he became Great Britain's foremost engineer. During his short life he tunneled under rivers, built water towers, tied continents together with railroads, built suspension bridges, and experimented with jet propulsion. His one uncompleted project lay in a shipyard at Millwall on the Thames, for Brunel had started to build the largest ship in the world. He called her the *Great Eastern.* Brunel quickly surmised that he had something in common with this uncommon American who wanted to lay the longest submarine cable in the world.

Field reached into his carrying case and removed a sample of the gulf cable. Brunel's fingers separated the twisted conductor strands and asked, "Why not have the outer covering of the cable formed of twisted strands as well as the conductor? By that means you'll have a stronger, lighter, and more flexible cable than if you make the outer covering of solid wire?" Field could not respond to the suggestion, but it became the design adopted by Charles Bright.

After the two men reached London, Brunel loaded Field into a carriage and took him to John Scott Russell's shipyard at Millwall on the Isle of Dogs. There against the riverbank lay the immense frame of *Great Eastern*, fed with material, one end to the other, by enormous steam cranes serving hundreds of workmen. Field had never seen such a ship. Brunel, observing Field's amazement, said, "There is the ship to lay the Atlantic Cable!" Brunel would not live to see his words come true, but on that day, while standing beside the "Little Giant" in his shipyard, Field suspected that no single ship could lay his cable but one the size of *Great Eastern.* He also knew she would never be ready to meet his self-imposed deadline of next summer. The relationship with Brunel, however, did not end at the Isle of Dogs. Field needed such men as Brunel and brought him into the company's circle of consultants.[11]

On October 20, 1856, with Berryman's survey and Whitehouse's trials to prop the promotion of the enterprise, Brett, the president; Field, the vice president; Bright, the chief engineer; and Wildman Whitehouse, the electrician, registered the Atlantic Telegraph Company, setting capital requirements at £350,000 ($1,750,000). On November 1 Cyrus Field, also acting as chief operating officer for the New York, Newfoundland, company, issued a circular titled "Atlantic Telegraph," announcing the formation of the new corporation. He then made a promotional tour through the greater cities of England and spoke before groups interested in the project.

Six days later the company issued their prospectus, offering 350 shares at £1,000 each. Believing that Americans would want ownership in the company, Field subscribed to 25 percent of the shares and became the largest stockholder in the company. Field hoped to sell most of his eighty-eight shares to investors in New York. Neither he nor Brett were concerned about relinquishing part of their interest because a nice stock bonus for organizing the company would be issued when the cable became operational. Field believed that because the British eagerly bought shares and put up most of the money, Americans would want a stake in the enterprise. In this he would be disappointed and remain as the company's principal stockholder. The Magnetic Telegraph Company bought most of the 106 shares sold in London. The remaining shares went to Liverpool, Glasgow, and other parts of England. In December the Atlantic Telegraph Company deposited the first installment of £70,000 in the bank.[12]

The timing seemed right for Field to lure the British government into the venture. A year ago, Lord Clarendon, the foreign secretary, had turned him down. After Whitehouse's successful trials in 1856, Field and Morse paid Clarendon another visit and received an altogether different response. Somewhat startled by the scope of the project, Clarendon asked: "But, suppose you don't succeed?" Field replied that he would "Charge it to profit and loss, and go to work to lay another." Clarendon smiled, attributing the answer to being "a truly American reply" and asked Field to present his proposal in writing.[13]

While waiting for an answer from Clarendon, Field traveled to Paris with the two Marys—his wife and his ailing sister. During the trip his sister unexpectedly died. Filled with sadness, he returned to London unfit to conduct business. James Wilson, the British treasury secretary, invited the Fields to his country home in Bath. Over the course of several days the two men discussed the Atlantic cable; Wilson digesting the information with growing interest, and Field using the opportunity to promote his project.

On November 20, after returning to his rooms at 37 Jermyn Street, Field received a letter from Wilson that restored his energies. Her Majesty's Government promised to furnish ships of the Royal Navy to "take what soundings may be considered needful" and to "favorably consider any request that may be made to furnish aid by their vessels in laying down the cable."

The government also agreed to pay the company £14,000 a year (4 percent on capital) as remuneration for government messages until such time as the net profits of the company attained 6 percent, after which the annual payment would be reduced to £10,000 per annum for the next twenty-five years "from the time of the completion of the line, and so long as [the cable] shall continue in working order." In the blink of an eye, the Atlantic Telegraph Company secured its first customer—providing the cable worked.[14]

While Field traveled about England, Morse continued to work with Bright and Whitehouse on electrical problems. For Morse, Bright acted as another Joseph Henry. He could solve problems that Morse could only discuss as concepts. The subject quickly turned to what kind of conducting wire to use. On October 10 Morse enthusiastically advised Field:

> There can be no question but that, with a cable containing a single conducting wire, of a size not exceeding that through which we worked, and with equal insulation, it would be easy to telegraph from Ireland to Newfoundland at a speed of at least ten words per minute . . . and allowing ten words for name and address, we can safely calculate upon the transmission of a twenty-word message in three minutes; twenty such messages an hour; four hundred and eighty in twenty-four hours, or fourteen thousand four hundred words per day.[15]

At this early stage, Morse clearly envisioned great profits flowing from his patented devices into his bank account. He no longer hedged his opinions with "practicable" or "practical." He became a man of unstinted optimism, writing: "I can no longer have any misgivings about the ease and safety with which [the cable] will be submerged. In one word, the doubts are resolved, the difficulties overcome, success is within our reach, and the great feat of the century must shortly be accomplished." Morse needed money, so he added, "I would urge you, if the manufacture can be completed within the time, (and all things are possible now), to press forward the good work, and not to lose the chance of laying it during the [forthcoming] summer."[16]

Field listened to Morse, perhaps a little too closely at times. He also listened to other advisers, among them Faraday, who differed with Morse over the conductor. In 1856 the laws governing the flow and retardation of current were not understood. The retardation of the flow of electrical current in a long wire covered by insulation and shielded by metal wires involved a new phenomenon that became the subject of research by Faraday, Morse, Whitehouse, and an eventual newcomer to the enterprise, Dr. William Thomson—a somewhat shy, scholarly professor of massive intelligence who became the foremost mathematical physicist of the day and eventually a director of the company.

Thomson, thirty-two years of age, had a slightly mousy and unassertive manner men like Whitehouse and Faraday squelched with authoritative bluster. Without the bravado of his peers, Thomson had quietly established one of the world's first experimental laboratories at Glasgow University. In 1846, at the age of twenty-two, the university appointed him to the chair in natural philosophy, a position he would hold for fifty-three years. By the age of thirty he was making major contributions in thermodynamics, geophysics, astronomy, optics, magnetism, and electricity. He entered the field of telegraphy through a study of transient currents and electric oscillations using mathematical analysis. When drawn into the small circle of the Atlantic Telegraph Company, he had yet to prove some of his theories and held no technical position in the enterprise, being subordinate to Bright

Professor William Thomson, who eventually became Lord Kelvin of Krags, as he appeared later in life when he taught at Glasgow University. Thomson became one of the pioneers in the dynamics of telegraphy. (From Edward Brailsford Bright, *The Life Story of the Late Sir Charles Tilston Bright*. Digitized by Debra Peffer.)

and Whitehouse. Giving Whitehouse precedence over Thomson would eventually prove to be one of the Atlantic Telegraph Company's greatest blunders. A hundred years later Sir Arthur Clarke summed up Thomson's capabilities by writing, "If one took half the talents of Einstein, and half the talents of Edison, and succeeded in fusing such incompatible gifts into a single person, the result would be rather like William Thomson."[17]

Unlike a bare wire strung on poles in the open air, long insulated cables created an inductive capacitance effect that retarded the flow of current. This question would not be resolved until Thomson formulated a law for the speed of telegraphic transmission, and when he did, not everyone agreed with him. The work of Faraday and Henry on electromagnetism proved that magnetism increased as more battery power was applied, and Whitehouse misapplied the same theory to pushing signals through extremely long submarine cables.

Morse believed that "large coated wires used beneath the water or the earth are worse conductors—so far as the velocity of transmission is concerned—than small ones; and, therefore, are not so well suited as small ones for the purposes of submarine telegraph signals." Faraday said, "The larger the wire, the more electricity [is] required to charge it, and the greater [is] the retardation of that electric impulse which should be occupied in sending that charge forward." Thomson said, though not emphatically enough, that for a given conductor diameter, the transmission speed decreased as the square of the cable length increased. His equation recognized the capacitance of a wire surrounded by an insulated cover and a metallic sheath, all laid in the conducting medium of salt water, which at the time neither Henry nor Faraday understood. Whitehouse challenged all three men, arguing that regardless of wire size, transmission speed depended upon supplying the line with sufficient voltage. Thomson considered Whitehouse's theory, which Faraday somewhat supported, fallacious, and so did Bright. They both lost the debate because of the distinguished reputations of Whitehouse and Faraday. Before Thomson became a director of the company, the cable specifications were already in the hands of the fabricators with delivery set for early July. Faraday was also partly wrong on the amount of current required, but his opinion did not adversely affect the viability of the cable so much as Whitehouse's theory on the application of voltage.[18]

Bright and Thomson were both too late in announcing their theories. Field was in too much of a hurry and began placing orders for cable materials before appointing a board of directors. After examining sixty-two types of cable, the Atlantic pioneers eventually chose one with a very light core composed of seven stranded copper wires weighing 107 pounds per nautical mile and insulated with 261 pounds of gutta-percha. Bright's copper core would have weighed 392 pounds per nautical mile, together with an equal amount of gutta-percha, adding 500 tons to the weight of 2,500 miles of cable ordered by Field. Whitehouse and Morse, the two men with the most questionable scientific credentials, overruled Bright. John Merrett observed: "It is very probable that many difficulties and disasters would have been avoided if Bright's suggestion had been adopted." Of the £350,000 raised for the enterprise, £225,000 went into manufacturing the cable.[19]

For directors of the company Field and Brett promoted some of the most influential bankers and merchants in Great Britain. From London came Samuel Gurney, T. H. Brooking, and T. A. Hankey. From Liverpool came the company's chairman, Sir William Brown, with Henry Harrison, Edward Johnston, Robert Crosbie, George Maxwell, and Charles W. H. Pickering. John Pender and James Dugdale came from Manchester, and William Thomson from Glasgow. Two American merchants living in England also became directors—George Peabody and Curtis M. Lampson. Peabody's firm subscribed £10,000; Lamson personally subscribed £2,000. On December 9, 1856, the directors met for the first time. The entire board was animated by the enterprise, so much so that they all agreed to accept no compensation. Into this mix of men came George Saward, the company's hardworking secretary and the organ of communication between the directors, the press, and the public.

With the organization in place and the design of the cable resolved, Field booked passage home. Before he departed he forwarded a copy of the company's agreement with Parliament to Cooper and asked him to draft a letter to President Franklin Pierce, indicating that the company wished to enter into a similar arrangement of rights and privileges with the United States. Cooper complied, and on December 15 sent the president a copy of the British agreement, stating the company's "earnest desire to secure for the United States Government equal privileges."[20]

Field made an interim stop at Newfoundland because steamers carrying messages to New York were not calling at St. John's; nor were projected revenues flowing into the company. Field wanted to increase the volume, even though he expected to have the Atlantic cable working by summer. Before leaving London he distributed a thirteen-page circular encouraging steamers to stop at St. John's and offered a subsidy of one dollar for each message they brought. Anticipating a sudden increase in volume, he wanted to make sure the Newfoundland telegraphers processed the messages expeditiously. Tired, weather-beaten, and frustrated, he returned to New York on Christmas Day after another turbulent voyage at sea.

Too many vice presidencies in too many companies combined with fatigue to make Field forgetful. After bringing the directors up to date with the British alliance, David Field reminded him that telegraphic landing rights in Canada only applied to the New York and Newfoundland company and not to the Atlantic Telegraph Company. Field gasped at the oversight. He wished the family a merry Christmas and returned to St. John's. The steamer pitched and pounded through winter storms all the way to Newfoundland. Too seasick to eat, he never left his cabin. Using the last of his strength, he put the Atlantic Telegraph Company before the Newfoundland legislature and collapsed. A local doctor prescribed bed and ordered him to stay there. When Field heard that a steamer was leaving for New York, he packed his bags and went home.

On January 9, 1857, New York Senator William Henry Seward introduced a bill asking for the same guarantees as offered by the British to the Atlantic Telegraph Company. Seward said, "My own hope is, that after the telegraphic wire is laid, there will be no more war between the United States and Great Britain. I believe that whenever such a connection as this shall be made, we diminish the chances of war." The words took on a more prophetic meaning when in 1861 Seward became secretary of state in the Lincoln administration and spent the Civil War years quibbling at long range with the British ministry over aid to the Confederacy. Seward's efforts brought little succor to Field's efforts to unload his surplus stock. Americans showed little interest in the enterprise and purchased only twenty-seven shares.[21]

At first the Senate opposed the bill, and Matthew Maury feared a deadlock in both chambers. He wrote Field, offering rooms at the observatory, "Bring Morse, Mr. Cooper and a few others. I think that by waiting on the President in a body we might well render the world . . . some service."[22]

Though still suffering from his Newfoundland voyage, Field accepted Maury's offer but Cooper declined. Cooper had been connecting the domestic lines of the newly formed Western Union and four other independent companies to the American Telegraph Company's network. To Morse's annoyance, Cooper standardized the continental telegraph on Hughes instruments that printed words on a paper tape. Fortunately for Field, Morse directed his venom at Cooper, who he considered the most treacherous man in the company. To Morse's attacks Cooper calmly replied, "It should be our ambition as well as our pride not to allow the paltry questions of *meum* and *teum* to dwarf the noble enterprise of working the electric telegraph around the world by the machinery best adapted to accomplish that end." Cooper's calming words did not change Morse's bitter attitude toward the American Telegraph Company. Though constantly complaining, Morse remained active in the enterprise, while Cooper, by holding Hughes patents, continued to buy access to Morse's lines at a cheap price.[23]

Cooper used his junior partner, Abram Hewitt, to urge members of Congress to support the cable. Field worked through Seward and the president, but he also worked the Senate chambers. His constant presence and his relentless badgering of senators came close to killing the legislation. There were men in the Senate from the South who wanted nothing to do with England or Englishmen. Other legislators ridiculed an expensive alliance with the British, against whom they had fought two wars and still seemed to be anticipating another. Fearing that Field's unremitting harassment of the Senate would kill the bill, Seward privately asked him to withdraw from the hallways and go to his room.

Southern senators condemned the legislation as unconstitutional. Senator Judah Benjamin of Louisiana, who four years later would become attorney general for the Confederate States and seek alliances with Great Britain, declared: “I should as soon think of questioning the constitutional power of the Government to pay freight to a vessel for carrying its mail-bags across the ocean, as to pay a telegraph company a certain sum per annum for conveying its messages by the use of the electric telegraph.”[24]

Peter Cooper had already covered this contingency in the company’s memorial to the president, writing: “Such a contract will, we suppose, fall within the provisions of the Constitution in regard to postal arrangements, of which this is only a new and improved form.” Senator Thomas F. Bayard of Delaware agreed with Cooper, explaining that a transoceanic cable

> is a mail operation. It is a Post Office arrangement. It is for the transmission of intelligence, and that is what I understand to be the function of the Post-Office department. I hold it, therefore, to be as legitimately within the powers of the Government, as the employing of a stage-coach, or a steam-car, or a ship, to transport the mails, either to foreign countries, or to different portions of our own country.

Attorney General Caleb Cushing declared the bill sound, throwing a few more coals into the fiery storm brewing between the North and the South.[25]

After six weeks of debate, the Senate passed the bill by one vote. The House eventually passed it by eighteen votes. At 10:00 A.M. on March 3, 1857, Field stood at Pierce’s side as the president, on his last full day in office, signed the bill. Field got what he wanted. The bill provided a maximum subsidy of $70,000 per year until the company’s profits equaled six percent of the investment; thereafter the annual subsidy would fall to $50,000. The term of the contract: twenty-five years.[26]

While Field attended to neglected affairs in the United States, the directors of the company in England proceeded with the manufacture of the cable. Like Field, they were in a rush to have everything ready by July 6, 1857, so the actual laying could commence during the July 20–August 10 calm period recommended by Maury. Such haste created compromises, and no single firm in England could produce 2,500 nautical miles of cable in the time allotted.

Brett wanted a cable more flexible than the one he lost in 1855 between Sardinia and Algeria—a cable so stiff and unwieldy that when it broke it whipped out the back of the ship with such velocity that no mechanism could check its fatal plunge into the sea. All was going well, Brett recalled, when suddenly “about two miles [of cable], weighing sixteen tons, flew out with the greatest violence in four or five minutes, flying around even when the drums were brought to a dead stop, creating the greatest alarm for the safety of the men in the hold and for the vessel.” Brett attributed the loss to tension on the paying-out machinery caused by irregularities in the seabed of the Mediterranean. The experience served as a warning to the company.[27]

Morse, Bright, and Whitehouse finally settled on the conductor, and the company adopted Brunel's recommendations of stranding the outer armoring. The final design provided for a cable not so heavy as to become unmanageable in the sea or so light as to lend itself to breakage. The cable would weigh a ton per mile, just enough heavier than the weight of water displaced as it sank.

On December 6, 1856, three firms each received a portion of the contract. At a cost of £40 per mile, Samuel Statham of the Gutta Percha Company agreed to supply 2,500 miles of copper conductor core covered with three layers of insulation. For the balance of the work the company split a £62,000 armoring contract, giving 1,250 miles to Glass, Elliot & Company of East Greenwich, and the other half to Newall & Company at Birkenhead. Neither firm could begin work until the Gutta Percha Company went into production and began shipping conductor.

The summer deadline drove the decision to split the armoring contract, and Field refused to wait another year. Bright and Thomson questioned whether it was possible to achieve uniformity of supervision if half the cable was armored at East Greenwich and the other half at Birkenhead. They also worried whether the cable's tensile strength or conducting power would be uniform, and whether two different companies would test the cable properly. Bright discovered too late that the armor twisted around the conductor ran right to left from one company and left to right from the other. This error could have been avoided, but as Bright wrote some forty years later, "the methods of those days were primitive as compared with present practice, and a system of electrical testing altogether wanting."[28]

Yet the work commenced. The cable adopted contained a central conductor composed of six copper wires twisted into a strand around a center wire. The strand itself was little more than a sixteenth of an inch in diameter, but 20,500 miles of .028-inch copper wire went into making the conductor. The center wire was drawn straight through a hole from a stationary drum behind a rotating horizontal table. Six drums on a steam-driven rotary table then wrapped .028-inch wire into a .083-inch strand around the center wire. The machine operated at great speed and only shut down when a drum ran out of wire. As the strands came off the production line, workmen rolled them up and fed them into a collection drum. The copper used to make the strand was periodically assayed for uniformity, but in 1857 chemical and mechanical properties of metal could not be accurately determined. The strand also received periodic break tests, and if stretched to 20 percent of its length without parting, the batch went to the gutta-percha coating area.

The twisted form of conductor offered many advantages over solid wire. With seven wires to conduct electricity, the little wires could break in hundreds of places, and unless they all broke in the same place, electric impulses would continue to flow.

Charles Bright, one of the pioneers of submarine cable technology, at the time of the first cable-laying expedition in 1857. (From Edward Brailsford Bright, *The Life Story of the Late Sir Charles Tilston Bright*. Digitized by Debra Peffer.)

Gutta-percha could be mixed in many consistencies. To diminish the influence of induction the company made the substance unusually thick. Workmen put the raw material through a revolving toothed cylinder to remove lumps before passing it through rollers into a mixer filled with hot water. When churned to the consistency of glue, the batch passed through a cold-water rinse before being heated to the temperature of boiling water and driven by hydraulic pressure through sieves fastened to the bottom of vertical pipes. The gutta-percha passed into a kneading machine where blades revolving in a trough masticated the material for hours to remove water. Once the material reached the desired consistency and purity, workers moved it into heated chambers where pistons, working inside cylinders, extruded the insulation through dies. Drums revolving around the cylinders fed the copper strands through the center of the die. The naked strand entered the die a bright copper color and issued from it a thick, dull-colored cord coated with gutta-percha. The seven strands making up the core received three coatings of insulation. The gutta trees of Malaya paid a dear price. Three hundred tons of their polymeric sap went into the cable.

As each batch came off the coating line, workers cut the core into two-mile lengths, immersed it in water, and tested the continuity and insulation. To test continuity, inspectors attached one end of the length to a low-power voltaic current, causing an impulse to register at the opposite end. To test the insulation they wound the core around a very sensitive horizontal galvanometer and turned the opposite end into the air. If the insulation was flawless, the battery would form one pole and the unattached end the other. If no current passed through the line, the galvanometer would not deflect. If current leaked through the insulation, it would go to ground, and the needle of the galvanometer—a term used to describe any instrument that measured the movement of electrical current—would deflect. The greater the deflection, the greater the amount of current passing to ground, and the amount of loss became a measure of the core's imperfection.

As each two-mile length passed inspection, workmen immersed it in a canal outside the Gutta Percha works. After fifty lengths had been tested, the company joined the ends together by brazing the core and insulating the joints. To splice the cable, workmen scraped the gutta-percha from the end of the strands of the two cores and overlapped them. A small piece of copper wire was placed on the joined strands and brazed to the ends. After the joint cooled, operators hand applied several layers of gutta-percha and sealed it using hot irons. Inspectors then subjected the 100-mile length to more tests before recutting it into two-mile lengths for shipment.

The company wound each two-mile length of core onto a flanged drum having wheels shod with tires. Covered by a protective coat of gutta-percha, the drums could be wheeled about or dragged without injury to the core and shipped to Greenwich or Birkenhead for armoring.

Both armoring firms—Glass, Elliot and R. S. Newell—operated much the same way. Laborers mounted the core-filled drums in rows on an axle so when one drum emptied the next could be quickly attached. When considering that each company had to connect and process two-mile lengths of core into 1,250 nautical miles of cable and have it ready by early July, they had to hurry.

As the core rolled off the drum, a machine of revolving bobbins wrapped it with hemp saturated with a composition of tar, pitch, linseed oil, and wax. The hemp protected the core from damage during the wrapping of the stranded metallic iron wires. Before a drum ran out of core, workers spliced the end strands to the next drum using exactly the same procedure as the Gutta Percha Company.

The cable-armoring operation consisted of a horizontal rotating table through which the wrapped core was lifted vertically by rollers onto a wide pulley turning overhead. Mounted near the outer edges of the table were eighteen bobbins feeding eighteen strands of bright charcoal iron wire. Each bobbin had two motions: one around its horizontal axis, and one around an upright pivot positioned to always deliver its strand in the same sequence to the passing conductor. The table rotated rapidly around the hemp-covered core, depositing an iron seven-strand wire in exactly the place with every rotation. The armor-feeding machine wrapped eighteen iron strands around the core in one revolution of the table.

Both companies operated several stranding machines, giving the work the appearance of many spiders spinning conical webs at great speed until the wires came together in a single strand. Had a single wire of the same diameter been used instead of a strand, the cable would not have been as flexible or strong.

Each stranding machine worked night and day spinning ninety-eight miles of wire into fourteen miles of strand. With all twenty-one machines working, the company could produce 294 miles of strand a day. The armoring machines could outproduce the stranding machines and produce thirty miles of cable a day. Using the 340,500 miles of wire that went into armoring 2,500 miles of cable 5/8-inch in diameter, the earth's circumference could have been girdled fifteen times.

As the finished cable came off the winding machines, laborers drew it through the factory wall and into a cistern filled with pitch and tar. They coiled the cable in tanks in the outer yard and brushed it again with pitch and tar. The two factories each produced four cables three hundred miles long, and there they laid, ready for transfer to a receiving ship. The cable weighed a ton per nautical mile—in water 1,340 pounds—and could withstand a strain of about 6,500 pounds before breaking, or about five miles of its weight suspended in water. When completed, inspectors spliced the entire cable together and tested it with a 500-cell battery—never realizing that a single-cell battery could have done the same.

Bright specified that the shore-ends of the cable be provided with extra protection. Instead of being armored with .083-inch strands, the cable makers used twelve wires of .340 inches, thereby increasing the weight of the shore-end to nine tons per mile. Ten miles of the heavier cable were to be laid from Ireland's shore, and 15 miles laid from Newfoundland's shore, where Dayman reported the coastal area filled with rocks.

All the company needed now were ships large enough to lay this immense investment safely on the ocean's floor.[29]

— Chapter 5 —

"In the Deep Bosom of the Ocean"

On March 18, 1857, Cyrus Field began another late winter voyage to London, but he departed in a happy mood, having become the father of his second son, four-day-old Cyrus William. Having lost his first son in 1854, the newborn came as a blessing from above. Distracted by the new arrival, Field left an important piece of cable business unresolved with the navy. Though armed with Matthew Maury's recommended course for cable layers to follow, Field had no American ships, only Maury's earlier letter suggesting that "we may be able to get the *Niagara* to lay the wire . . . it will be the best service ever yet rendered by a man of war steamer."[1]

The Senate debated the use of naval vessels to lay cable with the same fervor that they had argued over the government subsidizing the wire. Stephen Douglas of Illinois wanted to accommodate cable layers and asked the Senate, "Will it cost any thing to furnish the use of one of our steamships?" Then he answered his own question, declaring,

> They are idle. We have no practical use for them at present. They are in commission. They have their coal on board, and their full armament. They will be rendering no service to us if they are not engaged in this work. . . . England tenders one of her national vessels, and why should we not tender one also? It costs England nothing, and it costs us nothing.

On so vital an issue as America's involvement in one of the most significant international projects of the century, Thomas J. Rusk of Texas laconically agreed, adding, "I think that it is better than to keep them rotting at the navy-yards, with the officers frolicking on shore."[2]

Heated opposition came from wary southern senators who believed the

United States would be relinquishing commercial advantages to a former foe. These were the same senators whose states in 1860–1861 would secede from the Union and attempt to form alliances with the British government. But in 1857 mention of England "had the same effect on them as a red rag waved before the eyes of a mad bull." They staunchly believed that England would somehow profit at America's expense. There were those who believed that "in this submarine cable England was literally crawling under the sea to get some advantage of the United States." Robert M. T. Hunter of Virginia argued that "this was not truly a line between England and the United States, but between England and her own colonies . . . [because] *both its termini were in British possessions*."[3]

Seward fought back, explaining that there was no other terminus on the continent to make a connection with Europe and that the British entered the enterprise because they anticipated no interruption of amicable relations between the two nations. In defense of the Newfoundland connection, Seward said, "There is no other route known on which the telegraphic wire could be drawn through the ocean so as to find a proper resting place as this." As to war, Seward replied

> I believe that whenever such a connection as this shall be made, we diminish the chances of war, and diminish them to such a degree, that it is not necessary to take them into consideration at the present moment. . . . The British Government, if it had such a disposition, would certainly have proposed to monopolize all this telegraphic line, instead of proposing to divide it.[4]

In addition to a monetary subsidy, and with influential help from Seward and Douglas, Field got his ships.

There were those in the House of Lords who believed Her Majesty's ministry should not have given the United States important advantages that belonged to the crown. Because both terminals were on British soil, their lordships contended that the entire project should have been financed by the ministry, and foreign governments excluded. Earl Granville, on the other hand, argued that the "telegraph was intended to connect two great countries, and, as the two Governments had gone hand in hand with regard to the guarantee, it seemed only reasonable that both should have the same rights as to transmitting messages." The House of Lords did not approve the Atlantic Telegraph Company's bill until July 20, 1857, but in Great Britain it made no difference. Unlike the legislative powers conferred by the Constitution upon Congress, in Great Britain the ministry took precedence over Parliament.[5]

When Field reached London he found cable factories spinning thousands of miles of wire with shocking swiftness. He was delighted and surprised that his English partners made such fine progress during his absence. But while running spot checks on the cable, Thomson had discovered puzzling variances in the conductivity. He attributed the problem to inconsistencies in the purity of copper and mentioned it to Field, who had approved the specifications. Field refused to stop work at the Gutta Percha works to investigate conductor problems.

Perhaps looking into the storage tanks at Glass, Elliot and seeing hundreds of miles of cable ready for shipment reminded Field that he had not received word whether the U.S. Navy would provide ships. In a hurried conversation with Charles Bright, Field agreed to return to the United States to bargain with the navy for the use of the USS *Niagara*, the best steamer, according to Maury, for the job. Bright volunteered to make arrangements with the Admiralty for the HMS *Agamemnon*, which Field had requested during a previous visit.

The sudden need to identify the cable-laying ships placed another burden on the company. Apparatus had never been designed for paying out 2,500 nautical miles of cable over water as stormy as the North Atlantic. To hurry mechanical drawings imposed another problem on the Magnetic Telegraph Company's designers because every delay threatened to extend the cable-laying timetable into the gales of late summer. Field pushed to have two paying-out machines built by the middle of April, one for each ship, though no one could tell the designers how to fit them to ships not yet committed to the expedition. Then he sailed for New York.

Launched on February 23, 1856, the 4,582-ton screw-propelled *Niagara* had not been assigned to sea duty when Field applied to Secretary of the Navy Dobbin for her use. She was the largest steam frigate in the world, bigger than any ship in the Royal Navy, and cost the government $969,736 to build. She had five boilers feeding three horizontal, direct-action engines driven by a seventy-two-inch cylinder with a thirty-six-inch stroke. In a test run she posted 14.5 knots under sail and steam. George Steers, the architect of the famous yacht *America*, which had won all the races in the English Channel, also designed *Niagara*.

Dobbin made *Niagara* available for cable laying, and to give her deck space, the secretary held up the installation of her twelve twelve-inch Dahlgren shell guns. Each gun weighed fourteen tons, threw a 130-pound shell three miles, and required a crew of twenty-five men. Without Dahlgrens her decks remained clear and unencumbered except for four signal guns. Relieving *Niagara* of her arms lightened her by 270 tons and created extra cable-carrying capacity. She would be on an enterprise of peace, and the cable-laying mission would give her a good shakedown cruise.[6]

Because one vessel would not be enough, Dobbin added the 2,450-ton USS *Susquehanna*, a seven-year-old side-wheel steamer with a bark rig. *Susquehanna* carried a full deck of guns—150-pounder Parrotts and twelve-inch Dahlgrens—and she would serve *Niagara* as a consort. Knowing that both ships would be in the company of the Royal Navy, Dobbin chose two of the most impressive vessels in the U.S. Navy's floating arsenal.[7]

The British government demonstrated far more interest in the Atlantic cable than the typical American. The Admiralty committed the screw-propelled, line-of-battle ship HMS *Agamemnon* the moment Bright asked for her. She had been Lord Lyons' flagship during the bombardment of Sevastopol during the Crimean War. Her name carried special significance to the rare historian who remembered that King Agamemnon executed the first sea-bridging system of telegraphy by announcing to his queen the fall of Troy—1,084 years before the birth of Christ—by using a series of fires on mountaintops to island-hop over the Aegean to his palace in Mycenae. The battle-scarred *Agamemnon* would now do more to bring peace among nations by uniting them with a telegraphic cord.

The Admiralty chose *Agamemnon* because her peculiar construction made her ideally suited for the work. Her enormous hold amidships—forty-five-feet square and twenty-feet deep—could store almost 1,200 miles of cable. To accompany *Agamemnon* the Admiralty added the HMS *Leopard* and the HM sounding-vessel *Cyclops*, which, having been over the cable course twice, would lead the way. The generous offer came at a time when Britain was at war in China and suppressing mutinies in India. The press mirthfully referred to the five vessels as the Wire Squadron, and the name caught hold.[8]

Maury had recommended that the two ships meet in the middle of the Atlantic, splice the cable, and depart: *Niagara* for Newfoundland and *Agamemnon* for Ireland. Bright suggested doing the same. After the splice, the two ships could remain in communication by wire as they steamed in opposite directions. Wildman Whitehouse overruled both men, arguing that it was more important to keep in contact with shore. Therefore, Whitehouse said, the cable must be connected at Valentia, the first half carried to the middle of the Atlantic by the *Niagara* and spliced to the *Agamemnon* for the final leg to St. John's. Whitehouse excused himself from the voyage, explaining that it would be better if he stayed in communication with the Wire Squadron from Valentia.

On April 22, 1857, Captain William L. Hudson, commanding *Niagara*, sailed for England from the Brooklyn Navy Yard. Field followed a few days later on the steamer *Persia*. While at Brooklyn, Hudson had carpenters knock down the bulkheads so the cable could be stored between the beams. Chief Engineer William E. Everett came along to supervise the building of *Niagara*'s paying-out machinery. Samuel Morse hitched a ride as electrician for the New York, Newfoundland company. The navy no longer allowed correspondents on board, but Morse brought John Mullaly, who posed as his secretary while doubling as a reporter for the New York *Herald*. Mullaly became the chronicler of the expedition, and on the voyage across the Atlantic, he wrote, "the long swells were scarcely felt on the ship—a walk upon the deck is a luxury which Broadway, with all its varied beauties and attractions, could not surpass." Two curious officers of the Russian Navy joined the cruise as observers, Captain Schwartz and Lieutenant Kolobin, who admitted having more than a passive interest in cable laying.[9]

On May 14 Captain Hudson cast anchor off Gravesend, twenty-five miles below London. Many years had passed since the last American warship entered the Thames. Huge crowds assembled along the bank to view her enormous proportions. Hudson made everyone welcome, and from morning until night a fleet of small boats ferried men, women, and children out to the ship. Among them came Lady Franklin, widow of Arctic explorer Sir John Franklin. She made a special visit to thank America for sending two expeditions to search for her husband, who had perished with his crew during a polar expedition to find the Northwest Passage. The visitors climbed the ladder, gawked at the gunless ports, chatted with the crew, and confessed surprise that the United States should have such a ship.[10]

A few days later the HMS *Agamemnon*, commanded by Captain C.T.A. Noddal, steamed into the Thames. She came up the river in grand style, and when her crew recognized the *Niagara* lying off Gravesend, they gave her a series of blood-stirring hurrahs that only British tars can give. American sailors replied in kind, renting the air with cheers. Had stubborn senators from the South been on hand to witness the hearty goodwill that existed between the two nations, they may not have argued so fiercely to block the cable legislation.

Captain Joshua R. Sands, commanding *Susquehanna*, steamed into Gravesend from the Mediterranean and anchored near *Niagara*. She was a fit companion and a worthy American representative. For the first time, the largest propeller ship and the largest side-wheeler of the U.S. Navy lay side by side, a cable length's apart, in England's famous Thames.

Like everything in the enterprise, engineers who designed the paying-out apparatus did so in a hurry. The only machines in existence were those used to lay a few hundred miles of cable in shallow water. None of them worked well. They ran too fast, braked too hard, and needed constant attention to keep from kinking or parting the cable.

For working in the rollers of the Atlantic, the company needed paying-out machines that could be modulated to the rise and fall of the ship's stern. Messrs. C. de Bergue & Company thought they had a design that would contend with the ocean's variables. Instead, they produced a powerful five-wheel arrangement festooned with sheaves that could break a cable if the handwheel operator suffered a lapse of concentration and overactuated the frame-clutch controlling the brake. The company also designed unique guards to fit over the ship's propellers to prevent fouling the cable if the vessel went astern. Sailors nicknamed the guard "crinoline" because

The USS *Niagara* (foreground) and the USS *Susquehanna* steaming out of Gravesend to lay the 1857 cable. *Niagara* carried 1,265 nautical miles of cable. (Courtesy of the U.S. Naval Historical Center. Digitized by Debra Peffer.)

it resembled the apron of iron bands that formed the popular hoopskirt in ladies' undergarments.

The mix-ups began shortly after *Niagara* arrived. At Glass, Elliot laborers waited to transfer the cable into her hold, but because of her great length Captain Hudson could not bring her alongside the company's wharf. Field sent *Niagara* around to pick up Newell & Company's cable at Birkenhead, which had been scheduled to go on *Agamemnon*. On June 5 *Niagara* sailed from Gravesend for Birkenhead but stopped at Portsmouth the next day for more alterations. Having seen the immense length of cable waiting for the ship at East Greenwich, Captain Hudson believed *Niagara* needed more scooping out. Carpenters at Portsmouth tore out the officer's quarters to make more room for cable, and Chief Engineer Everett fitted the paying-out machinery to the afterdeck.

On June 22 *Niagara* reached Liverpool and cast her anchor in the Mersey. The town turned out to greet the American vessel, and once again thousands of sightseers clambered aboard for a tour. The Mayor of Liverpool gave a dinner, the Chamber of Commerce another, and on the Fourth of July Americans in Liverpool organized a grand banquet—the first public celebration of America's national holiday ever held in the city.

Most of the crew spent endless hours in the ship pulling cable into the hold and carefully arranging it in one continuous coil. Stalwart sailors numbering 120 formed the cable-coiling party. Hudson divided them into two groups of sixty and subdivided each group into two watches of thirty men.

In a gut-wrenching hand-pulling effort that lasted three weeks, the watches relieved each other until the last strand of cable flopped into the hold. To celebrate the occasion, the four directors of the Atlantic Telegraph Company residing in Liverpool feted the officers of *Niagara* and *Susquehanna* to a final dinner. The weary tars missed the banquet but enjoyed one last fling in the city.[11]

At East Greenwich, the sailors drawing the Glass, Elliot half of the cable into *Agamemnon* finished about the same time. They received help from a steam donkey engine that fed the cable into the ship. Sir Culling Eardley, though not financially involved in the project, hosted a festival on the picturesque grounds of his private park. Glass, Elliot chipped in, raised tents on the lawn, and invited their employees and the sailors to the affair. Sir Culling arranged the tables in a great semicircle, with three center tables for the crew of *Agamemnon*. The chairman of the banquet prepared a long list of toasts. Samuel Morse added his comments, extolling the great event about to occur on the high seas. Cyrus Field read a letter from President Buchanan, suggesting that the first message "be one from Queen Victoria to himself," and that he "would endeavor to answer it in a spirit and manner becoming a great occasion." T. H. Brooking, one of the company's directors, praised Field and the men of *Agamemnon*. With each toast jack-tar drank liberally from his three pints of beer. The mugs emptied long before the toasts ended, leaving jack with a good feeling but still thirsty.[12]

When *Agamemnon* weighed anchor and started down the Thames, thousands of spectators thronged the banks as far as Greenwich Hospital. To a brisk salute fired by the man of war, the crowd responded with deafening cheers. As smoke cleared, jack-tar manned the gunwales and with lusty lungs returned the cheer. The revelry never stopped until the ship steamed out of sight.

After the festivities ended, the next phase of work began. The cablemen on *Agamemnon* tested the paying-out machinery on their way to Queenstown, located on the southeastern coast of Ireland. The crew attached a thirteen-inch shell to the end of a spare coil and dropped it into the sea to check the strain on the dynamometer. After paying out cable at different speeds, a donkey machine retrieved the wire. Trials continued the following day with *Agamemnon* running at six knots, "all on board being more than ever satisfied at the success of the enterprise."[13]

At Liverpool *Niagara* and *Susquehanna* weighed anchor, steamed down St. George's Channel, and set a course for Queenstown to rendezvous with the Wire Squadron. On July 30 the British ships arrived, and on the following day electricians took a cable end off *Niagara* and connected it to the cable on *Agamemnon*, thereby joining together for the first time all 2,500 nautical miles of wire for a final test. For two days electricians performed a variety of experiments and declared the cable in perfect working order. Thomson demurred and expressed guarded concern over the continuity of the conductor, but Whitehouse and his experts disagreed, voicing the equivalent of "all's well."

To Whitehouse's credit, his electrical staff consisted of seven men who would one day become the foremost authorities on submarine cables in the world, but on this expedition they were still creeping up the learning curve. Men like C. V. de Sauty, Benjamin Smith, and Frank Lambert already knew more about telegraphic transmissions than Whitehouse. Whitehouse diminished Thomson, who probably knew more about electricity than all the experts combined, to the role of consultant and told him to do or say nothing unless asked. He also relegated the resourceful de Sauty, who had been the principal figure in laying the Black Sea cable during the Crimean War, to the role of electrical technician. De Sauty had also helped Canning lay the Gulf of St. Lawrence cable. Whitehouse, pleading illness, begged off the expedition, leaving shipboard oversight to his subordinates.

On the mechanical side, Bright's engineers consisted of Canning, perhaps the best cable layer in the world; William Henry Woodhouse, who had laid cables in the Mediterranean; and Henry Clifford, a mechanical engineer whose name would be linked to the cables of the future. Both teams, mechanical and electrical, were equally divided between the two cable-laying ships. Field still thought the ships should meet in the middle of the Atlantic, but Whitehouse prevailed and the decision to begin the expedition at Valentia remained unchanged.

On July 30 the cable layers sailed into Doulus Bay, where Valentia Island, located on the southwestern shore of Ireland, provided the staging area for the Wire Squadron. There they found the tender *Advice* and the steamtug *Willing Mind*, both sent by the Admiralty to assist in bringing the cable ashore. On the following day *Cyclops* arrived and the work commenced.

Across the Atlantic at Trinity Bay, Lieutenant Berryman waited with *Arctic* and the paddle wheeler *Victoria*. The crew at Newfoundland expected the Wire Squadron to already be well across the Atlantic. Canning had picked the site in Newfoundland, the beautiful pine-girded waters of Bull's Arm Bay, eighty miles long and thirty miles wide, with a cozy sandy beach nestled at the far end. Inland from the beach carpenters built a frame structure to house the instruments that would connect the cable to St. John's. There the technicians waited, watching the bay for the smoke of the Wire Squadron.

Maury picked the starting time, July 20, but fourteen days had already passed. Field and Bright wanted to get to sea, but Lord Lieutenant, Earl of Carlisle, who had journeyed from Dublin to act as the queen's representative, and Sir Peter Fitzgerald, the Knight of Kerry and lord of the manor for many miles around, waited at Valentia with hundreds of spectators to wish the expedition success. Fitzgerald flung open the doors of his estate to members of the historic gathering.

At night the rocky heights above Doulus Bay blazed with bonfires, and from *Niagara* sailors could hear the sound of country people singing their Gaelic songs as they danced on shore. In the morning, officers and their crews came ashore to attend a festive public breakfast given in their honor. To a toast given in recognition of his hospitality, the Knight of Kerry responded by saying:

> We are about, either by this sundown or by to-morrow's dawn, to establish a new link between the Old world and the New. Moral links there have been—links of race, links of commerce, links of friendship, links of literature, links of glory; but this, our new link, instead of superseding and supplanting old ones, is to give a life and intensity which they never had before.[14]

Loud cheers echoed across the bay. The stirring speech deserved to be read in the U.S. Senate to mollify southern senators, but in 1857 such eloquence seldom strayed far from the locality of its origin.

The Earl of Carlisle added disconcerting but prophetic words, though he meant no harm, when he declared: "Though disappointment might be in store for the promoters, it would be almost criminal to feel discouragement [when] the pathway to great achievements has frequently been hewn out amidst perils and difficulties, and that preliminary failure is ever the law and condition of ultimate success." Cyrus Field understood the truth of the statement. At great expense he had suffered those "perils" before and wanted no more visitations of the same.[15]

On August 4 the directors and engineers met and decided how to lay the cable at Valentia, carry it to midocean, splice it, and have *Agamemnon* carry it to Newfoundland. But first they had to get the massive shore end, which weighed ten tons a mile, out of *Niagara* and hauled over the rocks into the cove of Ballycarberry where Whitehouse's telegraph station stood. Choosing an American vessel to land the line in Ireland was more ceremonial than necessary, but the gesture did not go unnoticed by the press.[16]

Preparations came to a halt during the afternoon when a fresh breeze began blowing off the ocean. The wind howled all evening, and the Wire Squadron lost another day getting the cable ashore. Work resumed on August 5, and at two o'clock sailors on *Niagara* began uncoiling the cable and passing it over the stern to boats below. Vessels filled with spectators converged on the work parties, and in their eagerness to help, got in the way.

Boats aligned themselves behind *Niagara*, the first taking the shore end. Others fell in behind the leader, each grasping a hold as a flotilla of navy and fishing boats pulled toward the cove. The lord lieutenant stood on the beach at White Strand with his staff and guests, awaiting the shore end. As the first boat bumped aground at the strand, an American sailor jumped into the surf holding a hawser tied to the cable and handed it to the lord lieutenant. More than a hundred men stepped out of the crowd to help pull the heavy shore-end up to the telegraph shack.

That evening, Whitehouse made the connection and sent a series of clear signals back to *Niagara*. The large crowd waiting at the shack gave a rollicking cheer. As night fell the lord lieutenant made another speech, but this time the crowd demanded a few words from Cyrus Field. "I have no words to express the feelings which fill my heart tonight," he said. "It beats with love and affection for every man, woman and child who hears me." He promised them all a true welcome if they ever came to America and presented themselves at his door. In words befitting a marriage of another kind, he closed by saying, "What God has joined together, let not man put asunder."[17]

The cablemen returned to their ships to sail in the morning, but in the village of Kingston the Knight of Kerry hosted a final grand ball. Field could hear the noise in his stateroom and could not sleep. He went topside and walked the deck. He peeked into the hold to make certain no diabolical spirit had stolen his treasure. Drums of coiled cable, stacked three high from the bottom of the hold to the deck, ran like giant anthills from the bow to the paying-out machinery aft.

August 6 dawned bright off Valentia, and the engines of the squadron began to softly throb. Sounds of the merrymakers could still be heard, carried to sea by the offshore breeze. A few revelers loitered on the beach. They huddled around bonfires and watched the ships weigh anchor. When they waved, a few sailors waved back, expecting good-byes to be the last for weeks to come.

For the cablemen on *Niagara* there had been little time to practice. As the ship got underway the wheels of the paying-out machinery clattered and rotated, drawing cable through pulleys strung from the forward hold down the vessel to the stern. The cable watch stood like sentries at each pulley, ensuring that every hank of cable reached the next station undamaged. As the machinery turned it emitted squeaks and groans, like a creature not yet awake. Mechanics squirted the gears with oil, and the drums and sheaves settled into a throaty rumble.

The cable lay in huge coils wound with care around a central core. To get the cable through the paying-out machine, it traveled around four grooved sheaves five feet in diameter, set vertically on a horizontal plane, one in front of the other. A friction drum between the second and third sheave acted as a clutch. The sheaves were geared together by cogs and bolted firmly on girders to stay in alignment. An engineer kept a wary eye on the needle that measured the tension on the cable. A mechanic stood by the handwheel that turned the screw that tightened or loosened the braking mechanism. The latter consisted of two blocks of hardwood that gripped the brake drum, and a turn of the wheel could accelerate or decelerate the rotation of the sheaves dispensing the cable.

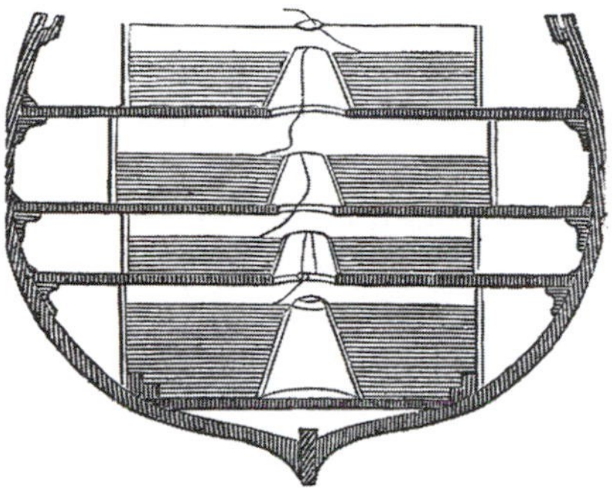

SECTION OF THE NIAGARA, SHOWING THE STOWAGE OF THE COILS IN THE FOREPART OF THE SHIP.

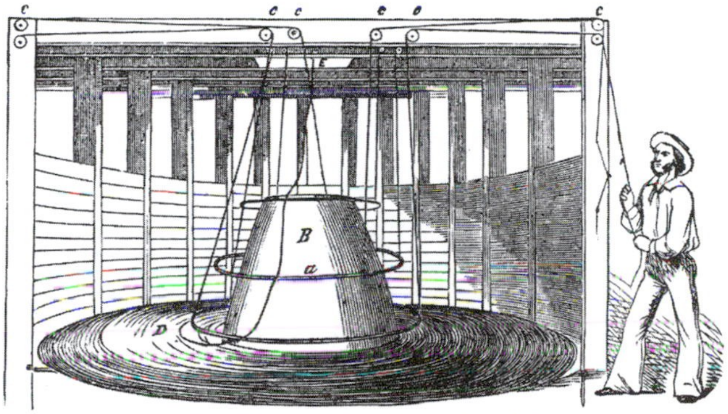

THE CABLE CIRCUS, THE CONE AND FAIR-LEADERS.

a—Large iron rings for fair-leaders and to prevent kinking.
B—Cone.
c—Pulleys with iron tricing lines for raising fair-leaders.
D—Portion of cone coiled.
E—Hatchway with the cable going up.

The four-deck stowage arrangement for the cable on the USS *Niagara*. The top figure shows the top end of each coil connected to the bottom end of the coil above. The bottom figure shows an arrangement of iron rings that prevented the cable from kinking. (From Charles Bright, *The Story of the Atlantic Cable*. Digitized by Debra Peffer.)

Controlling the paying-out machinery became a two-man job with an engineer relaying orders to the brakeman. From this apparatus the cable passed several feet above the poop deck to a fifth sheave cantilevered on rigid arms protruding over the stern. There the cable made its plunge into the sea. As the wire descended into the deep, the electrical department transmitted signals every second, back and forth, between the cable ship and Whitehouse's electricians on shore.

The paying-out machinery worked best when the ship maintained a constant speed. To measure the speed of *Niagara*, a patent log dragged in the water off the ship's beam. A wheel in the immersed log generated an electric impulse with each revolution. A wire covered with gutta-percha transmitted signals to an instrument on deck that translated the impulses into the ship's speed. As long as the sea remained calm, a brakeman encountered no problems, but in rough weather everything changed, making it necessary to constantly adjust the handbrake to the rise and fall of the stern.

The engineers established a procedure for slipping the cable off the paying-out machinery in an emergency. The decks of both cable-laying vessels contained two large reels with five miles of wire rope capable of holding ten tons of weight. Engineers believed there would always be enough time to cut the cable, clamp the end to the wire rope, hold the ship in the area until the emergency passed, and then reel the line back into the ship. Engineers and electricians believed they had considered all the possible hazards and could do no more. Two men worried more than the others—William Thomson, whose warnings about the conductivity of the wire aroused no concern; and Samuel Morse, who lay in bed with an injured leg listening to the rumble of the paying-out machinery and an occasional thump of a splice rolling through the sheaves.

At Queenstown, when transferring from *Agamemnon* to *Niagara*, Morse barely escaped going overboard. Using the wobbly legs of a landlubber, he had to crawl across several boats to reach *Niagara*. Three inches of skin scraped off his shin when his leg slipped between the gunwales of two boats. "It pained me a little," Morse recalled, "still I knew from experience that . . . I should be laid up the next day and possibly for several days."[18]

The seas had risen before *Niagara* got underway, and Morse, after struggling to his cabin, wrote his wife:

> The deck is a bewildering mass of machinery, steam-engines, cog-wheels, breaks, boilers, ropes of hemp and ropes of wire, cylinders of wood and cylinders of iron, meters of all kinds, anemometers, thermometers, barometers, electrometers, steam-gauges, speed-measurers, strain-gauges . . . and, thus freighted, we expect to disgorge our [cable] before reaching mid-ocean.[19]

The ink had barely dried on the letter when, after paying out five miles of cable, the wire slipped a sheave and broke. Hudson stopped the ship and hailed the *Willing Mind*. Morse hobbled to the deck grimacing with pain. *Willing Mind* returned to White Strand, grappled the cable, underran (picking up at the bows and relaying over the stern) its length back to *Niagara*, and on August 7 passed the severed end to the ship. Morse sat in a chair and supervised the splice. Electricians cut the end clean, brazed the connectors together, wrapped the spliced ends in gutta-percha, and added armoring. Morse tested the connection and, finding the circuit sound, signaled the captain to get underway. A quartermaster, watching as the splice splashed into the sea, turned to a gathering of observers and said, "I tell you what, that was a hard tug, and I hope we won't soon have . . . another." In his journal Morse wrote: "I have seen enough to know now that the Atlantic Cable is sure to be established, *for it is practicable.*" Then he added, rather forebodingly, "*We may not succeed in our first attempt.*"[20]

To avoid a second accident, Hudson steamed ahead slowly, feeling the ship's way at two knots. Field walked the deck, seldom leaving it. He acted as the unofficial flag officer of the fleet, and Hudson rarely took exception to his wishes. The sea having calmed, the ships of the Wire Squadron kept in sight, close enough to hear each other's bells. *Susquehanna* stood a half-mile off *Niagara*'s starboard quarter; *Leopard* roamed five hundred yards off the port; and *Agamemnon*, with her massive and warlike hull, steamed slowly a mile beyond *Leopard*. *Cyclops* led the way, skittering back and forth like a playful porpoise.

To save coal, the ships unfurled their sails, but the breeze died. Even the ensigns hung from the peaks in folds. The hours passed slowly, and all went well. Far behind, the high rocks of the Skelligs were still visible above the horizon, one of Ireland's many landmarks that the mariner sees when he is looking for Dingle Bay. As the sun dropped below the horizon, the soft translucent clouds overhead turned from rose to violet, and then the stars came out. On that first day at sea barely anyone slept. Every man on board, stockholder and sailor alike, took a personal interest in getting through the night.[21]

Henry Field wrote in his narrative:

> All through that night, and through the anxious days and nights that followed, there was a feeling in every soul on board, as if a friend in the cabin were at the turning point of life or death, and they were watching beside him. There was a strange unnatural silence in the ship. Men paced the deck with soft and muffled tread, speaking only in whispers, as if a loud voice or a heavy footfall might snap the vital chord. So much had they grown to feel for the enterprise, that the cable seemed to them like a human creature, on whose fate they hung, as if it were to decide their own destiny.[22]

The constant rumble of the paying-out machinery became a salve to one's consciousness. If eyelids closed to grasp an hour's nap, the steady thrum of the sheaves, which resonated throughout the ship, became a tonic for sleep. Morse recalled that when coming awake the machinery sounded like "the purring of a great cat." Bright called it "the old coffee-mill, and, his fears being relieved, he would go to sleep again." Mullaly wrote, "The sound became as familiar to us as that of our own voices, and so long as we heard it, we knew that everything was safe."[23]

On August 8 *Niagara* carved a steady wake on a windless sea, the log reading four-and-a-half knots. The cable paid out faster than the speed of the ship, adding slack as the ocean deepened. The cablemen began to relax. To Valentia they telegraphed messages to friends and family to be carried by Liverpool steamers bound for New York.

The cable slithering out of the hold came topside without a kink, unwinding easily as it passed over the stern and into the sea. In its brief encounter with the warm sun an occasional glob of tar and pitch oozed through the armoring. It caked on sheaves, filled the grooves, and threw off the cable. Mechanics spread oil on the tar to soften it and scraped the grooves without shutting down the machinery, but the annoying problem persisted. "At our mess table," wrote Mullaly,

> [the paying-out machine] was the principal subject of conversation, and all were of the opinion that the laying of a cable across the Atlantic was not only feasible, but that it would be accomplished in the present month of August . . . Those brakes are the only things that we have to dread.[24]

During the first two days, the Wire Squadron steamed 200 miles, passing over the gradually deepening shelf off Ireland's coast. On Sunday, August 9, Berryman and Dayman's charts showed *Niagara* approaching the edge of the eastern shallows where the seabed dropped from 3,300 feet to 10,500 feet over a span of ten miles. Morse examined the charts and noticed the "depth of the ocean gradually increasing up to four hundred fathoms, and then . . . a sudden and great increase to seventeen hundred fathoms, and a further increase to two thousand and fifty, nearly the greatest depth with which we should meet in the whole distance." Such depths worried him, but before the day ended, the cable rested peacefully on a soft cushion of microscopic shells, its circuits pulsing every second through water two miles deep. Those who could be spared for Sunday services joined Captain Hudson topside and prayed to "Him who spreadeth out the heavens and ruleth the raging of the sea."[25]

The ruling sea had not been a problem. As Maury predicted there had been no storms, just gentle rollers tipped by light summer breezes. Maury's window of opportunity—July 20 to August 10—would end the following day.

At 4:00 A.M. on the morning of August 10, as the wire descended into 12,300 feet of water, Bright watched as the strain on the cable jumped from 700 pounds to 1,500 pounds. He attributed part of the tension to deepwater drag. With the paying-out machinery working well, Hudson had also increased the ship's speed to five-and-a-half knots. "We could check the speed," Morse wrote, "but it is a dangerous process." However, too little restraint could cause kinking and wastage, but allowing the cable to run beyond controllable limits might also cause it to break if paying-out

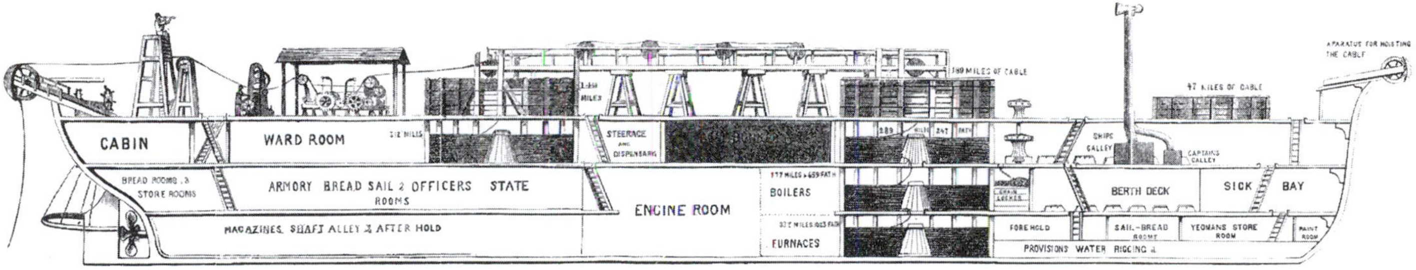

Sectional view showing cable stowage arrangement on the HMS *Agamemnon*. Note dangerous placement of coils on forward upper deck. (From Charles Bright, *The Story of the Atlantic Cable*. Digitized by Debra Peffer.)

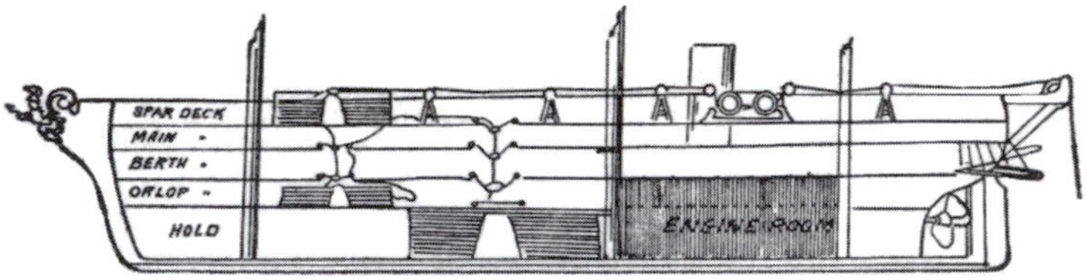

Sectional view of the USS *Niagara*, showing seven cable holds distributed between the forward holds and the paying-out machinery aft. (Courtesy of the U.S. Naval Historical Center. Digitized by Debra Peffer.)

speed was checked. Morse spoke for everyone when he said, "Hence our anxiety."[26]

During the day the breeze grew stronger, the swells increased, and the strain on the cable registered 2,000 pounds. At 6:00 P.M. the cable jumped the sheaves when a splice hurdled over a lump of dried tar. So many splices had been made during continuity tests at the factories that they became a constant hazard when winding through the sheaves. Hudson stopped the ship and hove to while mechanics, holding the cable by stoppers, cleaned the sheaves and reoriented the guards. Hudson ordered *Niagara* forward at three knots, and the cable, recovering some of its elasticity, whipped into the ocean at six knots.

At 9:00 P.M. the regular impulses suddenly ceased. Morse, fighting seasickness, hobbled down to the electrician's room with de Sauty and for several hours could not coax a signal from the instruments. The men discussed cutting the cable, or finding a way to rewind it, when suddenly the circuit came alive, making the interruption even more mysterious. Morse ventured an explanation, speculating that at some point the gutta-percha insulation had been stretched apart when the cable jumped the wheels but had resealed after reaching deeper ocean pressure. Others hypothesized that unknown creatures lurked at the bottom of the ocean and somehow disrupted the current. At least one man shed tears: the cable had become like a pet, and he did not want it to die.[27]

The unexplained incident shattered Field's nerves, and for a while he could not sleep. The constant rolling of the ship combined with the ominous incident to make him nauseous. He shook off the sensation and lapsed into troubled sleep. Morse returned to his cabin, distressed by the odd behavior of the cable. He gave up trying to explain it and wrote, "The more I contemplate this great undertaking, the more I feel my own littleness, and the more I feel the hand of God in it."[28]

The weather continued to worsen, and strain on the cable crept from 2,000 pounds to 2,250 pounds. At 2:00 A.M., August 11, the wind began driving the vessel at an angle, causing the cable to payout at twice the forward speed of the ship. To reduce flow of slack, the mechanic on the brake increased tension on the cable to 2,600 pounds. Bright had been watching the machine since midnight, and after satisfying himself that the mechanic knew how to control the brake, he went forward to make sure nothing obstructed the cable feeding out of the hold. He also planned to stop in the electrician's room, but before he reached either, the rumble of the paying-out machinery inexplicably stopped. Bright ran aft hollering, "Relieve the brakes! Relieve the brakes!" When he reached the machine he saw the cable had parted. More than 380 nautical miles of precious wire lay at the bottom of the Atlantic. He examined the brake and found that it had not been released, and that the mechanic, in a state of semipanic, had turned the handwheel the wrong way. Others believed the mechanic had applied the brake when the ship was stern-down in a wave, causing a sudden jolt to the cable when the stern lifted. Bright entered Field's cabin and reported the accident.[29]

Captain Hudson stopped the ship and signaled the Wire Squadron, "The cable has parted." A few minutes later Captain Wainwright of *Leopard* and Captain Sands of *Susquehanna* came on board *Niagara*. There was nothing they could do. *Niagara* flew her flag at half-mast; the others did the same.[30]

For several days Field kept the squadron bunched together to run a series of experiments. *Cyclops* took soundings in the morning and verified the depth at 12,300 feet. Electrical technicians on *Niagara* and *Agamemnon* ran successful conductivity tests on the cable on their ships, but with more than $500,000 of wire swallowed up by the ocean, there was not enough cable to chance a second effort.

Engineers and mechanics ran trials on the paying-out machinery, making notes for improving the apparatus. Field wanted answers he could take to the directors. He knew the problems could be solved, and he knew the cable could be laid. Then he remembered that Whitehouse would wonder what had happened to the circuit, so he asked Dayman to go back to Valentia and report the accident. Twelve hours earlier Whitehouse had sent an optimistic message to George Saward in London, "Nearly 360 miles have now been successfully laid down into the sea. . . . All are well on board, in excellent spirits, and hourly becoming more and more trustful of success."[31]

Bright performed a postmortem on the possible causes of the cable's breakage. As long as the sea remained calm, the ship's stern remained steady. Once swells built, the stern heaved up and down, easing the strain as it fell and increasing the strain as it rose. Deep water added more strain, and strong breezes blowing from the quarter created another problem, forcing the mechanic watching the brake to react to too many variables. Even the mechanic could not say what had happened. One brutal fact remained. After paying out 380 nautical miles, the cable snapped and ended the Atlantic Telegraph Company's 1857 effort to connect Europe with America.

Morse blamed the accident on Bright, writing:

> Mr. Bright spoke to the man in charge of the brakes, asking him what strain was upon the cable, to which the answer was . . . about 3,000 pounds. Mr. Bright directed him to put 100 lbs. more . . . upon the brakes to check the speed of the cable. This was demurred to by the man for a moment, who expressed a fear that it would not be prudent. Mr. Bright, however, persevered in his orders. The brakes were applied with additional force, which suddenly stopped the wheels of the paying-out apparatus . . . [and] when the stern was lifted by the irresistible power of the succeeding wave the force exerted upon the cable under such circumstances, would have parted a cable of 4 times the strength . . . I feel sorry for Mr. Bright.[32]

Finger-pointing began and ended in less than twenty-four hours. Field at first accepted Morse's version of the disaster, but he later learned that Bright was not at the machine when the cable snapped. All the quibbling made no difference. Field recovered from the shock, writing:

> The successful laying down of the cable is put off for a short time, but its final triumph has been fully proved by the experience that we have had since we left Valentia. My confidence was never so strong as at the present time, and I feel sure . . . we shall connect Europe and America with the electric cord.[33]

Morse voiced a vote of confidence, writing: "There is no insurmountable difficulty that has for a moment appeared, none that has shaken my faith in it in the slightest degree." Such words of confidence coming from Morse fortified Field's resolve.[34]

The Wire Squadron returned to Plymouth and unloaded the cable into storage tanks at Keyham (Devonport Dockyard). Bright offered to make arrangements to recover the lost cable, but it stayed where it lay on the bottom of the ocean.

Field made hurried plans to go to London to confer with the directors. Among other things, he needed money to buy 600 miles of cable, and he also needed money to improve the paying-out machinery. The trip back to England gave him time to recover his spirits. Showing disappointment could be fatal.

In a letter written to his family on August 13, Field said, "Do not think I feel discouraged, or am in low spirits, for I am not: and I think I can see how this accident will be of great advantage to the Atlantic Telegraph Company."[35]

But could he raise enough money for another expedition? Turning a disaster into an opportunity required a powerfully positive attitude. As *Leopard* steamed for Southampton, Field prepared to meet with the directors. With more than $650,000 of his capital invested in the enterprise, he was not ready to cut his losses and go home. Field knew he must go on.

CHAPTER 6

OCEAN RENDEZVOUS

Field disembarked at Southampton and immediately called for the directors to meet on August 15 in London. Instead of referring to the aborted mission as a colossal disappointment, he called it an "experience . . . of great value to the Atlantic Telegraph Company." He attributed the difficulties to the paying-out machinery, which he said could be corrected with slight alterations. He asked the directors for funds to replace the lost cable and for approval to try again "or wait until another summer." Bright added his support, knowing nothing could be done that summer, and despite Field's intimation that the paying-out machinery needed only a "slight alteration," he knew it needed much more.[1]

Field's arguments persuaded the directors to sustain the company and open subscriptions for more capital. They restrained him from attempting to squeeze another expedition into 1857. The directors had neither enough money, which they depended upon him to raise, nor the ships, which had returned to their respective duties after landing the company's cable at Plymouth.

Raising money in England for a second expedition became a frustrating experience. British investors felt they had already sacrificed too much on a hopeless venture. Charles Bright took the pulse of the country and wrote:

> The first expedition had opened the eyes of the public to the vastness of the undertaking, and led many to doubt who did not doubt before. Some began to look upon it as a romantic adventure at sea, rather than a serious commercial undertaking. This decline of public faith was felt as soon as there was a call for more money.

From a "current of popular enthusiasm" in early 1857, Bright now acknowledged a "growing tide of popular distrust."[2]

With money tight, Bright traveled to Valentia in October and hired the paddle-wheel steamer *Leipzig* to recover as much cable as possible. Gales hindered the work, but the crew salvaged fifty-seven miles of wire before being blown off the ocean. Bright sent the lot over to Keyham for storage. *Leipzig* underran the shore end and buoyed it twenty miles offshore. Bright intended to splice to it the following summer, but the 1857 shore-end was never used again.[3]

While Bright sought ways to save money, Whitehouse continued to spend it. Having never proven his theory of retardation, Whitehouse still believed that impulses sent over long distances had to be boosted with more voltage to flow faster through the conductor. He began buying instruments, but the transmission tests he made on the cable soaking in vats at Keyham did not produce answers that corresponded with his theory. He refused to believe that weak voltage could transmit signals better than strong voltage. So Whitehouse decided to postpone his study until the Atlantic cable was laid.[4]

Field returned to New York in mid-September to find the city's financial institutions crumbling. The crash threatened to bankrupt some of the city's richest men. The trouble started in 1836 when President Andrew Jackson banished America's central bank, and with it the nation's opportunity for a sound monetary system. New York's financial crisis rippled across the nation. Too harried by cable problems to follow America's economic woes in the London press, Field arrived home during the height of the panic. Cooper said he sold some of his cable stock at a quarter of its value because he feared that if the economy continued to collapse, there could be mass starvation. Hard-hit City Bank took most of Moses Taylor's wealth. The next shock came from Field & Company's managers, who warned that payments had been stopped and the company owed $600,000, with half that amount overdue to them in uncollectable receivables.[5]

Field hurried to the company's telegraph office and found it swarming with Wall Street brokers trying to expedite messages to Europe through the Newfoundland line. The breathtaking tumult punctuated the need for fast communications with Europe. By now the cable should have been working, carrying those messages to England and returning a profit to the company. Instead, he was back in America in the midst of a stock market crash trying to raise money from the very men who, under financial duress, were selling their shares in the telegraph company.

Field felt an even greater urgency. Without the solvency of Field & Company his own flow of cash would end. He called the company's creditors together and offered them notes at seven percent interest. Most of them took the deal, a few men accepted shares instead. He made no progress raising $500,000 to replace the lost cable.

Once again, the money came from the original British stockholders of

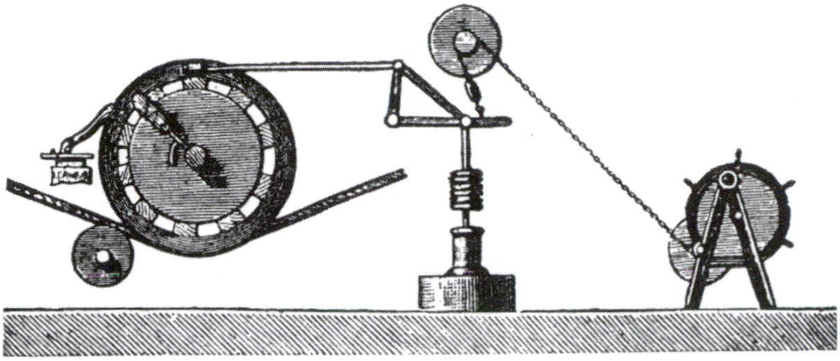

Sketch of the Appold brake that Charles Bright adapted to the paying-out machinery. (From Charles Bright, *The Story of the Atlantic Cable*. Digitized by Debra Peffer.)

the Atlantic Telegraph Company. Bright issued contracts for manufacturing 700 miles of replacement cable. With one exception, the new cable could not be distinguished from the old. Thomson had never been satisfied with the purity of copper used in the 1857 cable. He finally won a battle with Whitehouse and wrote a purity clause into the contract with the Gutta Percha Company. He tested every hank of wire coming off the stranding machines and rejected any length that fell below his criteria. Though the higher quality conductors would be spliced to those already made, Thomson established a new industry standard that applied to copper conductors for many years to come.

Bright and Field each knew that the paying-out machinery needed improvement. Bright took the problem to Easton & Amos, a machinery manufacturer, and suggested a braking mechanism similar to a counterbalanced cranking apparatus designed by John G. Appold, which was used on heavy doors in British prisons. Field, during a trip to Washington, called upon Secretary Toucey to ask again for a pair of naval vessels for next year's expedition. He also requested the services of William Everett, who had worked with the paying-out machinery on *Niagara*. Everett said the contraption had too many wheels and predicted more trouble if not redesigned. On December 13, 1857, Toucey handed Field an official letter, and said, "There. I have given you all you asked."[6]

Morse, however, began sending signals of personal disenchantment, informing his brother Richard "I intend to withdraw altogether from the American Telegraph enterprise, as they who are prominent on this side of the water [meaning Field and Cooper] in its interests are using it with all their efforts and influence against my invention." Morse had been made an honorary director, not a voting director, and never anything more than a minor stockholder, yet he felt the company owed him a special emolument.

Morse blamed his situation mostly on Cooper and would, from time to time, spend the next years sniping at him in correspondence with friends and relatives.[7]

Amos Kendall, Morse's attorney, cast roadblocks into Cooper's efforts to gain control of the eastern seaboard and expand inland. He and Francis O. J. "Fog" Smith, owner of the New York & New England Union Telegraph Company, petitioned Congress asking that a law be passed to restrain acquisitions of other telegraph companies when the ostensible purpose was to suppress competition and gain monopolistic advantages. Kendall feared that the American Telegraph Company, already linked to the New York, Newfoundland, and London Telegraph Company, would eventually combine with the Atlantic Telegraph Company, and through its sheer weight, size, and capital, absorb every telegraph company in America, including the Western Union. So while Morse continued to serve as an unhappy honorary director for the New York, Newfoundland company, Kendall and Smith, who used Morse patents, gave enthusiastic support to Shaffner, one of the few promoters in the business who labored each day in opposition to the American Telegraph Company by expanding telegraph lines into the South and West. Congress did nothing to slow down the American Telegraph Company's assimilation of smaller companies, but Shaffner, over time, used Kendall and Smith's support in an effort to undermine Field and Cooper's efforts in America and Great Britain.[8]

On January 6, 1858, Field and naval engineer Everett sailed for England on the steamer *Persia*. On arrival, Field learned the directors had named him general manager with control of the entire staff, including the engineers and electricians. He accepted the position but turned down the salary, even though £1,000 that came with the job would have helped him financially.[9]

When in Washington, Field had spoken with Maury, who looked at the latest sample of the cable and again declared it too heavy. When Field reached England, he found the replacement cable already in production at the Gutta Percha works. Bright informed him of Thomson's improvement in copper purity, and Field let the matter of cable size drop.

Everett moved over to Easton & Amos in Southwark to collaborate with C. E. Amos in designing new paying-out machines. The two men worked for three months experimenting with designs before settling on a concept that required fewer wheels and incorporated Appold's concept of a self-regulating braking mechanism.

Everett believed the new brake would never allow a cable to snap, even though an emergency handwheel came with the mechanism. The maximum tension on the cable could never exceed 2,400 pounds, this being well below the cable's 6,200-pound test strength. The tension on the cable depended upon the number of weights attached to a bar that delivered tension to a lever that adjusted the braking force. Adding weights decreased the tension while removing weights increased the tension on a pair of grooved hardwood blocks fastened to the outside circumference of a wheel through which the cable passed. Bright added a dynamometer to read the actual strain on the cable. Even without a dynamometer, the brake was calibrated to eliminate severe force on the cable.

The dynamometer consisted of a wheel that moved up and down as the cable passed through the brake. If the strain on the cable were slight, the wheel would bend the cable downward. If the strain were considerable, the cable would force the wheel upwards. An indicator needle worked off the rise and fall of the wheel and read the tension in hundredweights and tons. The designers calibrated both the dynamometer and the weights, and if wear occurred during the voyage across the Atlantic, Everett had prepared a procedure for recalibrating the entire mechanism without stopping the machinery.

The new paying-out machine was half the size of the contraption used in 1857. Cable coming from the coils in the hold passed under a lightly weighted jockey pulley that fed the wire into a four-groove drum on the paying-out machine. The cable wound three times around each of two drums, passed over a grooved sheave, traveled through the dynamometer and braking mechanism, passed over the stern sheave, and dropped into the sea. This design, with minor modifications, became the standard system for laying submarine cables for decades to come.

Willoughby Smith solved the problem of the tar and pitch buildup experienced on the 1857 machine by inventing a new insulating and adhesive compound to replace the coal-tar naptha wrapped around the core. Smith came by his job with the Gutta Percha Company quite by accident. He began his career running growlers of beer from a nearby tavern to men working overtime at the plant. He learned about the problems by chatting with the workmen and made a few suggestions. Someone recognized his abilities, and in 1848 the company hired him as a junior engineer. A year later he became a supervisor and in 1850 laid Brett's Channel cable.

Had the cable been successfully connected to Newfoundland during the summer of 1857, one of the most important discoveries may have gone unrecognized for years. Thomson wore a monocle, and one spring day in 1858, while twirling the glass in his laboratory, he noticed how swiftly light beams danced about the room. He wondered whether a beam of light could be used to interpret electric impulses and developed what he called a "mirror-speaking instrument." He also called it a marine galvanometer, but in those days every instrument involved with electricity was called a galvanometer.

The simple device consisted of a minuscule light steel magnet with a tiny mirror fixed to it, together weighing less than an ounce. A filament of silk suspended the free-swinging magnet between an insulated coil of very thin

Sketch of the operation of the paying-out machinery that William Everett designed for the USS *Niagara*. A similar machine was also used on HMS *Agamemnon*. (From Charles Bright, *The Story of the Atlantic Cable*. Digitized by Debra Peffer.)

copper wire. A weak current passing through the coil caused a shift in the suspended magnet. A ray of light from a lamp directly behind a slotted screen reflected off the mirror and cast a beam onto a horizontal scale containing the letters of the alphabet. The instrument contained no mechanical parts and once calibrated required no adjustment.

Any movement of the reflecting mirror indicated the presence of a current. The strength of the current determined the amount the mirror deflected. When the mirror sent a ray of light through a lens focused on the alphabetical scale, the operator simply recorded the letter marked by the light beam. The system required very little voltage and sharply reduced the length of time required to record a message. Wildman Whitehouse never understood the simple sophistication of Thomson's mirror-speaking instrument.

Whitehouse still believed the only way to overcome retardation across 2,000 miles of submerged cable was to hammer it through using lots of power. Thomson's device demonstrated that messages could be transmitted with the weakest of voltage. The two men could not agree, and General Manager Field found himself in the middle of a battle without having the technical knowledge to take sides.

Whitehouse, being less of a scientist but a more assertive technocrat,

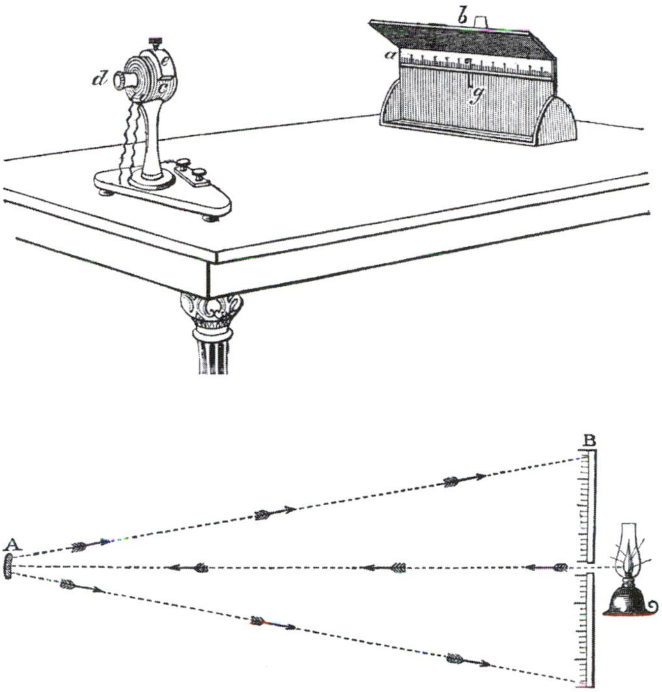

Professor Thomson's unique "mirror-speaking device" enabled a telegraph receiving clerk to transcribe a message from alpha characters that were one by one reflected by light through a small lens onto a scale containing those characters. (From Charles Bright, *The Story of the Atlantic Cable.* Digitized by Debra Peffer.)

usually got his way. He could not accept that the younger Thomson might know more than he, and his favorite tactic was to ignore the professor's advice. Throughout these scuffles Thomson maintained a full workload at the University of Glasgow and could not take time for a scientific spat with a man as obstreperous as Whitehouse. Even Field began to question his chief electrician's competence and considered buying his eight shares.

Recent improvements in cable design gave substance to claims that Field rushed too impetuously to lay the 1857 cable. Competing telegraph companies in the United States added to Field's recklessness. The 1857 debacle only raised the ante, as Shaffner began lobbying Canada to reconsider their agreement with Field and open the door for competition. For Field's two American telegraph companies to maintain monopolistic rights, the success of the 1858 cable became crucial.

On March 12, 1858, Morse attempted to exculpate himself from the devious designs of the American Telegraph Company, while at the same time warning Field that competitors wanted a piece of the action:

> Many of my assignees . . . deem the success of the laying of the cable to be the basis . . . for monopolizing and controlling all the Telegraph lines of the United States.
>
> I wish you to distinctly understand, however, that I am not responsible for the schemes or plans . . . of those interested in the established lines, whom the antagonistic course of the American Telegraph Company has aroused in opposition. I hear of plans, the details of which are not imparted to me . . . which may well occasion you some uneasiness in regard to your anticipated profits.[10]

Field left no record of how he responded to Morse's warnings, and Bright refused to be rushed. The latter was partly accommodated by *Niagara*. Captain Hudson did not arrive in Plymouth until late March to load *Niagara*'s share of the cable.

During April, Bright organized an experimental expedition using *Agamemnon*, now commanded by Captain George W. Preedy, and *Niagara* for cable maneuvers. The Admiralty added the HMS *Gorgon*, commanded by Lieutenant Dayman, and the survey-steamer *Porcupine*. Field became moderately embarrassed when he learned that the navy would not make *Susquehanna* available because an outbreak of yellow fever had quarantined the ship. He hired a cab and went straight to Sir John Pakington, First Lord of the Admiralty. "I am ashamed to come to you," he said, "after what the English Government has done for the Atlantic Telegraph. But here is our case." He explained conditions on *Susquehanna*, and asked, "Can you do anything for us?" Pakington said he would see what he could do, and a few hours later sent word to the company that the paddle-wheeler HMS *Valorous*, commanded by Captain W. C. Aldham, would join the squadron and act as *Niagara*'s consort.[11]

Bright's cable-laying exercises included a series of tests on the paying-out machinery, splicing procedures, and retrieving and buoying cables in deep water. He also wanted to run the mechanical and electrical crews through their work assignments, this time using Thomson in a more assertive role. He ignored Whitehouse's demand to have the cable run from Valentia, instead favoring a splice in mid-ocean, *Agamemnon* running to Ireland, and *Niagara* to Newfoundland.

The directors waited patiently while 160 men began transferring 2,800 miles of wire into the two cable ships—a task that took from the beginning of April until the middle of May. The 1857 cable had been recoated with tar, pitch, linseed oil, and beeswax to preserve it over the winter: it stuck together and came out of the tanks grudgingly. Workmen coiled the cable around a series of large cones, which took extra time. Divided into four gangs of forty men, each gang coiled about fifteen miles of cable a day. Bright wanted every section retested before it went on board, every length

The USS *Niagara* (right) and the HMS *Agamemnon* (center) assemble in the Bay of Biscay to perform trials on the new paying-out machinery. (Courtesy U.S. Naval Historical Center. Digitized by Debra Peffer.)

tested after being spliced, and the whole lot connected and tested before sailing for rehearsal in the Bay of Biscay, where the seabed was a mile deeper than the telegraphic plateau.

The Wire Squadron sailed on May 29 and bore southward 300 miles. Two days later they met over the deepest section of Biscay. *Niagara* hawsered her end of the cable and passed it to *Agamemnon* for splicing. The splice required an elaborate iron and wood, twelve-foot long coupling frame. One ship carried cable with armor spiraled to the right, the other ship with armor spiraled to the left, and the frame provided the means for keeping the two ends clamped together. At 5:30 P.M. the mechanics on *Agamemnon* lowered the 300-pound frame into the sea. *Niagara* and *Agamemnon* separated, and without the slightest difficulty paid out miles of cable. Eight hours later the wire parted. This came as no surprise because Bright used cable condemned at Glass, Elliot. *Agamemnon* began the retrieval exercise and recovered most of the cable, including the splice frame.

Bright continued the tests, paying-out cable at different speeds while manipulating tension on the braking mechanism. The cable flowed smoothly with the ship running at five-and-a-half knots and with 2,300 pounds registering on the dynamometer. The mechanics expressed shock when the cable suddenly jammed in the machinery and broke. After making adjustments to the mechanism, Bright made another trial run. At seven knots the cable paid-out smoothly, and despite being a condemned section, the wire continued to transmit strong signals. On June 3 the Wire Squadron returned to Plymouth to load coal before sailing for the midocean rendezvous. The moment of truth had arrived.

Henry Field rejoined the squadron at Plymouth and became shocked by the appearance of his brother. "The strain on the man was more than the strain on the cable, and we were in fear that both would break together."[12]

For Cyrus Field, the last few weeks had become a test of emotional and physical endurance. He barely slept, and every business demand drained a few more ounces of energy. He looked forward to a respite when on Thursday, June 10, he threw his bags into his stateroom on *Niagara*. The Wire Squadron sailed immediately "with fair skies and bright prospects" and headed for a rendezvous at 52°2'N, 33°18'W in the middle of the North Atlantic. The barometer read steady at 30.64 inches of mercury. If Field had any reservations about laying the cable before July 20—Maury's recommended starting time—the pristine weather calmed his nerves. Besides, British nautical authorities disagreed with Maury. They declared the first weeks of June "the best time of the year for the Atlantic."[13]

The squadron passed through the Plymouth breakwater and into the open sea. Bright, Canning, and Thomson watched from the deck of *Agamemnon*: Field, Everett, and de Sauty from the deck of *Niagara*. Once again Whitehouse pled illness and remained ashore at Valentia. Disillusioned, Morse never left New York, leaving the electrical work to de Sauty.

Not a wisp of wind ruffled the surface of the water. "The second day was like the first," recalled Henry Field. "There was scarcely wind enough to swell the sails. The ships were all in sight, and as they kept under easy steam, they seemed bound on a voyage of pleasure, gliding over a summer sea to certain success." The first three days confirmed the opinions of the British wise men of the sea who predicted pristine weather, and those on board, being among the true prophets, shook their heads with the satisfaction that comes from being right. With each vessel laden with 1,500 tons of cable and tons of extra coal, the fine weather came as a blessing, especially to the overladen and smaller *Agamemnon*.[14]

On Saturday, June 12, a fair breeze began to blow. The Wire Squadron hoisted the screws, shook out the sails, raked out the fires, and bowled along under royals and stunsails. Skippers wanted to conserve their coal for cable laying, especially Preedy of *Agamemnon*.

First the barometer staggered and then on Sunday plunged as squally weather produced boisterous symptoms of an Atlantic gale. Jack-tar gritted his teeth: he knew the signs. The leaden sky shed a wretched mist and spattered rain. The squadron's vessels loomed like shadows as they pounded through heavy swells. Gale winds intensified, and by late afternoon the cable ships beat through hissing white-horses under close-reefed topsails and foresails. Field clutched the rail of *Niagara* and stared across the storm-swept Atlantic at *Agamemnon*. From a mile away he could see the big ship pitch and roll in an unnatural way. He went to the bridge and asked Hudson to keep *Agamemnon* in sight. With her extraheavy load she had less freeboard, making her a dangerous ship in a storm.

At nightfall the winds steadily increased, stacking up the seas. Most of the squadron dispersed; only *Agamemnon* and *Niagara* had the strength to sail against the wind and stay in sight. Bright went topside, clutching the rail, and scanned the seascape. "The ocean resembled one vast snowdrift," he recalled, "the whitish glare from which—reflected from the dark clouds that almost rested on the sea—had a tremendous and unnatural effect, as if the ordinary laws of nature had been reversed."[15]

On June 20, after seven days of fighting gales, as fierce a storm that ever struck the Atlantic bore down upon the squadron. The barometer sank to twenty-nine-inches, and by nightfall every ship began to look after itself. Men on *Agamemnon* feared she would break apart. Overloaded with coal and cable, she labored in thirty-foot swells. The massive beams under her upper-deck coil creaked and cracked, drowning out the hideous roar of wind screaming and howling through the rigging and clawing at the storm sails.

Men lay in their hammocks unable to sleep, listening as planks of the upper deck worked loose. They heard the seas crash violently against *Agamemnon*'s bow, felt the wash as it seeped through the ports, flooding the floor of their deck. Old tars that sailed the ship before said she carried too much weight forward, which brought the ship down by the head, plunging the bow into towering waves that swept the deck. Others expected the mass of cable to slip from its ties and plunge through the vessel's side. Correspondent Mullaly wrote:

> Nobody thought of these things when on the morning of the 10th of June the squadron quitted Plymouth. It was to be a yachting cruise—a mere summer-trip—and any talk of waterproofs and sou'westers would not have been more out of place in a drawing-room than on the deck of the *Agamemnon*.[16]

On Monday morning the barometer plummeted, the wind blew harder, and monster seas grew to frothing mountains of water tipped with a stinging spray that horizontally flailed the deck. At noon the sun suddenly broke through the clouds. For thirty minutes it shined with magnificent brilliance, and then suddenly disappeared in a column of clouds having gusts of wind that shattered the eardrums and almost sent *Agamemnon* boring into the combers under bare poles.

The gale suddenly shifted to the southwest, driving the ships off course. The coil on the upper deck, put there to help stabilize the ship, did the opposite. Having shifted to starboard, it now began shifting to port, and once again the beams groaned in protest. Men rushed below to shore up the hold. Others rushed into the bunkers to keep the coal from shifting. The old man-of-war pitched and yawed, moaning in agony, and water continued to cascade into the bilge at a rate that tested the endurance of the clanking pumps.

On Tuesday the barometer crept back to 29.3 inches, but the wind switched to the west and maintained its intensity. With cooperation from the sun the captain took a noon reading and reported the ship's position 563 miles from her midocean destination. After five days at sea *Agamemnon* had come less than halfway. For the first time in three days Captain Preedy caught sight of *Niagara*, but the other vessels were nowhere in sight.

The sudden shift of wind plunged *Agamemnon* into troughs with such force as to break her back and heap her cable on the ocean floor. In desperation, Preedy ordered the boilers lit and the engines started. Beams cracked on the lower deck, and sailors rushed to shore them up with jackscrews. But the ship never faltered and Preedy plunged ahead, hoping for an improvement in the weather as he steamed slowly westward.

By Saturday, June 19, the bleak seascape began to clear. The barometer crept upwards, and the seas dropped. For the first time in many days men ate hot food and walked the deck. From a comparative calm during the afternoon the sky darkened to the west, the glass fell abruptly, rain began to fall, and the wind began to howl, not in gusts but with steadily increasing force. The sea, being "ready-built" by the first storm, caught the screaming tempest and by midnight tore into *Agamemnon* with such violence as to roll her thirty degrees from one beam to the other. Men scrambled to the tops, clutching flapping wet canvas with bloody hands as the ship canted until her yards nearly nipped the crests. With every roll the masts bent, working loose and stretching the shrouds. By daylight the ship was almost as wet inside as outside, everything going awash from the upper deck to the galley. *Agamemnon* pitched and shuddered, boring into troughs and slamming into mast-high combers. Men on board having nothing to grasp wedged themselves into corners or held onto beams to keep from being tumbled across the deck.[17]

The violent motion of *Niagara* made Field sick. He stayed on deck for a while and watched *Agamemnon* slide down one wave and stagger up another. Spray as cold as ice bit his face and stung his knuckles. A spar snapped in the bow, another tumbled down from overhead, bringing sails and shrouds with it. A capsized lifeboat floated past, ripped from the davits of some hapless ship. Wet and chilled, Field went back inside, only to be met by a sea of chairs, tables, and accessories cut loose by the pitch and roll of the ship. He clawed his way forward to where the company's 1,500 tons of cable lay quivering in its coils. Carpenters stumbled about, bracing the precious cargo with beams, for if the cable broke its bonds, the ship would be doomed.

At 10:30 A.M. on Sunday morning, a lookout on the bridge of *Agamemnon* reported several gigantic waves bowling down on the ship.[18] Correspondent Nicholas Wood of the London *Times* wrote that he saw them:

> coming slowly on through the mist nearer and nearer, rolling on like hills of green water, with a crown of foam that seemed to double their height. The *Agamemnon* rose heavily to the first, and then went down quickly into the deep trough of the sea, falling over as she did so, so as almost to capsize completely on the port side. There was a fearful crashing as she lay over . . . for everything broke adrift, whether secured or not, and the uproar and confusion were terrific for a minute, and then back she came again on the starboard beam in the same manner, only quicker, and still deeper than before.[19]

Masses of water cascaded across the decks, forcing its way through ports, pouring down hatchways, crashing through skylights and into the engine room. One hundred tons of coal stowed on the main deck broke loose, smashed everything in its way, and washed through the scuppers. Before the helmsmen at the wheel could right the ship, *Agamemnon* careened to port and coal on the starboard side of the lower deck gave way, and like a roaring avalanche of black billiard balls collected everything in the way.

Aware that another lurch like the last could dismast the vessel, Captain Preedy shouted from the poop, "Hands, wear ship!" Officers standing near him passed the word, but barely anyone could hear above the storm's roar. With ladders smashed and debris choking the decks below, jack-tar responded slowly, slipping and falling to get topside. With the vessel heeling back and forth, no one on deck could keep his feet without holding something. The ship's barge broke loose from its lashings on the main deck, and anyone passing it took his life in his hands. As men tried to wear ship on the starboard tack, five enormous waves attacked the ship in succession, heeling her over forty-five degrees. The upper-deck coil strained the ship to the utmost but remained secure. The coil in the main hold broke loose, strewing fifty miles of cable in a tangle that resembled an invasion of eels.[20]

Niagara, buried in the trough of the same waves, righted herself without difficulty. On two occasions Captain Hudson observed *Agamemnon* heel sharply and feared she would go under. Then he saw her wear around and wore also, bearing down to render assistance. Preedy signaled that *Agamemnon* remained seaworthy, which was providential because Hudson could not risk getting closer. Both ships rode with the storm, but *Agamemnon* continued to get pummeled. A heavy sea struck her stern, partially smashed the "crinoline" guarding the propeller, and left just enough of the cage hanging off the stern to threaten the rudderpost and the screw. Men risked their lives passing hawsers to the broken frame. They succeeded in keeping the crinoline away from the rudder but could not prevent the cage from banging against the vessel's beam, creating concern that the frame would punch a hole beneath the ship's waterline.

Preedy looked again to his masts. Stretched by the ship's rolling, the shrouds no longer gave the masts full support. With every roll the lower masts tottered as if ready to go over the side. Nothing could be done to relieve the strain, and Preedy knew if the masts went, the ship would likely go under. So with his officers he solemnly watched, and when the wind subsided slightly at dusk, he brought the ship about under steam and put her back into the wind. As the ship wore around, she fell into another trough and rolled. A pipe broke, flooding the engine room with steam and disabling a boiler. Kegs of copper sulfate broke apart and smothered the lower deck with toxic fumes. Barrels of oil overturned on the spar deck and sent sailors sprawling as they tried to regain their feet.[21]

There were men on board who believed the ship could not survive further battering. London *Times* correspondent Wood wrote:

> of all on board none had ever seen a fiercer or more dangerous sea than raged throughout that night and the following morning, tossing the *Agamemnon* from side to side like a mere plaything among the waters. The night was thick and dark, the low black clouds almost hemming the vessel in; now and then a fiercer blast than usual drove the great masses slowly aside and showed the moon, a dim, greasy blotch upon the sky, with the ocean, white as driven snow, boiling and seething like a caldron.[22]

Agamemnon's crew waited for the one staggering blow that would topple the ship. No form of dying terrified sailors more than death by shipwreck. The men who gripped the rail on the poop with the captain stared ahead into the darkness for that one wave to end it all. Towering white-horses formed in echelons to attack, and the ship's bow thudded against alpine slopes. Beams and knees groaned under the strain, water flooded into the ship through hawseholes and hatches faster than it could be carried away through the scuppers, but the waves, one after the other, went hissing past and into the darkness aft.

Daylight brought no reprieve, but through the scud Preedy could see *Niagara* in the distance—one moment topping a comber and the next moment gone from sight. Hudson had the better vessel, being heavier by 2,000 tons displacement, but Preedy could see her bow plunge into the waves and ship-heavy seas. The two ships tried to pass signals, each concerned about the other, but suddenly it grew darker and thicker, and *Niagara* disappeared from sight.

After one massive wave took *Agamemnon* into a trough and the next threatened to carry her under, Preedy considered his options. He could wear around and try her on the starboard tack, as he had done before; he could run before the wind; or, he could lighten the vessel by jettisoning the

The HMS *Agamemnon* heeling over during the fierce North Atlantic storms during June 1858. (From Charles Bright, *The Story of the Atlantic Cable*. Digitized by Debra Peffer.)

upper deck cable that made his ship unstable. If he came about, he could fall into a trough and lose the ship's masts. If the upper-deck coil shifted, he felt certain the ship would go under in less than ten minutes. By attempting to run before the storm he risked the stern being smashed and hundreds of tons of water added to her burden until she finally filled and sank. He decided to take his chances and issued orders to wear ship.

Bringing her around placed *Agamemnon* broadside against the running seas. At first the combination of steam, sail, and helm could not bring her about. Of 200 men topside, more than 150 of them were knocked to the deck and scattered about as they sought for a handhold. Preedy expected the masts to go and that the last hour of the stout ship had come. Every time she pitched, water flooded the lower decks. Coal crashed through the bunkers, carrying everything before it, rolling in waves into the engine room. The 250-ton main-deck coil shifted again but held, though four men trying to secure it with beams were tumbled to the deck.

Preedy finally brought the vessel about, and with full steam, a foresail, and a foretopsail to lift her head, he ran at a gallop before the storm. The battered man-of-war crested the combers, rolling and tumbling over huge crests at tremendous speed. Waves infallibly poured over her stern, one washing through the wardroom and floating two seasick officers off a sofa.

On Monday, June 21, the barometer began to rise, but the storm continued to blow with the same ferocity. At 4:00 A.M. on Tuesday Preedy, now exhausted, ordered the vessel back into the wind and set a course for midocean, which was now 200 miles farther away than a week ago. The ship gained little against the wind, so on Friday morning—sixteen days after leaving Plymouth—Preedy found his ship still fifty miles from the rendezvous, a trip that should have taken four or five days. As he approached the meeting place, *Valorous* hove in sight at noon; during the afternoon *Niagara* came in from the north; and in early evening *Gorgon* came up from the south.

As if the curtain had finally descended on a tragic opera, the sea became as tranquil as Plymouth harbor on the day the squadron sailed. The cable crew woke to a gentle sea, a bright cloudless sky, and not a breath of wind. Henry Field considered the change uncanny, writing: "This evening the four vessels lay together side by side, and there was such a stillness in the sea and air, as would have seemed remarkable in an inland lake; on the Atlantic, and after what we had all so lately witnessed, it seemed almost unnatural."[23]

Officers lowered boats and made the rounds, visiting each other to review damage and discuss their experiences. Dayman and Aldham declared it had been the worst weather they had ever experienced in the North Atlantic. *Niagara* suffered the least, but she lost her jib boom and the buoys she carried for marking the cable.

Agamemnon suffered the most. The rough seas had shaken the ship and the cable. More than 100 miles lay twisted and tangled so badly that the wire had to be dragged to another part of the vessel before a splice could be made. The storm had opened waterways, rendering the vessel in a dangerous condition. One marine, literally frightened out of his wits, remained insane for several days. Forty-five men lay in the sickbay, many with fractured limbs. When Field visited *Agamemnon* he found her usual white decks littered with debris and impregnated with coal dust.

The day passed, and what new adventures lay ahead for the Wire Squadron had to wait until Saturday. Had Maury, now a commander, been watching from the Naval Observatory, he might have wondered why the squadron sailed in early June instead of waiting for the better weather of late July. But now the ships had come together in the middle of the Atlantic, and the spliced cable, with a bent sixpence fitted into the splice for good luck, lay in readiness for the morning plunge. The vessels rocked restfully in a soothing night breeze, waiting for daylight.

CHAPTER 7

BACK AND FORTH ACROSS THE OCEAN

On Saturday morning, June 26, 1858, the weather turned cold and foggy. A stiff breeze flailed the decks of the squadron with an unseasonable dose of sleet. No one cheered when the splice frame with the lucky sixpence splashed over the side and began its descent to the featherbed of microscopic shells on the ocean's bottom. For men like Cyrus Field, Charles Bright, William Thomson, Stephen Canning, and the mechanics and electricians who joined the expedition, the atmosphere was reminiscent of mariners attending a burial at sea. Sailors standing at the stern of *Niagara* gave a polite wave to men on *Agamemnon* as both vessels steamed in opposite directions.

Electricians filtered back to testing rooms and began exchanging signals between the ships. The vessels vanished in the fog. After paying out three miles of cable, a mechanic on *Niagara* allowed the feeding mechanism to run slack. The cable overrode the pulley feeding the drums, snagged in the apparatus, screeched to a halt, and broke. Electricians on *Agamemnon* informed the captain that impulses had stopped. Preedy ordered the ship to come about and return to the rendezvous.

When Captain Hudson learned of the break, he hurried aft, took one look at the frayed end, stopped *Niagara*'s engines, and ordered the signal gun fired. While waiting for *Agamemnon* to return, he penned a comment in the ship's log: "The cable, being hauled in the wrong direction, through the excitement and carelessness of one of the men, caught and parted in the *Niagara*'s machinery."[1]

Once again the cable-laying vessels came together in the middle of the ocean. Swells interfered with passing the cable between ships, but by late afternoon the electricians completed the splice and lowered the wire into

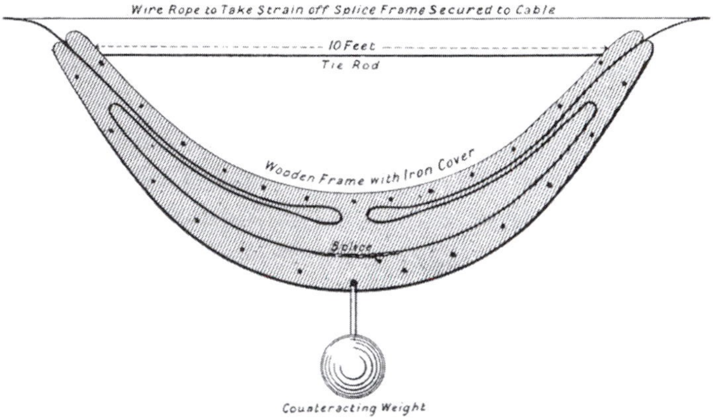

A huge splice frame was necessary when coupling the cable between the USS *Niagara* and HMS *Agamemnon* because the armoring on the conductor twisted in opposite directions. (From Edward Brailsford Bright, *The Life Story of the Late Sir Charles Tilston Bright*. Digitized by Debra Peffer.)

the water. This time no one bothered to wave when the Wire Squadron separated. *Agamemnon* and *Niagara* started down their courses at two knots, and as they faded from sight, accelerated to four knots. With the machinery on both vessels running smoothly, and with the needle on the dynamometers steady at 2,000 pounds, the ships moved through the night at five-and-a-half knots. Barring further accidents, the two captains expected to reach their respective destinations in five days.

At midnight the wire began to take a more horizontal slant as it peeled off the machinery and started to settle on the bottom. The mechanics and the watchers began to relax, and those off duty moved into their cabins to rest.

At 3:40 A.M., after forty miles of cable had rolled through the sheaves of each ship, Thomson reported the line dead. Finding the machinery in perfect order on *Agamemnon*, he believed the cable parted on *Niagara*. Preedy stopped the *Agamemnon*, mechanics applied the brakes to the machinery, and electricians cut the wire. Thomson took the end and connected it to his instruments to determine where the break occurred. He suspected the cable, though dead, may not have broken, and while considering his options, a stiff breeze combined with a heavy swell lifted the ship's stern and pushed the dynamometer to 4,000 pounds. A few fathoms below the stern-wheel the cable parted.

The signal gun fired, and a blue light flashed the grim news to the *Valorous* that another break had occurred.

On Sunday morning the ships' heads came about to return to the rendezvous. Once again, *Agamemnon* began the weary work of beating up against the wind. Preedy now faced other problems. Storms had prolonged the cruise, eaten away his coal reserve, and loosened his masts. Much of the ship's food had been contaminated by seawater and could not be eaten. The exasperated British crew blamed the Americans for causing a second accident. As the two vessels hove in sight on Monday, June 28, the men on *Agamemnon* waited for an explanation. *Niagara* astounded Preedy's crew by running up the interrogatory, "How did the cable part?"[2]

Field and de Sauty went to *Agamemnon* to compare data recorded in minute logs by both electrical departments. De Sauty reported that when the wire went dead, the machinery on *Niagara* was working perfectly and everyone on board believed the break had occurred on *Agamemnon.*

De Sauty suggested that the cable parted at the bottom of the ocean about ten miles from one of the ships, but he could not say which vessel. From the logs, however, Thomson found that both ships recorded a loss of continuity at the same split second of time. Thomson understood the rate of resistance on each mile of cable and ran more tests, concluding that the break occurred nowhere near either vessel but midway between them. The data also showed leakage through the insulation occurred seconds before the break. Other accidents could be explained, this one could not. The discovery renewed questions about Berryman and Dayman's surveys. Were sharp-pointed rocks on the supposed plateau, or had the storm damaged the insulation? Nobody could say. The only alternative was to make a third splice and try again.

The loss of eighty miles of cable (forty from each vessel) caused concern, but each ship started the expedition with several hundred yards of extra cable. Field, Thomson, Bright, Canning, and Everett agreed to continue the expedition, but not indefinitely. Conscious of food and fuel problems on *Agamemnon*, Field told both captains, "Should any accident occur to part the cable before the ships have run a hundred miles from rendezvous . . . the ships shall return to rendezvous and wait eight days, when, if the other ships do not appear, then proceed to Queenstown." Despite a shortage of food and fuel, Preedy agreed.[3]

On the evening of June 28 *Agamemnon* lowered the third splice into 12,000 feet of ocean and vanished in a cold blanket of fog. This time Bright and Canning kept watch on *Agamemnon*, and Field did not go to bed on *Niagara*. Both vessels, after traveling several miles, increased their speed to five knots, the dynamometer reading a safe and consistent 2,000 pounds. When the dynamometer unexpectedly slackened to 1,300 pounds, Bright knew the ship was passing over a rise in the ocean bed not recorded on Berryman or Dayman's charts. After an hour the strain on the cable increased, as did its rate of speed through the machinery, indicating that the wire was descending down an underwater slope.

By midday Tuesday, June 29, both vessels had traveled about sixty miles from the rendezvous and paid out seventy-six miles of cable. Continuity checks remained strong, and the spirits of the men on the cable ships continued to improve with each passing hour. Mechanics and electricians alike began to sleep again in shifts, and when they awoke the first question asked concerned the status of the cable. At breakfast a new enthusiasm harmonized their conversation. On *Agamemnon* even Preedy cheered up when he noticed the troublesome heavy coil on the upper deck was nearly gone.

Henry Field made the rounds on *Niagara* and took the pulse of the engineers and electricians, writing:

> The scene at night was beautiful. Scarcely a word was spoken; silence was commanded, and no conversation allowed. Nothing was heard but the strange rattling of the machine as the cable was running out. The lights about the deck and in the quarterdeck circle added to the singularity of the spectacle; and those who were on board the ship describe the state of anxious suspense in which all were held as exceedingly impressive.[4]

On June 30 the fog cleared and the weather became magnificent. Bright turned his attention to the next problem. After nightfall the cable would have to be changed from the upper deck to the main hold, and the crew would have the delicate job of making the transfer in weak lantern light. The only time this had been attempted was once during the full light of day in the Bay of Biscay. As the time approached, Preedy ordered the ship's speed reduced to three knots. The rotation of the propeller slowed from thirty revolutions a minute to twenty. More than 150 miles of cable had been paid out. As the vessel slowed, the dynamometer eased from 2,100 pounds to 2,000. Without any warning, or any single incident to account for it, the cable inexplicably parted twenty feet from the stern of the British ship.

A blast from *Agamemnon*'s gun brought the entire crew topside. The bad news spread like wildfire. The Brits could not blame this one on the Yanks. Bright rushed to the machinery and found it idle. The severed end of the cable hung over the stern-wheel, swinging loosely back and forth. No one on the machinery could explain what had happened. The break occurred instantaneously, and though the mechanics suggested a number of ingenious reasons, Bright and Canning remained mystified. In an investigation of the upper-deck storage area, Canning discovered that the storm had worked the flooring loose, and the joints had chafed the protective armoring on the bottom coils.

Signals on *Niagara* also abruptly stopped. Called from his bed, Field rushed to the electrician's room. De Sauty shrugged, waiting and watching, hoping for the resumption of impulses. Hudson joined the meeting to ask what he could do. Minutes passed, and then an hour. Since the last splice, *Niagara* had paid out 111 miles, and Field suspected that *Agamemnon* had dispensed the same. Because of his agreement with Bright to abort the expedition if the cable failed more than a hundred miles beyond the rendezvous, Field asked Hudson to bring the ship about and return to Queenstown. Never did defeat taste so bitter.

Instead of cutting the cable, or attempting to recover it, Field let it drag off the stern of *Niagara*. The mechanics applied the brakes to the cable and locked down the paying-out machinery. The wire refused to part and held the whole weight of *Niagara* by its slender cord. "Although the wind was quite fresh," Hudson wrote, "the cable held the ship for one hour and forty minutes before breaking, and [withstood] a strain of four tons." The test made on the *Niagara* corroborated the opinion of engineers on *Agamemnon* that the upper-deck cable probably suffered fatal damage during the storm.[5]

While Field and Everett performed break tests on the cable, *Agamemnon* stood exactly 225 miles to the east. Bright realized that the ship had passed the abort point, but by only fourteen miles. By his count, both ships should still have at least 150 miles of extra cable on board—as much as they carried during the 1857 expedition. Knowing how Field's mind worked, he expected his partner to have arrived at the same conclusion. Despite being short of coal and provisions, Preedy accepted Bright's proposal to sail back to the rendezvous in the likely prospect of finding *Niagara* there. Bright expected Field to make the same calculation and wait eight days, as agreed, but in this he would be disappointed. He also hoped Everett would find a way to recover some of the cable, even though no arrangement had been made for reversing the paying-out machinery.

As *Niagara* sailed for Queenstown, *Agamemnon*, for the fifth time, began beating under sail for the old rendezvous. On Wednesday, June 30, the breeze blew from the southwest, bringing mist, rain, and mounting seas. On Thursday the wind intensified. Waves grew in strength, and a wet fog smothered the seascape, making it so dense that a person standing on deck could not see the mastheads. The chilly conditions reminded Bright of a wintry day in London.

Late that afternoon heavy seas lashed at the ship, but with 250 tons of cable gone from the upper deck, she rode into the storm under double-reefed topsails, pitching and rolling as before, but under no strain. Bright observed that she handled the waves "as buoyant as a lifeboat, and no one cared how much she took to kicking about, though the cold wet fog . . . penetrated everywhere, [making] the ship as wet inside as out."[6]

Bright now believed that the nautical sages in Great Britain who advised sailing in June really knew nothing about weather in the North Atlantic. In such thick, stormy conditions he doubted whether it would be possible for *Agamemnon* and *Niagara* to meet unless the ships ran into each other—then the "cable-laying would have gone on wholesale." To avoid such a mishap, and to keep from bungling into *Valorous*, Preedy ordered the ship's guns fired at regular intervals, fog bells rung, and a bugler stationed forward to warn off approaching vessels.[7]

The gale blew without cessation for two days, but quite unexpectedly on Sunday morning, July 4, *Agamemnon* sailed into the rendezvous and found the weather clear and bright. Once again it seemed to Preedy that the only tranquil spot on the entire North Atlantic lay in mid-ocean. Dayman came over from *Valorous* and reported that for two days the fog had been so thick that the ship "had scarcely seen herself, much less anything else until Sunday."[8]

For two days *Agamemnon* and *Valorous* cruised about the area looking for *Niagara*. The weather remained pleasant and uncommonly clear. On Tuesday the British ships cruised far and wide, sailing into another storm so thick with fog that the whole Royal Navy could have been a half mile away and never been seen. Preedy signaled *Valorous* to return to the rendezvous for one more look, and if failing to find *Niagara*, to sail for Queenstown. At 8:00 P.M. Preedy turned the ship's head homeward. Under full sail *Agamemnon* rode a stiff southwesterly breeze and on July 12 cast anchor in Queenstown harbor.

The delayed arrival of *Agamemnon* produced a universal deep breath of relief among the crew of *Niagara*. When the American ship arrived at Queenstown on July 5, Field had expected to find *Agamemnon*, enjoying a 200-mile head start, rocking at anchor. Knowing of the battering she suffered during the June storms, the concern for her safety mounted as each day passed. Field waited at Queenstown, but he felt equally obligated to meet with the company directors in London. Torn between two responsibilities, he knew the bad news would reach London by cable long before he could appear in person. He needed something reassuring to tell the directors, but he wanted Bright and Thomson by his side when he faced them. He did not know what had happened on *Agamemnon*, but making calculations during the voyage back to Queenstown, he became aware that if *Agamemnon* had lost no more cable than *Niagara*, he would still have enough to span the Atlantic.

Field cabled the directors explaining his reasons for remaining in Queenstown. Each day that passed added more anxiety to the wait. Ships coming east reported unseasonably thick fog and high winds in the mid-Atlantic. Field knew about *Agamemnon*'s strained mast, her shortage of coal, and the punk food. British correspondents insinuated that after the weather turned foul, *Niagara* deserted the British ship and fled for safety. Londoners would not know the story until *Agamemnon* returned, and after a week passed, some of them never expected to hear from her again. They damned Cyrus Field, damned the cable, and damned the directors for becoming involved in such foolishness with an American.

On July 12, while the British continued to look for someone else to damn, *Agamemnon* slipped into Queenstown. Field conferred with Bright and Thomson and wired the directors that they were on the way. The directors thought the expedition had been abandoned and felt the same way themselves. Chairman Sir William Brown decided it would not be worth his time to leave Liverpool and attend the meeting. He sent his resignation, adding, "We must all deeply regret our misfortune in not being able to lay the cable. I think there is nothing to be done but dispose of what is left on the best terms we can." He recommended that the proceeds be divided equally among the shareholders and the company liquidated.[9]

On July 13 Field, Bright, and Thomson met the directors in the same room where they had convened with so much optimism six weeks before. The mood had drastically changed to one bathed with dour expressions. Bright wrote: "Most of the directors looked blankly into one another's faces." Without giving Field an opportunity to state his case, Vice Chairman Brooking read Sir William's letter and walked out of the meeting. The next day he tendered his resignation, stating that he intended "to take no further part in an undertaking which had been proved hopeless, and to persist in which seemed mere rashness and folly."[10]

After Brooking resigned, the remaining directors said they were ready to listen if Field had any positive remarks to make. At first, Brown and Brooking's defections staggered Field, but the company's resilient general manager did not go to the meeting without preparing a strategy. The mere intimation of the board's willingness to listen brought Field to his feet. He could see that the remaining directors did not want to liquidate the company for a pittance if there was still a chance of banking a profit.

Field did not have to concoct a story to hold their attention. What he said he emphatically believed. The company's loss of only three hundred miles of cable did not represent a catastrophic financial blow: liquidating the remainder of the cable would. The ships waiting at Queenstown still carried enough cable to cross the Atlantic. To set out again, all the ships needed were coal and supplies. Bright confirmed that the mechanical aspects of the expedition had been finely tuned for a second effort. Thomson explained how the accidents occurred and what caused them. Bright blamed most of the problems on storm damage to the cable stored on *Agamemnon*'s upper deck, which all now lay on the bottom of the ocean. The two British experts stated emphatically that the cable could be laid. According to Maury's recommended cable-laying window of opportunity, July 20 was rapidly approaching, and if a second effort were to be made, Field stressed that the expedition must be launched immediately.

As Field spoke, he rekindled the fires of success in the bellies of the directors. They unanimously agreed to retain the company, replacing Sir William with James Stuart-Wortley as chairman, and replacing Brooking with Curtis Lampson as vice chairman, whose perseverance Queen Victoria would one day reward with a baronetcy. Before the meeting ended, Field, Bright, and Thomson received a typical parliamentary vote of confidence along with an order to set out on one last expedition as soon as possible. If that failed, the directors would dissolve the company. Samuel Gurney, one of the faithful board members, and Field went directly to the Admiralty and obtained approval to dispatch the ships immediately. Field telegraphed the outcome of the meeting to Hudson and Preedy at Queenstown and asked them to be ready to sail as soon as he arrived.[11]

The company directors made their position perfectly clear. They would never back another expedition. For Cyrus Field and his team, all other options had expired. There must never be another failure.

—— Chapter 8 ——

An Affair to Remember

On Saturday, July 17, 1858, Field and de Sauty held their last discussions with Thomson and Bright before going on board their respective ships. The second start drew no crowds. There were no words of encouragement, rather the opposite. No lord lieutenant came to Queenstown to make a speech. Peter Fitzgerald, the Knight of Kerry, threw no banquets. Nobody got drunk and sang through the night. Wildman Whitehouse went back to the telegraph station at Knightstown. Bright heard the locals speak of the second expedition as a "mad freak of stubborn ignorance." They had read Nicolas Wood's account of the storm in the London *Times*.[1]

Wood observed the absence of well-wishers. From small ships anchored in the harbor, barely a sole looked up as *Agamemnon* steamed by. "Everyone seemed impressed with the conviction that we were engaged in a hopeless enterprise, and the squadron seemed rather to have slunk away on some discreditable mission, than to have sailed for the accomplishment of a grand, national scheme."[2]

Sailors of the Wire Squadron voiced their opinions in the sanctity of the forecastle, calling the hurried departure just another "fool's errand." They placed bets with odds running against the cablemen. They said "the Company was possessed by a kind of insanity" and predicted "they would soon be cured by another bitter experience." Cyrus Field remained optimistic, ignoring such talk. Bright shielded his worries from the others. The only creatures as cheerful as Field were a flock of gulls that circled the ships and squawked at jack for scraps of salt horse.[3]

The squadron agreed to not keep together but to sail at their own speed to the rendezvous. With her bunkers full and no wind in her sails, *Niagara* steamed the entire distance and reached the starting gate first. A week later

Valorous arrived; followed by *Gorgon*. Neither vessel reported seeing *Agamemnon*. Once again the old man-of-war seemed to have been swallowed by the ocean. Field became anxious, offering a cash prize to the first man to sight her. A sudden rash of sightings, including such apparitions as the ghostly *Flying Dutchman*, did not bring her any faster.

To conserve coal, Preedy bent his canvas and sailed most of the way. He arrived last, this time delayed by too little wind rather than too much. Preedy could have used coal to get out of Queenstown, but he stuck with sails and never cleared the harbor until July 18. A light southwest wind held him back, so he never rounded Cape Clear until five o'clock in the afternoon. At dusk the rocky heights at Bantry Bay finally dropped out of sight. At the same hour, *Niagara* had steamed 200 miles into the Atlantic.

Jack-tar voiced no objection to the lazy cruise. Unlike the first expedition, the sea shimmered in sunlight during the day, skies glimmered with majestic reddish hues at sunset, and at night a full moon danced upon the ocean, casting silvery beams on a tranquil sea. The dark hull of the ship barely moved through the calm. Overhead, drooping white sails hung like slack clouds, now and then slapping at a wisp of wind. Men gathered on deck to enjoy the night. No one cared and no one worried, but as one day passed and another began with no change in the wind, Thomson and Bright began to lose admiration for the stellar days of summer. Such pristine cable-laying days should not be wasted.

The weather never changed, and Preedy finally burned a little coal. The voyage became an endless tedium of changing from sail to steam, and then from steam to sail, back and forth, over and over again, just to save fuel. On a good day *Agamemnon* logged eighty miles headway. Grubbing gulls that joined the ship at Queenstown enjoyed a free ride and regular meals. They clung to mastheads, squawked at dawn, took a dip in the Atlantic after breakfast, hovered about the ship all day, and returned during the afternoon for a serving of garbage from the galley. The gulls showed no inclination to fly home, serving as indicators of continued fine weather.

While *Niagara* drifted listlessly in midocean, Captain Hudson became daily more alarmed by the absence of the Wire Squadron. Finally on July 26 the *Valorous* hove in sight, followed a day later by the *Gorgon*. Hudson hailed the latter, asking, "Have you seen the *Agamemnon*?" The captain replied, "No. Have you any coal to spare?" Hudson, having burned much of his coal, replied, "No, none at all." Field, listening to the conversation, wondered if the next problem would be a coal shortage.[4]

On Wednesday evening, July 28, eleven days after sailing from Queenstown, *Agamemnon* approached the area marked by a tiny dot on Commander Moriarty's navigator's chart. Bright climbed into the shrouds and before sunset spotted the three ships of the Wire Squadron. The night passed quietly. For the first time since the beginning of the voyage the usual scuttlebutt on deck and yarning in the forecastle gave way to renewed rounds of wagering. Jack-tar placed bets on how far the ships would travel before the next accident, and barely anyone staked money on the cable making it across the ocean.

For five days the crew of *Niagara*, having arrived at the rendezvous on July 23, had speculated on the possible causes for *Agamemnon*'s delay. One source put her on the rocks off Queenstown. Though the weather remained tranquil, Preedy faced a storm of questions when in the morning Field and others from the squadron met on *Agamemnon*.[5]

Fearing that such perfect cable-laying days could not much longer last, Field pressed everyone to get started. At daylight on July 29, *Niagara* and *Agamemnon* closed within shouting distance. Both ships lowered boats, passed hawsers, and made fast to each other. *Niagara* passed her end of the cable to *Agamemnon*. Thomson's electricians made the splice at 12:30 P.M., using the heavy frame that worked like a splint to hold the splice. The electricians attached a lead sinker to carry the frame to the bottom, but the weight broke free and plummeted overboard. Sailors blamed the mishap on failing to braze a lucky sixpence to the splice. The cable crew hauled the contraption back on board and anchored it with a thirty-two-pound shot. They tossed the splice into the sea together with a loose sixpence, and both descended into the deep. Nobody mentioned whether this small oversight influenced the oddsmakers. On this day, however, no spectators gathered to witness the weary formality. As correspondent Wood observed, "those on board the ship had witnessed so many beginnings to the telegraphic line that it was evident they despaired of there ever being an end to it."[6]

Field experienced a tremor of rare gloom, writing:

> When I thought of all that we had passed through, of the hopes thus far disappointed, of the friends saddened by our reverses, of the few that remained to sustain us, I felt a load at my heart almost too heavy to bear, though my confidence was firm and my determination fixed.[7]

After 216 fathoms of cable descended into the deep, the two cable ships set a course in opposite directions and steamed slowly away.

Field, who had become a nautical perfectionist for detail, noted in his journal:

> Thursday, July twenty-ninth, latitude fifty-two degrees nine minutes north, longitude thirty-two degrees twenty-seven minutes west . . . sea smooth; light wind from S.E. to S.S.E., cloudy. Splice made at 1:00 P.M. Signals through the whole length of cable on board both ships perfect. Depth of water fifteen hundred fathoms; distance to the entrance of Valencia harbor eight hundred and thirteen nautical miles. . . . Distance to the entrance to Trinity Bay, Newfoundland, eight hundred

The USS *Niagara* (right) and the HMS *Agamemnon* (left) part company in the middle of the North Atlantic to lay the 1858 cable. (From Charles Bright, *The Story of the Atlantic Cable*. Digitized by Debra Peffer.)

and twenty-two nautical miles, and from there to the telegraph-house at the head of the bay of Bull's Arm, sixty miles, making in all eight hundred and eighty-two nautical miles. The *Niagara* has sixty-nine miles further to run than the *Agamemnon*. The *Niagara* and the *Agamemnon* have each eleven hundred miles of cable on board, about the same quantity as last year.[8]

For three hours the cable ships proceeded cautiously, allowing the cable to settle on the ocean's floor. After the wire took a horizontal slant, they accelerated to five knots. Cable spun off the sheaves at six knots, and the dynamometer recorded 1,700 pounds tension.

On both vessels the engineers let the electricians run the show. If the testing room reported a problem with the cable's continuity, the engineers and mechanics marked the cable at the paying-out machine and suspended operations until the electricians decided how to proceed. The ship's testing room contained what correspondent Wood called Thomson's "mysterious apparatus by which electricity is weighed and measured." The instruments transmitted and received signals through the entire length of the cable, one ship to the other, and never ceased.[9]

The ships exchanged signals every ten minutes. The impulses not only tested the continuity and insulation of the wire from end to end, they provided a means to communicate between vessels. Every time one of the ships laid ten miles of cable, electricians notified the other ship, enabling them to track each other's progress. If one ship stopped to splice or to shift to a fresh coil, another message went across the wire. The current carrying the message passed through an electromagnetometer, a fancy word for a simple instrument invented by Whitehouse to detect the passage of electric current. The current flowing through the detector exited at the end of the cable through Thomson's mirror reflecting instrument. Electricians recorded any deflections on the instrument's scale, and also the degree of charge and discharge registered by the electromagnetometer. Hence, if a defect in continuity or insulation occurred, it could be pinpointed by comparing the collected data.

The New York *Herald*'s special correspondent on the *Niagara* overheard a sailor remark, during the end of a rather unscientific discussion with his messmates:

> Darn the continuity. I wish they would get rid of it altogether. It has caused a darn sight more trouble than the hull (sic) thing is worth. I say they ought to do without it and let it go. I believe they would get the cable down if they didn't pay any attention to it.[10]

The well-meaning sailor envisioned continuity as a diabolical infestation that bewitched the expedition.

At 4:00 P.M. a very large whale approached *Agamemnon* at great speed off the bow, rolling and stirring the surface into foam as it passed down the starboard beam. "For the first time," wrote correspondent Wood, "we felt a possibility . . . that our second mysterious breakage of the cable might have been caused, after all, by one of these animals getting foul of it under water." Observers on deck began shouting, "Look! It's heading straight for the cable!" To the relief of all, the whale passed astern, grazing the cable where it entered the water but miraculously did no damage.[11]

Four hours later a cable inspector discovered an injured section of wire about two miles ahead of the paying-out machine. Canning, the engineer on duty, had about twenty minutes to repair the damage before the section reached the machinery. Checking the speed of the ship had caused problems in the past, so Canning wanted to make the repair without stopping the engines. Just as the mechanics finished lapping the joint, Thomson reported a dead short in the wire, meaning the conductor wires had broken and the cable had to be cut and spliced. Without a moment to lose, the mechanics severed the cable to make a splice, but Thomson's instruments indicated that the fault lay overboard, fifty miles from the ship. How much of the cable had been damaged no one could tell, for the entire coil had been shaken during June's storms.

With the cable flowing through the paying-out machine at six knots an hour, not a second could be lost. Thomson finally hailed the bridge to stop

The cablemen on HMS *Agamemnon* received a shock when a huge whale suddenly appeared off the ship's beam and grazed the cable flowing into the ocean. (From Charles Bright, *The Story of the Atlantic Cable.* Digitized by Debra Peffer.)

the ship. The moment the propeller stopped rotating the stern of the vessel began lifting and falling in the waves, gradually pulling more cable through the braking machinery. Nearly all of the officers of the ship, and those connected with the enterprise, gathered in the main hold to watch as the wire slowly unwound from the coil, lurching in jerks and spasms toward the paying-out machine while electricians raced against time to make the splice.

When it became apparent that the electricians were losing the race, Thomson sent a runner to the paying-out machine with orders to set the brake. For several minutes the ship hung by the cable, and as each minute passed, the indicator on the dynamometer crept higher. When Thomson signaled the splice made, the dynamometer read 4,000 pounds. The mechanic released the stoppers on the brake and the splice whipped through the machinery and into the deep.

Thomson returned to the electrician's room and learned, after so narrowly saving the cable, that the wire was still dead. Preedy cut back *Agamemnon*'s engines to save as much cable as possible while Thomson waited the mutually agreed upon six hours in the hope that the fault, whatever it might be, would mend itself. No signals returned, the magnetic needles on the receiving instruments never budged, and Thomson calculated that a total breakdown of insulation occurred somewhere very close to *Niagara*. While the electricians furtively watched the instruments and debated whether to cut the cable, the impulses suddenly returned as strong as ever. In a "perfect fever of nervous excitement, shaking like an aspen leaf," Thomson eventually composed himself but continued to fret over the cause of the interruption. Through the nerve-shattering ordeal Bright stood "like a boy caught in a fault, his lips and cheeks smeared with tar, biting his nails and looking to the professor for advice." They later learned that a defect had occurred in the battery bank used on *Niagara*, which for several hours baffled de Sauty's electricians as well as Thomson's.[12]

When the circuit went dead, Cyrus Field absorbed the shock courageously, again anticipating the worst. He joined de Sauty in the electrician's room, who believed the problem might have occurred on *Agamemnon* because he could not detect a breakdown of insulation. Nobody bothered to check the erratic battery, which somehow corrected itself. Field noted in his journal: "Kept on paying out from the *Niagara* very slowly, and constantly applying all kinds of electrical tests until ten minutes past nine, ship's time, when again commenced receiving perfect signals from the *Agamemnon*." The unexplained incident merely added more anxiety to the emotions of the cablemen who spent every hour of each day anticipating another expedition-ending catastrophe.[13]

On *Agamemnon*, Bright stationed more inspectors around the reel feeding the cable-laying machinery. Toward morning he received a report of another damaged section coming off the coil. Discovered in time, Canning's mechanics repaired the joint. Preedy had no need to stop the ship, and at noon on Friday, July 30, he reported *Agamemnon* ninety miles from her starting point.

The *Niagara* also made good headway, but for unaccountable reasons ran sixteen miles off course during the night and wasted twenty miles of cable. *Gorgon* came abeam in the morning and informed Hudson that *Niagara* was headed in the wrong direction. Hudson concluded that the mass of iron-armored cable in the hold caused the compass to deviate, so he asked *Gorgon* to take the lead and he would follow. Had the compass error not been discovered, or if the British had not loaned *Gorgon* to the expedition, the *Niagara* would have exhausted her supply of cable before reaching Newfoundland.

During the afternoon Captain Preedy noticed a disturbing drop in the barometer, and by evening a gale began blowing out of the east—a rather uncommon occurrence for late July. At sundown *Agamemnon* labored at four knots against the wind. He ordered topmasts lowered and every stick and spar aloft sent down to reduce the wind's resistance. The ship burned an enormous amount of coal to keep the cable on course with Valentia. "If the wind lasted," wrote the London *Times* reporter,

> we should be reduced to burning the masts, spars, and even the decks. . . . It seemed to be our particular ill-fortune to meet with head-on winds whichever way the ship's head was turned. On our journey out we had been delayed and obliged to consume an undue proportion of coal for want of an easterly wind, and now all our fuel was wanted *because* of one.[14]

The gale did not last, and on Saturday, July 31, the breeze swung abruptly back to the southwest. From messages transmitted by *Niagara*, both ships had paid out 300 miles of cable, and Bright estimated that the two steamers now lay 450 miles apart with each ship keeping pace with the other.

On *Agamemnon*'s side of the ocean, the southwesterly breeze soon formed into another gale. On the other side of the Atlantic, *Niagara* steamed westward, hindered only by a sea of passive rollers. By evening tremendous waves ran before the southwest tempest, pitching and tossing *Agamemnon* to the extent that Bright feared the cable would not hold through the night. With Canning and Henry Clifford at his side, they stood by the machinery through the storm, one watching the sheaves, the other manning the brake; everyone making small adjustments to compensate for the rise and fall of the ship's stern.

Early Sunday morning the wind increased again, blowing itself into a gusty gale. Bright assigned two more engineers to the relieving wheels of the dynamometer, one spelling the other every four hours. Every time the stern dropped into a trough, the operator had to ease the tension on the brake moments before the next wave heaved the stern upwards. Any lapse of concentration or any misstep would tear the cable apart. Every so often a curious sailor ambled aft to peer over the taffrail, unable to comprehend how such a small thread could withstand the ravages of the surging seas. At night they watched as the cable carved a narrow wake, spreading a thin phosphorescent glow upon the enormous waves sweeping under the stern.

Those that crawled into their cots expected at any moment to hear the sharp report of cannon, signaling the cable had snapped, but the thin cord held. In the morning the sky remained black and stormy to windward. Violent squalls of wind and rain hammered the ship throughout the day. Having now passed over the deepest part of the ocean (14,400 feet), Bright made a quick assessment of the cable in the hold. Not so much slack would be required the rest of the way. A noon observation put *Agamemnon* about 350 miles from her midocean starting point, and unless the bad weather continued and cast the ship off course, Bright counted more than enough cable to reach Valentia.

Monday afternoon, while Bright and Thomson ate their meal, their hearts took a tumble when they heard a report from *Agamemnon*'s gun. Thomson rushed to the electrician's room and found the impulses steady as ever. Bright careened down the deck to the paying-out machine and found the drums running smoothly. Canning pointed to the American schooner *Chieftain*, which had just dipped her colors after coming in from the east. While tacking, the schooner nearly collided with the cable ship. Warned off by three shots from *Valorous* and one from *Agamemnon*, she passed in a daze.

The unexpected roar of guns came as a thunderbolt to more than a hundred sailors eating their meal. As they pushed through hatches to the deck, they heard another gun, which usually meant that someone had fallen overboard. When the crew of *Chieftain* realized why they had been warned off, they gave three hearty cheers to the cable ship, which *Agamemnon*'s crew with understandable hesitation returned. Those who expected to collect on their bets returned to finish their meal. The cable continued to pay off the stern, oblivious to the danger narrowly escaped.

Thomson returned to the testing room because signals from *Niagara* were becoming weaker. He sent a message to de Sauty asking why signals could not be read. He received no answer, and at 3:00 P.M. electrical impulses ceased altogether. For more than two hours Thomson and Bright sat in the dimly lit testing room hoping to see a flicker of light register on the mirror reflecting instrument, but none came.

In the electrician's room on *Niagara*, Field noted at noon "imperfect insulation of cable detected in sending and receiving signals from the *Agamemnon.*" For the balance of the afternoon men on both vessels looked for clues to explain the problem. Inspectors on *Niagara* discovered a fault about sixty miles from the lower end of the coil stored in the wardroom. Having emptied the holds of so much weight, *Niagara* became lighter and began rolling in the swells, and the motion crimped a hank of cable. The mechanics cut out the damaged area and brazed a splice. At 5:40 P.M. signals stronger than ever flowed once more between the cable ships.[15]

Thomson became convinced that most of the problems with the cable occurred above the sea rather than below it, so he posted extra watches on the coils and wired de Sauty, asking him to do the same. Thomson now knew that the cable's insulation improved in the deep, where cold water and pressure squeezed out air bubbles, hardened the gutta-percha insulation, and corrected any small manufacturing faults in the copper conductor.

With the weather moderating and the signals again strong, Thomson and Bright crawled into their bunks at midnight. At 3:00 A.M. a gun boomed. Both men, followed by a hundred more, rushed to the deck to ascertain the cause of the disturbance. In the dim light of the sea they could see *Valorous*, rounded to in a warlike attitude, firing gun after gun at an American bark standing directly off *Agamemnon*'s stern. Unable to comprehend why a British warship would be firing at her, the bark threw her sails aback and hove to. Whatever the American shipmaster might have thought of having his flag outraged will never be known. He remained hove to until

Agamemnon and *Valorous* passed out of sight, never knowing how close his ship had come to fouling the cable.

On Tuesday afternoon, August 3, Thomson wired Field that *Agamemnon* had paid out 780 miles of cable. An hour after Field received the message *Niagara* began dodging icebergs, some a hundred feet high with peaks topped by a corona of fleecy white clouds. At sunset Thomson wired Field that *Agamemnon* had just brought the cable up the slope and onto the shallow plateau off the Irish Coast and was now paying cable into 1,200 feet of water. De Sauty replied that *Niagara* had ascended onto the continental shelf and by Wednesday hoped to be in sight of Newfoundland. The company crews on both vessels, though dead tired, could barely sleep through the night. The thought of being so close to land with circuits strong made everyone's heart beat faster.

At noon on Wednesday, August 4, the *Agamemnon* lay eighty-nine miles from the telegraph station on Valentia. The sun glittered brightly over a calm and placid sea. The cable rolled through the machinery with little tension on the line. The mechanics had only one more hurdle, to make a second change from the upper-deck coil to the small coil on the orlop deck. The transfer went smoothly, but Bright became mystified when he discovered far less cable in the hold than his last estimate. He discovered that operators had been paying out an excessive amount of slack since reaching the plateau, so much, in fact, as to alarmingly reduce the amount of wire needed to reach Ireland. He stopped the practice, increased the tension on the brake, and hoped he would still have something to splice to the shore end at Valentia.

From the other side of the ocean Field wrote: "Weather beautiful, perfectly calm. *Gorgon* in sight. . . . Sixty-four miles from the telegraph house." At 12:30 P.M. the *Niagara*, after passing another field of icebergs, entered Trinity Bay. Never did the rocky shores of Newfoundland, with its scrub pines and velvet moors look so good to weary travelers. After sunset, Field could not sleep or relax. He had to stay awake and see it through to the end.[16]

Unlike *Agamemnon*, *Niagara* sailed through marvelous summer weather all the way to Newfoundland, fulfilling at least part of Commander Maury's prediction that the best time to lay the cable was between the end of July and the beginning of August. Captain Otter, commanding the HMS *Porcupine*, sent by the Admiralty to watch for the Wire Squadron, came alongside *Niagara* and put a pilot on board to guide her into Bull's Arm Bay. At 1:45 A.M. on Thursday, August 5, she dropped anchor between *Porcupine* and *Gorgon* at the head of the bay.

Agamemnon and *Niagara*, each having traveled half the distance across the Atlantic, made landfall within hours of each other. As the pilot from *Porcupine* brought *Niagara* into Bull's Arm Bay, *Agamemnon* came in sight of Skelligs Light on Ireland. The crew of *Valorous* gave a cheer and steamed ahead, firing rockets at intervals to guide *Agamemnon* inshore. At dawn Thursday morning the rocky heights surrounding the wild, picturesque neighborhood of Valentia Island loomed into view, and Bright could distinctly see the dim lights of Knightstown nestled along shore. The London *Times* reporter spoke for everyone when he wrote: "Never, probably, was the sight of land more welcome, as it brought to a successful termination one of the greatest, but at the same time most difficult, schemes . . . ever undertaken."[17]

No one noticed the approach of *Agamemnon* until Dayman took *Valorous* into the harbor and woke the sleepy villagers by firing a gun. At 6:00 A.M. *Agamemnon* came to anchor off Beginish Island. By then hundreds of Valentia's inhabitants had taken to boats, shouting and waving at the cable ships. The Knight of Kerry came around from Dingle in Her Majesty's gunboat *Shamrock*, and before Thomson and Bright could make the splice, the celebration began.

Thomson went to the electrician's room and wired Field, reporting *Agamemnon* off Valentia Bay after paying out 1,020 miles of cable and preparing to splice to the shore end. De Sauty replied that *Niagara*, after paying out 1,030 miles of cable, was ready to do the same. The signals between both vessels remained clear and strong.

At 2:00 A.M. Field's restlessness got the better of him, and he asked the officer of the deck to lower a boat and lend him a pair of oarsmen. Though uncertain whether he could find the telegraph shack in the dark, he still wanted to go ashore. A half hour later the bow of the boat ground against the beach, and finding an open stretch of skyline through the woods, Field started up what he believed to be the trail to the station.

He had never been there before, but he knew the building lay in woods about a half mile from the beach. He stumbled up the trail, kicking aside branches and brambles, and stomping through mud holes. He soon spied a dark structure that suddenly loomed in front of him, but he could not find a door. He stopped to listen and heard heavy breathing from men asleep. He hollered, "The cable is laid," and two dark objects gave a snort, lit a lamp, and came to the door.[18] Their dirty clothes looked like they had been dragged through the bed of the forest on a wet day. When dawn brightened the landscape, Field observed that the two-story clapboard station lay on the side of a hill in a perfect wilderness. The building had only one door but inside contained a comfortable parlor, kitchen, several bedrooms, and a telegraph room. Of eleven men assigned to the station, those there claimed to be maintenance men. None of them knew how to send a message. Field also noticed that none of them knew much about cooking, making beds, or sweeping the floor. The nearest station capable of transmitting a message to New York lay fifteen miles away at St. John's. Two of the men, learning that their early morning visitor was no other than Cyrus Field, volunteered to take his dispatches to the city.[19]

The telegraph station at Trinity Bay, Newfoundland, depicted during the winter of 1857–1858. (From William H. Russell, *The Atlantic Telegraph, 1865*. Digitized by Debra Peffer.)

To his wife, Field wrote: "Arrived here yesterday. All well. The Atlantic telegraph cable successfully laid. Please telegraph me here immediately." He then sent a message to the Associated Press. It contained a brief description of the voyage, intimating that before the day ended the two continents would be connected. The message took the entire country by surprise. Relay stations from Canada to America flashed a condensed version of the news to every telegrapher in North America. One would have thought a war had been won, and in a sense it had: not a war against nations but one against the sea and the stumbles encountered in perfecting a new technology.[20]

He also sent a cable to the White House, advising President Buchanan, "as soon as the two ends are connected with the land lines Queen Victoria will send a message to you, and the cable will be kept free until after your reply has been transmitted."[21]

After the first wave of euphoria passed, Field sent a message to Cooper, writing: "We landed here in the woods; until the telegraph instruments are ready, and perfectly adjusted, communication cannot pass between the two continents, but the electric currents are received freely. You shall have the earliest intimation when all is ready, but it may be some days before everything is perfected."[22]

At 5:15 A.M. a detail from *Niagara* dragged the cable ashore and connected it to the land end, which lay covered in a ditch at the edge of the woods. De Sauty and Woodhouse made the connection and tested the line. Signals flowed through the conductor to *Agamemnon*, the impulses stronger than ever. A few minutes later Thomson replied. "Very strong currents of electricity through the whole cable from the other side of the Atlantic."[23]

Bright went ashore, and using the telegraph station at Knightstown, wired the directors, "The *Agamemnon* has arrived at Valentia, and we are about to land the cable. The *Niagara* is in Trinity Bay, Newfoundland. There are good signals between the ships." The unexpected message shocked the jubilant directors, but probably to a lesser degree than it shocked Sir William Brown and T. H. Brooking, who had liquidated their shares.[24]

At 3:00 P.M. Bright's mechanics, led by Canning and dozens of boatmen from the *Valorous*, headed ashore at Knightstown with the cable. Sir Peter Fitzgerald, Knight of Kerry, after hurrying over to Valentia from Dingle, jumped into the surf to bring the wire ashore. The crowd on shore joined with men on the boats to clutch the cable. Together with a thoroughly drenched Sir Peter they laid the wire in a prepared trench and carried the end to the telegraph station. Whitehouse made the connection, and the first telegraphic message sped its way across the ocean to Bull's Arm Bay. A royal salute from *Agamemnon* and *Valorous* loosened a few rocks and made the rugged hills reverberate, communicating to the neighborhood that the Old World and the New World are joined.

On the other side of the ocean *Gorgon* fired a twenty-one-gun salute. The *Niagara* remained silent. She had not yet received her guns. Captain Hudson offered a prayer, made a few appropriate remarks, and let his marines celebrate the occasion by firing their muskets.

Correspondent Wood disembarked at Valentia and telegraphed the London *Times*: "End of cable landed safely, close by pier, at Knightstown, being carried on paddle-boxes of the *Valorous*—expect to be open to public in three weeks."[25]

For the first time in the history of man, telegraph lines connected two rivers at opposite ends of the world, the Missouri River in America and the Volga River in Russia. Much work still needed to be done at both ends of the line before commercial messages could be sent, but the celebration had already begun.

CHAPTER 9

JUBILATIONS BEFORE DEATH

The successful connection of the cable took people on both sides of the Atlantic by surprise. After the fiasco in June 1858, the public agreed with the "croakers" who infested the alehouses and street corners of London and New York. Assuming the stance of wise prognosticators, the June expedition gave them the opportunity to say, "I told you so," or words to that effect. Even Abram Hewitt, who could never understand why Peter Cooper invested in the enterprise, admitted, "I regarded the investment of so much money in a doubtful enterprise as a piece of folly. I am forced to acknowledge the superior wisdom of Mr. Cooper."[1]

Morse was en route to England when a sailboat stopped the steamer *Fulton* and delivered the news that the first messages had been passed on the Atlantic cable. The announcement came quite unexpectedly. Morse turned to his brother Richard and said, "This is very gratifying, but it is doubtful whether many more messages will be received." Richard asked why, and Morse replied, "The cable has been so long stored in an improper place that much of the coating has been destroyed and . . . in other respects injured." Morse wanted the cable to work because his patented lines would carry part of the volume.[2]

When the good news came in August, press announcements electrified two continents in more ways than one. Since the early 1850s, men on both sides of the ocean predicted that if the Atlantic telegraph ever became a reality, which they doubted, it would rate as the "greatest feat of the century." Having happened, that is exactly what the press called it. The London *Times* compared the accomplishment to the discoveries of Columbus "linking the Old World with the New," but this time "annihilating space."

The *Times* enclosed a few words for the croakers, calling them "antiprogressives by nature."[3]

The *Times* also added a curious statement, easy to misinterpret in the United States: "More was done yesterday for the consolidation of our empire, than the wisdom of our statesmen, the liberality of our Legislature, or the loyalty of our colonists, could ever have effected." There were some readers who wondered whether the *Times* still thought of American "colonists" as part of the British Empire.[4]

On August 6, with Cyrus Field on board, *Niagara* put into St. John's for coal. The governor and the chamber of commerce arranged an honorary dinner and hosted a ball at Colonial Hall. Called upon for a speech, Field gave great credit to the contributions of his associates, who more than deserved it, and he even had a few good words for those who deserted him, such as the company's former chairman and vice chairman. But he made a curious comment that a few days later crept into the London *Times* when he said, "We have had many difficulties to surmount, many discouragements to bear, and some enemies to overcome, whose very opposition has stimulated us to greater exertion." Exactly who those enemies were Field did not say, and his statement may have caused him trouble had his words been broadcast beyond the readership of the *Times*.[5]

The good news created a stunning effect at a somber religious convocation of alumni at the Andover Theological Seminary, which was too far away to hear bells ringing and guns booming on Boston Common. During the group's semicentennial anniversary dinner, Rev. Dr. Adams rose, and holding a message over his head, announced the news. A thousand men of the cloth rose to their feet, rent the air with cheers, wet their cheeks with tears, and danced about with unrestrained jubilation. They suddenly remembered the great event "as from the hand of God" and sang the doxology.

Rev. Dr. Hawes added, "We have now consecrated this new power, so far as our agency is concerned, to the building up of truth." There were no guarantees that only truth would flow across the wire, but such an imposing gathering of the Lord's servants could not be expected to pray for anything less.[6]

Henry Field wrote, "Much to his own surprise, Cyrus awoke and found himself famous. In twenty-four hours his name was on millions of tongues."[7]

President Buchanan cabled Field at Trinity Bay, writing: "I congratulate you with all my heart on the success of the great enterprise with which your name is so honorably connected. Under the Blessing of Divine Providence I trust it may prove instrumental in promoting perpetual peace and friendship between kindred nations." At the time, Buchanan was experiencing difficulties with his own kindred nation as the battle in Congress between pro and antislavery factions threatened to dissolve the Union.[8]

Throughout August, the New York papers never stopped eulogizing Cyrus Field and members of the Atlantic Telegraph Company for their great achievement. After denigrating the June expedition for failing, the press outdid itself with platitudes of praise. Having not yet returned home, Field missed the early celebrations. During his absence guns boomed across the nation, fireworks arced through the dark skies of summer nights, and newspapers kept the spotlight on the weary traveler by running such headlines as "Cyrus the Great" and "The Columbus of America." William M. Evarts, later attorney general and secretary of state, said, "There is one world, let there be two." Field replied, "There are two worlds, let there be one." The entire country, thirty million people from Bangor, Maine, to San Francisco, knew his name. During his absence, every banquet, parade, celebration, and popular demonstration became an important news item.[9]

While Great Britain and America celebrated, electricians on both sides of the Atlantic worked frantically to perfect transmissions for commercial use. On August 10 the Trinity Bay station cabled Ireland: "Coil currents have been received—forty per minute easily. . . . Please send slower for the present."[10]

Four days later the Trinity Bay station transmitted a clear message of fourteen words, stating the wire could now be used at the pleasure of the company. On August 16 the directors in London spoke to their brethren in the western hemisphere: "Europe and America are united by telegraphic communication. 'Glory to God in the highest, on earth peace, goodwill towards men.' " The message took fifteen minutes to cross the ocean.[11]

The prearranged message from Queen Victoria to President Buchanan came next and took more than sixteen hours to transmit and receive:

> To the President of the United States, Washington
>
> The Queen desires to congratulate the President upon the successful completion of this great international work, in which the Queen has taken the deepest interest.
>
> The Queen is convinced that the President will join with her in fervently hoping that the Electric Cable which now connects Great Britain with the United States will prove an additional link between the nations whose friendship is founded upon their common interest and reciprocal esteem.
>
> The Queen has much pleasure in communicating with the President, and renewing to him her wishes for the prosperity of the United States.[12]

By the same agreement and on the same day, August 16, 1858, Buchanan replied with a 149-word message that took ten hours of cable time:

> To Her Majesty Victoria, Queen of Great Britain
>
> The President cordially reciprocates the congratulations of Her Majesty the Queen on the success of the great international enterprise accomplished by

the science, skill, and indomitable energy of two countries. It is a triumph more glorious, because far more useful to mankind, than was ever won by conqueror on the field of battle.

May the Atlantic Telegraph, under the blessing of Heaven, prove to be a bond of perpetual peace and friendship between the kindred nations, and an instrument destined by Divine Providence to diffuse religion, civilization, liberty, and law throughout the world. In this view will not all nations of Christendom spontaneously unite in the declaration that it shall be forever neutral, and that its communications shall be held sacred in passing to their places of destination, even in the midst of hostilities.

James Buchanan[13]

The exchange of messages signaled the soon-to-come opening of the cable for commercial use and started a fresh series of demonstrations. New Yorkers fired a 100-gun salute in City Hall Park at daybreak and another at noon. Bells tolled throughout the day as if to announce the coming of the Messiah. Flags flew from every public building. Stores, hotels, and businesses displayed banners, posters, and images of Field and Morse, calling them the "Wire-Pullers of the 19th Century." Even the city's crowded tenement dwellings joined in the celebration, their proud occupants dangling small flags and streamers from upper story windows. At night gaslights and bonfires illuminated the streets and kept the fire companies on alert until dawn. Torch carriers converged on City Hall to join the celebration and accidentally set the cupola on fire. The fire department arrived in time to save the building.

New Yorkers held no exclusive patent on celebrations. Cannon boomed and bells rang in every city and hamlet from the eastern seaboard to the Golden Gate. Nothing seemed too extravagant for the public's expression of popular rejoicing. Even abolitionists and slaveholders found an event upon which they could both agree.

Poets, good and bad, appeared across the nation and vented their patriotism in newspapers, magazines, town halls, and religious gatherings. One anonymous individual, who perhaps like Francis Scott Key wrote only one worthy poem during his lifetime, gave to posterity his finest work:

'Tis done, the angry sea consents,
  The nations stand no more apart,
With claspèd hands the continents
  Feel throbbings of each other's heart.

Speed, speed the cable: let it run
  A loving girdle round the earth,
Till all the nations 'neath the sun
  Shall be as brothers of one hearth;

As brothers pledging, hand in hand,
  One freedom for the world abroad,
One commerce over every land,
  One language and one God.[14]

On August 18 *Niagara* arrived at Castle Garden with Cyrus Field and received a national salute, setting off another round of celebrations. Field said a few words and extricated himself from the crowd. He hurried home in desperate need of rest. Cables from Great Britain lay waiting on his desk; one from director George Peabody, who felt vindicated for leaving his money in the company; others from Sir Charles Wood and Sir John Pakington, successive First Lords of the Admiralty who supported the expedition with ships of the Royal Navy. Field received offers of $5,000 a share for stock he could not have sold for $100 a month earlier.

During the voyage to New York from St. John's, Field attempted to close another chapter on his life. After three harrowing years of mental and emotional exertion, he needed a reprieve. To the company directors in England, he wrote:

> At your unanimous request, but at a very great personal sacrifice to myself, I accepted the office of General Manager of the Atlantic Telegraph Company, for the sole purpose of doing all in my power to aid you to make the enterprise successful; and as that object has been obtained, you will please accept my resignation. It will always afford me pleasure to do anything in my power, consistent with my duties to my family and my own private affairs, to promote the interests of the Atlantic Telegraph Company.[15]

A letter arrived from George Saward, the company's secretary in London, who wrote:

> At last the great work is successful. I rejoice at it for the sake of humanity at large. I rejoice at it for the sake of our common nationalities, and . . . I most heartily rejoice with you . . . for the name of Cyrus W. Field will now go onward to immortality, as long as that of the Atlantic Telegraph shall be known to mankind.[16]

From Field's perspective, he had already experienced too much rejoicing, but he did not object to a little overexuberance from his British partners.

Field longed for privacy and rest. He could go nowhere without becoming the object of immediate attention. People clapped their hands as he walked by, and though he appreciated their gratefulness, such public demonstrations embarrassed him. He learned with amusement that dance halls now featured the latest popular tune, the "Atlantic Telegraph Polka."

As a gesture of appreciation, Mary kept the doors of her home open to Captain Hudson and the officers and crew of *Niagara*. The Fields also included Captain Aldham and the crew of *Gorgon*, without whose help

Cyrus Field's reception in New York created a celebration that lasted for a month and made the cover of *Harper's Weekly*. (From *Harper's Weekly*, August 21, 1858. Digitized by Debra Peffer.)

Niagara may have wandered off to Labrador because of compass error. He also cabled London and received permission from the Admiralty to retain Aldham's crew in New York for a celebration of triumph at Palace Gardens.

Friends and acquaintances, members of the American Telegraph Company, and directors of the original New York, Newfoundland company stopped by at all hours to congratulate and hail the new king. Tiffany & Company, jewelers of New York, begged Field to sell them leftover cable. He sold some of it, but not all. A few days later Tiffany enjoyed a brisk business in souvenirs, and New Yorkers found peddlers on street corners selling images of Cyrus Field framed in a strand of cable and tied with a blue ribbon.

Reporters from New York camped on his doorstep asking when the cable would open for commercial use. He told them soon, explaining that the

Atlantic Telegraph Company's directors, by prior agreement, insisted that the electricians be given the opportunity to perfect transmissions before determining tariffs.

The lengthy time required for the exchange of messages between Queen Victoria and President Buchanan worried him. He kept in constant touch with de Sauty, who remained at Trinity Bay to work on the line with Whitehouse at Knightstown. Signals had grown inexplicably weaker, but de Sauty kept those worries to himself.

When two overdue passenger ships, the Cunarder *Europa* and the *Arabia*, thickly freighted with human lives, collided off Cape Race on the night of August 14, all were feared lost. Friends on both sides of the Atlantic despaired after waiting a week without word. Two days later *Arabia* limped into St. John's. Fourteen days would have elapsed before the arrival of the next steamer. Field authorized a cable to be sent, and in short order de Sauty alleviated the concerns of friends and family with a single telegram, which read: "Newfoundland:—*Arabia* in collision with *Europa*, Cape Race, Saturday. *Arabia* on her way. Head slightly injured. *Europa* lost bowsprit, cutwater; stem sprung. Will remain in St. John's ten days. . . . No loss of life or limb." Five days later the Newfoundland office spoke again: "*Persia* takes *Europa*'s passengers and mails. Great rejoicing everywhere at success of cable. . . . Pray give some news for New York: they are mad for news."[17]

William E. Dodge, a merchant from New York, numbered among those waiting in Liverpool for *Europa*. "Any delay in the arrival of the ship would have caused great anxiety," Dodge recalled. "But one morning, on going down to the Exchange, we saw posted up this dispatch received the night before by the Atlantic Telegraph. All then said that if the cable never did anything more, it had fully repaid its cost."[18]

On August 27 George Saward squeezed a message through the Valentia station that read like a collage. New York papers printed it the same day:

> —News for America by Atlantic cable:—Emperor of France returned to Paris, Saturday. King of Prussia too ill to visit Queen Victoria. Her Majesty returns to England, August 30th. St. Petersburg, August 21st—Settlement of Chinese Question: Chinese Empire opened to trade; Christian religion allowed; foreign diplomatic agents admitted; indemnity to England and France.[19]

The settlement of the "Chinese Question" occurred two months earlier with the signing of the Treaty of Tientsin, but word had just arrived in England by ship. Saward's telegram reached the United States by cable on the same day, sped by the breakthrough in telecommunications. The complete message took two minutes to receive, dispelling Field's concerns and renewing his confidence that the puzzling number of transmission problems had been solved. To those who asked, he replied: "The cable works splendidly." Such positive news convinced Mayor Daniel F. Tiemann that the daily celebrations in New York would never cease without organizing a grand finale. With city council, he set aside September 1 and 2 for one "General Celebration of the Laying of the Atlantic Cable"—the greatest victory celebration the city ever held, but mostly to get New Yorkers back to work.[20]

In addition to Field's distinguished circle of associates, the city fathers invited the crews of *Niagara* and *Gorgon*, and from Washington, three scientists who each shared in the success—Matthew Maury, Alexander Dallas Bache, and Joseph Henry. The mayor knew nothing about the feud between the three men over the question of who produced the better science. The argument had gathered steam ever since Lieutenant Berryman's questionable Atlantic soundings, which under Bache's influence proved to be faulty. Nor did Tiemann know of Morse's quarrel with Henry over credit for inventing telegraphy. Having Maury and Morse at the banquet disconcerted Henry, so he dodged the affair. In a brief explanation to Bache, he said, "I might be called out and in the heat of the moment say something which would not be in good taste or in proper keeping with the occasion."[21]

On August 31, the eve of the two-day celebration, de Sauty received two important messages from the British government. The mutiny in India had ended, and Her Majesty no longer needed two regiments from Canada to fight the Sepoy rebellion. De Sauty forwarded the first message to General Trollope in Halifax: "The Sixty-second Regiment is not to return to England." The second message went to Montreal: "The thirty-ninth Regiment is not to return to England." The two messages contained a total of twenty words and saved the British government $250 to $300,000 in transportation costs, giving both sides of the Atlantic something to celebrate.[22]

The Lord Mayor of Dublin had also chosen Wednesday, September 1, to host a grand banquet for Charles Bright, who contributed far more to the technical success of laying the cable than did Field or anyone else—a possible exception being William Thomson, who had returned to Scotland to see his wife. Bright remained in Valentia for several days while Whitehouse attempted to improve the signals. When Thomson returned, he discovered that in place of his delicate instruments Whitehouse had substituted his own devices using banks of batteries to form a power grid. Thomson demanded that the batteries be removed and his instruments restored. Whitehouse departed in a huff, leaving Thomson with the chore of attempting to restore good signals.

A few days before the Dublin banquet, signals between de Sauty and Whitehouse inexplicably weakened. The trouble seemed to be at the Valentia end. De Sauty sent messages that read: "We can't read . . . currents too weak to read." After Whitehouse's adjustments, de Sauty would reply:

"Very good currents but we can't read." De Sauty knew the problem occurred at Whitehouse's end of the line, but he could not explain the varying strength of currents received at Newfoundland. Instead of seeking assistance, Whitehouse continued to apply his own energies, mostly in the form of greater voltage.

Though gravely concerned about problems at the Knightstown station, Bright began his trip to Dublin. Cheering crowds met him along the way, and everywhere he stopped they called for a speech. The lord lieutenant did most of the talking, forever extolling the expedition's great accomplishment. He compared the landing of cable on August 5 to significant moments in history dating back to 1583 when

> Sir Hugh Gilbert, a worthy countryman of [Sir Walter] Raleigh and [Sir Francis] Drake, steered his good ship the *Squirrel* to the shores of Newfoundland and first unfurled the flag of England in the very bay where this triumph has now taken place. . . . Let the 5th [of] August be a day ever memorable among nations.[23]

The lord lieutenant, feeling much like Mayor Tiemann in New York, understood that all great accomplishments deserved one grand celebration to get everyone back to work. Bright's banquet occurred exactly one day before Field's massive affair across the ocean. Being a reserved young man, the time Bright spent with the lord lieutenant during the trip to Dublin barely prepared him for the lord mayor's immense reception. The banquet included every civil authority and guests for miles around. Somewhat to his amazement, Cardinal Wisemann appeared "in most tremendous costume," Bright wrote his wife,

> just like Kean in *Henry VIII*, with a large jeweled cross around his neck, and an immense sparkling ring of office on his white hand, which contrasted strongly with his red face and dress. However, I found him a very pleasant man, full of scientific knowledge and interest in the Atlantic line. He pressed me to come and see him in London.[24]

The occasion held special meaning for Bright. Queen Victoria, being abroad, delegated the lord lieutenant to honor Bright with the ceremony of knighthood on her behalf. She had made the decision a few days after *Agamemnon* landed the cable, so Charles Bright, at the age of twenty-six, became the youngest man to become a knight for many generations past.

After the lord mayor spoke of Bright's contribution to science, a subject on which he was poorly informed, the assemblage demanded a few words from the Queen's new knight. The moment he rose, cheers rocked the hall. Bright preferred responding to engineering problems, but the lord mayor's clamorous guests wanted a speech. Reporters lost Bright's words in the commotion, but they heard him "thank the assemblage for their hearty welcome" and express his gratefulness for having his name associated with the "great work of the Atlantic Telegraph." He complimented all the men who made the cable possible and then proposed a toast to "the health of Cyrus Field." Some days later Bright learned that no one attending the New York banquet thought to propose a toast to him except as one of the directors. Though such oversights did not go unnoticed by Bright, his close relationship with Field continued for years to come.[25]

The Admiralty elevated Captain Preedy of *Agamemnon* and Captain Aldham of *Valorous* to C.B. (Companions of the Bath), and officers engaged in the expedition all received promotions in grade. William Thomson, despite his unique mirror-reflecting apparatus, seemed to be the only forgotten member of the expedition despite his many contributions, but his greatest achievements still lay in the future. Wildman Whitehouse, chief electrician of the expedition, also received no particular recognition, though he believed his electrical "detector" surpassed in importance any other instrument of telegraphy. Thomson and Whitehouse skirmished over the latter's use of the "detector." Thomson believed it had a purpose, but not in the manner applied by Whitehouse.

Thomson returned to the telegraph station at Knightstown on September 2, the last day of Field's great testimonial banquet in New York.

During the days leading up to the grand celebration at New York's Metropolitan Hotel, Field privately fretted over the erratic signals from Valentia. He hoped the problems would be solved, and on August 31, when de Sauty reported improvements in the signals, Field began the two-day celebration in a better frame of mind.

On September 1 the sun cooperated and brought magnificent summer weather for the first day's celebration. Field felt a strong sense of vindication. A few weeks ago the same men now praising him were among those who had called him a crank, a charlatan, and a "sharper" promoting an idiotic idea for financial gain.

The day got off to a splendid start. As a special guest of Mayor Tiemann, Field attended services at Trinity Church, where flags of all nations garlanded the sanctuary with bright color. At 10:00 A.M. Bishop William H. Doane of New Jersey delivered a service of thanksgiving before 1,000 persons and 200 members of the clergy. After a reception, Field rode with the mayor in a carriage drawn by six white horses to the Battery. Before he stepped into the carriage a man from the telegraph office put a message into his hand from George Saward, who had sent it from Mallow Station, Ireland. Field smiled and tucked the cablegram into his pocket, making a mental note to read it to the public at a more propitious moment. The procession forming at the Battery spread all the way back to where the New York Public Library now stands. Sprinkled among the crowd were a hundred veterans from the War of 1812, officers and men of the army and the navy, and dignitaries from the British ministry. From the Battery the parade marched to the Crystal Palace, New York's grand hall for special occasions, located at Fifth Avenue and 42nd Street. After many addresses, David Dudley Field, who had served throughout the years as the company's legal counsel, delivered the closing speech, the "History of the Ocean Telegraph," and began with the story about his brother's chance meeting with Frederick Gisborne.[26]

Followed by immense crowds, the procession wound through the streets of New York and came to rest at Bryant's Park, where Field received from the city an engraved gold coffer. He thanked the mayor, thanked the crowd, and then drew from his pocket Saward's message announcing that the London directors were "on their way to Valentia, to make arrangements for opening the line to the public." He referred to Mallow Station as "a little [Irish] village, now a suburb of New York." Such good news could not have provided a better climax to the daylong celebration. The crowd roared its appreciation. Bands replied with patriotic melodies, and when they played the "Atlantic Telegraph Polka," guys grabbed their gals and did a few turns on the grass. The city replied after dark with a rousing display of fireworks, eclipsing anything ever witnessed on the Fourth of July. Captain Hudson received a gold medal, and the local British consul presented testimonials to the officers and crew of the *Gorgon*, after which thousands of people rose to their feet and sang "God save the Queen."[27]

On the evening of September 2, six-hundred guests crowded into the ballroom of the Metropolitan Hotel, stumbling over the many vases of flowers lining the walkways. Officers from *Niagara* and *Gorgon* received invitations, but with wine flowing the Common Council of the city wisely excluded the ships' crews. The organizers of the affair tried to keep everything nautical, right down to flags and cable ships fashioned out of hors d'oeuvres, cakes, and frosting. If an attendee could not find enough to eat from the seven courses and twenty entrees offered on the three-page menu, he could choose at his pleasure from forty different desserts. Wine loosened many tongues, and the toasts delivered during the dinner became as numerable as the dessert selections on the bill of fare.

In his speech at dinner, Field paid tribute to those who had done so much to lay the cable. He then proposed a special toast to "Those never-to-be-forgotten philosophers, Lieutenant Maury (who was now a commander), Professor Morse, Professor Faraday, Professor Bache and Professor W[illiam] Thomson who have rendered most efficient aid without receiving any compensation." For inexplicable reasons, he made no toast to Bright or Canning, or to the dozens of mechanics and electricians without whom the expedition would not have been possible.[28]

Field's toast to Bache and the United States Coast Survey, followed by his toast to Maury as "The indefatigable investigator of the courses of winds and currents, and of the ocean depths" inadvertently rekindled the feud between the two men over Lieutenant Berryman's soundings in 1856. At least the two scientists had the good manners not to mention their differences at the banquet and appeared to get along guardedly well.

Throughout the banquet and the loud, prolonged applause, Field alone suffered doubts. As he sat listening to the endless stream of eulogies, he held in his pocket the last cable from Valentia. Though de Sauty warned him that very afternoon that signals were continuing to weaken, Field went ahead with his plans to have sending and receiving instruments installed in the hotel.

Before dinner a single message arrived from Ireland. The telegrapher handed it to Field as he went into the ballroom. It read: "C. W. Field, New York: Please inform . . . government we are now in position to do best to forward—" Field read it and stuffed it in his pocket. Forward what? he wondered. The rest remained blank. He had planned to declare the Atlantic telegraph open for business. Once or twice during the evening he glanced at the message, wondering what omen it portended. As he sat at the head table reflecting, the words of others penetrated his thoughts. He probably remembered the mayor's flattering address from yesterday and the gift of the gold coffer. He remembered his own reply: "This will be a memorable day in my life; not only because it celebrates the success of an achievement with which my name is connected, but because the honor comes from the city of my home—the metropolitan city of the new world." Now this puzzling cable. Not until the following morning would he learn that de Sauty's incomplete message would be the last intelligible words transmitted over the 1858 cable.[29]

Consternation on both sides of the Atlantic took the place of jubilation. For the next three days electricians ran tests on Whitehouse's detector, Thomson's reflecting apparatus, and the batteries used to electrify the conductor. Undecipherable signals spewed back and forth across the Atlantic, losing strength as each day passed.

Field sulked. He suffered a lingering dread that the young line, behaving like a feeble old horse, was slowly dying. He did not know why. A letter written by George Peabody, a company director in England, arrived a few days later. It contained a curiously foreshadowing message with an ominous connotation:

> I read the accounts in the New York papers in celebration of the great event of the year and age with great interest, and although I think in some respects that they are a little too enthusiastic, yet so far as it regards yourself they cannot be so, for if the cable should be lost tomorrow you would be fully entitled to the high honor you are daily receiving.[30]

He did not see the gut-wrenching letter written by George Saward, the company secretary, to the London *Times* until many days later, which read: "owing to some cause not at present ascertained, but believed to arise from a fault existing in the cable at a point hitherto undiscovered, there have been no intelligible signals from Newfoundland since one o'clock Friday, the 3d inst." Saward assured the *Times* that electricians "are investigating the cause of the stoppage, with a view to remedying the existing difficulty. Under these circumstances, no time can be named at present for opening the wire to the public."[31]

During the first weeks of September Field brooded. He sought shelter from the public and remained in daily contact with the Newfoundland telegraph station. For three weeks de Sauty tried to bolster Field's morale by sending him messages containing words of guarded optimism. The other telegrapher at Newfoundland, a man named Mackay, answered Field's inquiries more brutally. When Field, on September 24, demanded a straight answer, de Sauty replied: "We have received nothing intelligible from Valentia since the 1st (actually the 2nd) of September, except feeling a few signals yesterday. I cannot send anything to Valentia. There has been very little variation of the electrical manifestations."[32]

In 1855 Field had promised Maury that the Naval Observatory would have first rights to use the line for establishing the true longitude of Washington, D.C. Maury believed the time had come, but he found himself pitted against Bache, who on September 28 applied to the Treasury Department for the same right. To get his way, Bache involved Joseph Henry in the skirmish, asking him to exert his considerable influence on the secretary in an effort to override Maury's claim. None of the quarreling scientists had received word of the difficulties and continued to battle each other for a privilege neither of them would ever obtain. The wrangling between Maury and Bache continued well into 1859, though by then both men knew their positioning for preference was pointless.[33]

By late September the public suspected the cable had failed. Already cries of "Hoax" echoed across the land, and Cyrus Field, once the worshipped hero became the scapegoat. The Maury-Bache dispute only made the situation worse, giving the public another reason to suspect a conspiracy. One writer called the telegraphic plateau a mere myth hatched to squeeze innocent investors of their life's savings. Using one of Maury's own maps he could show "that the bottom of the ocean was jagged and precipitous; and that the cable passed over lofty mountain chains, and had hung suspended from the peaks of submarine Alps, till it broke and fell into tremendous depths below." Maury had produced maps exactly like that for the area of the Atlantic crossing over the Azores, not for the section of ocean forming the telegraphic plateau.[34]

In his chronicle Henry Field morosely wrote: "Alas for all human glory! Its paths lead but to the grave. Death is the end of human ambition." The cable may have given "its last throb," but the promoter still lived, and Cyrus Field wanted to know precisely what had happened to kill the currents that gave his cable life.[35]

Chapter 10

Accusations and Inquest

"The Atlantic Cable is Dead!" In September 1858, words to that effect blackened the headlines in newspapers on both sides of the Atlantic. The public's image of Cyrus Field and his cable scheme drifted to a new low in America when Charles O'Conor, a distinguished New York lawyer and personal friend of David Dudley Field, "proclaimed that this apparent sleight-of-hand stunt, a deception from start to finish, was a classic demonstration of how easily the public could be fooled." The Boston *Courier* claimed that pretense of success had been Field's way of dumping $350,000 of worthless stock on gullible investors. The London *Daily News* produced a Royal Navy lieutenant who offered to give evidence under oath that "the cable had broken in mid-ocean in July and had never been respliced." Another inquisitor remarked, "Now that the great cable glorification is over, we should like to ask one question—How many shares of his stock did Mr. Field sell during the month of August?"[1]

Though exactly 366 readable messages had been passed through the cable (269 contained 2,840 words from Newfoundland to Ireland, and 97 contained 1,102 words from Ireland to Newfoundland), the majority of them were technical exchanges between electricians and of no value to the public. During the cable's short life, it never functioned perfectly, but it did send messages. Solid proof of the wire's working ability were two cablegrams passed between Queen Victoria and President Buchanan, but skeptics believed that even those had been fabricated.[2]

The public advanced countless theories, following the tendency of an excited populace to rush from one extreme to the other. Calmer minds waited for a scientific explanation. Morse, having withdrawn from the project, cast his own sagacious opinion into the muddied affair by declaring that in handling the cable, it had been overexposed to the sun, thereby melting the gutta-percha insulation and causing leaks. Morse put his finger on one of the contributory problems, but most Americans had never heard of gutta-percha. His dispute with the American Telegraph Company over patent infringements did not make him particularly sympathetic towards Field's crushing embarrassment. He could have stepped forward to strongly assert the legitimacy of the cable, but chose otherwise.[3]

Morse blamed the failure of the 1858 cable to not being invited on the expedition because

> Mr. Field had represented to the Directors that I was hostile to the company. . . . I ought to have been with the cable squadron last summer. It was no fault of mine that I was not there. I hope Mr. Field can exculpate himself in the eyes of the Board, before the world, and before his own conscience, in the course he has taken.[4]

At the time of the expedition, Morse had been antagonistic toward the company, and Field had enough problems without courting another.

While the public railed against the cable layers from both sides of the Atlantic, Bright and Thomson systematically reverted to their electricians' logs and began running tests from Valentia. Thomson noticed that after July 29, the day of the mid-ocean splice, cable deflection tests between *Agamemnon* and *Niagara* continued to improve the farther the two vessels moved apart. Contrary to Morse's opinion, tests proved that the insulation on the cable dramatically improved after submersion, and on August 5, when Whitehouse made the connection at Valentia, the transmissions back and forth across the Atlantic flowed with clarity and strength. Part of the improvement resulted from disconnecting the cable from the Daniell seventy-five-cell batteries on *Niagara* and reconnecting them to fresh batteries at the Newfoundland station. Whitehouse, who still believed that signals could be jammed through the line at greater speeds by applying higher voltage, urged de Sauty to increase the voltage at Newfoundland.[5]

After Thomson landed at Valentia, he went home to see his wife. He left cable refinements up to Whitehouse, who wanted no help. Toward the latter part of August, Thomson began receiving messages from Bright about transmission problems. He hurried back to Knightstown and discovered that Whitehouse had replaced his sensitive instruments with enormous induction coils five feet long and electrified with 500 cells that emitted up to 2,000 volts. Whitehouse had also inserted his own relay and Morse's electromagnetic recording instrument because he never understood Thomson's instruments well enough to use them. By the time Thomson restored his own instruments to the cable, Whitehouse's powerhouse had burned so many faults into the conductor that Thomson's devices would no longer work on lower voltages. To send a signal, Thomson had no recourse but to boost the voltage, and this continued to degrade the conductor by burning the insulation.[6]

The seventy-five-cell Daniell battery carried by *Niagara* contained sawdust to prevent sulfuric acid from slopping over during the ship's tossing. Each cell developed 1.1 volts. The battery in the Valentia telegraph station, like the battery in Newfoundland, contained eighty-four cells and no sawdust. Using the batteries provided, neither site could generate more than 92.4 volts. Why Whitehouse set up 500 large cells, each capable of supplying four volts, mystified everyone connected with the project.

Whitehouse experienced difficulty working the line with his special induction apparatus but reported no problems to the board for more than a week. Instead, he sent an occasional message assuring company directors that "signals were highly satisfactory, and . . . the adjustment of instruments was progressing." The insulation, however, could bear the strain of thousands of pounds of pressure on the seabed but not 2,000 volts. The dangerously overheated electrical current that Whitehouse pumped through the tiny stranded wires of the conductor ate away the insulation. Contrary to Thomson's repeated warnings, Whitehouse still believed that more voltage would push the signals through the cable faster and stronger, even though Thomson had on several occasions demonstrated the opposite was true.[7]

On August 13 Whitehouse received the first clear and complete message from Valentia. The one-week delay occurred because de Sauty, at Trinity Bay, experienced difficulty setting up Thomson's mirror-reflecting instrument, which worked so well on *Niagara*. Whitehouse's gradual destruction of the cable with high-potential currents began a few days later. De Sauty could not monitor Whitehouse's experiments from Newfoundland, but his daily log mentioned an instance where the response to a message sent to Ireland came back in two minutes. De Sauty used such encouraging anomalies as this to keep Field advised of small successes without disclosing the more troublesome problems.

Thomson worked with the line for more than a month. The flashes of light that once reflected beams on his mirror-speaking device slowly diminished to flickers and soon extinguished altogether in the eternal darkness of the deep Atlantic. After a period of confused signals on October 20, 1858, the line went dead. The last intelligible word, sent directly to Field during the grand banquet on the evening of September 2, read "forward."

Whitehouse blamed the failure of the cable on a violent thunderstorm that ripped through Trinity Bay on the morning of August 26 and remained overhead for most of the day. At 3:00 P.M. the lightning became so severe that the technicians disconnected the cable and for ninety minutes put it to earth for protection. Serious problems with the cable began occurring about the same time, but when the telegraphers reconnected the cable at 7:00 P.M., they found the erratic signals no different from those the day before.

Though Whitehouse would never blame himself for destroying the line, others did.

After removing Whitehouse from the telegraph station, Bright and Thomson began searching for faults. Based on Bright's calculations, the problem lay off the Irish coast. This did not preclude the existence of faults beyond that point. Thomson's diary noted a number of minor faults, none of them fatal, along the entire length of the cable laid by *Agamemnon*. An area about 300 miles off the Irish coast became especially suspect because soundings showed that the seabed dropped sharply.

At Bright's request, the Royal Navy dispatched Captain Hoskins with the HMS *Porcupine* to run additional surveys on both sides of the Atlantic. Soundings subsequently revealed that in the vicinity of the fault a steep range with a sloping bank existed, falling 7,200 feet over a span of eight miles. Though some self-declared experts asserted that an insufficient amount of cable had been paid out while crossing the ridge, Bright recalled the excessive amount of slack going into the sea and knew the opposite was true.

Though gravely disappointed by the destruction of the cable, Bright found ample reason to be proud of the effort of his engineers. They laid more than 2,050 nautical miles of cable in a single length in depths approaching three miles. In those depths and distances electricians transmitted distinct and regular signals. After the 1857 cable broke, Bright lobbied for heavier cable with a larger conductor and with a corresponding increase in the gutta-percha insulation, but Field, being in a rush, vetoed the suggestion. In the end it probably made no difference. The enormous currents applied by Whitehouse would have destroyed any conductor, but Thomson may have been able to save the wire had it been wrapped with more insulation.

On cable design, Morse agreed with Bright, writing: "large-coated wires used beneath the water or the earth are worse conductors—so far as velocity of transmission is concerned—than small ones; and therefore are not so well suited as small ones for the purposes of submarine transmission of telegraphic signals." Field accepted the opinion of Morse, the pioneer of electric telegraphy, but he had refused to listen to Bright's demands for more insulation. Later experiments would prove that small conductor wires worked better than large wires, and a heavier cable with more insulation worked better than the cable designed in 1857, but Field did not wait to run the tests required to confirm or to reject the opinions of his experts.[8]

Even Faraday was partly wrong. He blandly stated before the Institution of Civil Engineers: "the larger the jar, or the larger the wire, the more electricity [is] required to charge it; and the greater [is] the retardation of that electric impulse, which should be occupied in sending the charge forward." It is no wonder that Whitehouse, armed with erroneous guidance, burned holes through the insulation and destroyed the cable.[9]

While Americans continued to wring their hands and castigate Field over the loss of the cable, the British public, being accustomed to cable mishaps, became more reflective. After all, the cable had saved the government up to $300,000 by being able to halt the transfer of two regiments from Canada to India. Experts got the shouting over early and accepted what many had already come to believe as inevitable. After learning about the problems, they declared the cable "mechanically good, but electrically bad."

To settle the expanding feud between Whitehouse and Thomson, the British government convened a commission of electrical experts to conduct an inquest, much like Scotland Yard assigns detectives to investigate a murder. The group consisted of Cromwell F. Varley, the Electric Telegraph Company's chief electrician; Edward B. Bright, the Magnetic Telegraph Company's general manager; and William T. Henley, who held several patents on telegraphic instruments. Their assignment: to work with Bright and Thomson, evaluate the causes leading to the death of the cable, and report to the directors. Many years would pass before the crown recognized the genius of Thomson. In 1896 Oliver Heaviside, in summing up Thomson's work, said, "Sir W. Thomson taught telegraph engineers the principles of the business (in its electrical aspects), and to a great extent the practice too."[10]

The commission used the telegraph station at Knightstown to begin work on the dead line. They installed Bright's patented apparatus for detecting faults and confirmed a breakdown of insulation 270 to 300 miles from Valentia. They discovered the line still passed a weak current, which meant that neither the cable nor the conductor had parted but that seawater had penetrated the insulation. No system existed for raising a cable from such depths.

After additional testing Bright and Thomson concluded that all of the cable problems lay at the Valentia end. Bright recovered a section of cable near shore and began underrunning it out to sea. After pulling several miles of cable onto a barge, and being unable to gather any more, he cut and tested it. Convinced that the fault still appeared to be on the seaward side, he abandoned the idea of repairing the cable and spliced it again.

With the conductors reconnected, Bright attempted to renew signals by using a large, improved magnetic telegraph invented by Henley and connected to curb keys invented by Edward Bright. The system sent currents of opposite character and of given lengths. Each impulse sent was instantly followed by one of opposite polarity that neutralized, by proportionate strength and duration, all that remained of its predecessor. The conductor was thus cleared for each succeeding signal, which varied from the first to form a letter. The new instrument, though still in development, proved the cable useless for transmitting signals.

Having confirmed the lifelessness of the cable, the commission turned its attention to the cause. Using de Sauty's daily log from Newfoundland in conjunction with the one kept by Whitehouse at Valentia, all agreed that the cable worked well on August 5, the day of its connection. De Sauty's electricians even " 'tasted' the current, and received a pretty strong shock, so strong that they willingly resigned the chance of repeating the experiment." This happened on the same day that Field cabled the Associated Press, writing: "The electrical signals sent through the cable are perfect." Four days later de Sauty sent another message: "Receiving good, recorded signals from Valentia. Perfectly satisfactory."[11]

At Knightstown, Whitehouse's records mirrored de Sauty's. On August 10 he added: "the line works as well as it did before it was laid." When giving evidence before the commission, Whitehouse said, "The signals were very strong: they made the relay speak out loud, so that you could hear it across the room." At the time, battery power employed at Newfoundland consisted of seven 12-cell batteries—ordinary portable copper and zinc batteries in a gutta-percha case. The batteries were slightly stronger than the ones used on board the ships, and as long as Whitehouse used the same batteries at Valentia, the cable transmitted signals with the same clarity as on the ships.[12]

Toward the middle of August Whitehouse unilaterally attempted to boost the transmission speed by attaching his coils and over the next several days gradually added more voltage. To simulate Whitehouse's methods, Varley brazed a short section of cable to a piece of wire covered with gutta-percha, and using a needle, punctured the insulation to let a tiny amount of water reach the conductor. He then bent the wire to close the pinprick, placed it in a large jar of seawater, and connected Whitehouse's induction coils to the cable. Varley sent a few signals through the test wire, noting:

> The intense current burst through the . . . minute perforation, rapidly burning a hole nearly one-tenth of an inch in diameter, afterward increased to half an inch in length when passing the current through the faulty branch only. The burned gutta-percha then came floating up to the surface of the water, while the jar was one complete glow of light.[13]

Two experts, one from each side of the ocean, read and gave opinions on Varley's experiment. David Hughes, the inventor of the type-printing machine used by the American Telegraph Company, pointed to Whitehouse's induction coils as the culprit that killed the cable. Professor Charles Wheatstone agreed with Hughes, writing: "That the force of the induction coils must have been enormously greater than that of a battery of 400 elements," adding that anyone who touched the conductor when current was being discharged from the induction coil "would receive a shock sufficiently strong to cause him to faint." Whitehouse never explained to anyone's satisfaction why he continued to increase the voltage on the line after

Thomson advised against it. The answer came down to the simple fact that the company's obstinate chief electrician knew no better.[14]

Thomson summed up the investigation in 1860, writing:

> It is quite certain that, with a properly adjusted mirror-galvanometer as receiving instrument at each end, twenty cells of Daniell's battery (about 22 volts) would have done the work required, and at even a higher speed if worked by a key devised for diminishing inductive embarrassment; and the writer—with the knowledge derived from disastrous experimentation—has now little doubt but that, if such had been the arrangement from the beginning, if no induction coils and no battery power exceeding twenty Daniell cells had ever been applied to the cable since the landing of its ends, imperfect as it then was, *it would be now in full work day and night, with no prospect or probability of failure.*[15]

Aside from Whitehouse's mismanagement of the power source, Varley discovered secondary causes that could have shortened the cable's life. In his opinion the Gutta Percha Company had manufactured the cable too hastily. In fairness to the owners, they had expressed concern over the scheduling deadline demanded by Field. Much of the 1857 section, which represented seventy percent of the cable laid in 1858, contained impurities in the copper wire and a thinner covering of gutta-percha insulation. The 1857 section had also been subjected to overhandling. The cable was taken out of ships, uncoiled and recoiled at Plymouth, and uncoiled and recoiled again in 1858, twisting and untwisting it as many as ten times. By storing the coils outdoors from one summer to the next, Morse and others observed that the insulation decayed when heated by the sun. The coils carried on *Agamemnon* in 1858 had been jostled and injured during the terrible storms of June, causing some sections to be cut out and condemned while other flaws passed into the ocean undetected. "Take all these things together," Henry Field wrote, "and the wonder is, not that the cable failed after a month, but that it ever worked at all."[16]

Peter Cooper never got the story quite straight and probably mimicked Morse's opinion when in 1863 he reported to the board of directors:

> Unfortunately, in the manufacture of the cable, when it was being passed out of the shop and into a vat, intended to be kept always overflowed with water, the water was allowed to flow off a little, and a part of it was thus exposed, on a hot day, to the sun, which melted the gutta-percha, leaving but a thin coating to protect the copper. That accounts fully for the cause of the disaster, but for which that cable, would be at work successfully today.[17]

Such ineptitude committed by Whitehouse, combined with Field's impetuosity to move the project forward, cost the company £379,029 ($1,895,000). The debacle stripped the company of its capital along with its public image and lost $140,000 in guaranteed annual revenue from the

British and American governments because the cable failed. No records were kept for the cost of the ships and crews, some of which could be placed on Whitehouse's ledger and some on Field's.[18]

Thomson never publicly condemned Whitehouse for destroying the cable or for wasting $60,000 of the company's capital on destructive experimental equipment. He defended his colleague's industry but not his methods. Thomson did admit, however, that after Whitehouse applied full power to his coils the only message he ever received from Newfoundland was the word "be." Far less gentle than Thomson, the company directors damned Whitehouse for being "pigheaded, insubordinate, and rash," accused him of foolishly wasting the company's money, and fired him.[19]

Whitehouse defended himself in a twenty-seven-page pamphlet published on September 27, 1858, four weeks after his dismissal. In his rejoinder, Whitehouse took a swipe at everyone and everything, including his own state of poor health. He lashed out at Thomson, his sole supporter, and blamed him for ignoring a fault in the cable "240 to 300 miles" from Knightstown. Whitehouse implied that Thomson, in his anxiousness to depart from Valentia to visit his wife, left the electricians to conduct experiments on a cable they both knew contained faults.

> Could Professor Thomson then expect to find the condition of the cable on the 21st [of August] as good as it had been on the 10th?—when for eleven days it had been subjected to these destructive influences, which might have been counteracted, but for the neglect of the Directors to protect the fragile cable.[20]

Whitehouse also defended the use of his recording instruments—which never worked—claiming he had used them together with Thomson's reflecting instrument, but because "currents from Newfoundland *were communicated direct* to my own apparatus," he saw no need to continue using Thomson's mirror-speaking device. Thomson and Bright both knew this was untrue.

Whitehouse then turned on Field, accusing the American promoter of giving him insufficient time to complete experiments, rushing him on the installation of equipment, pushing to get everything done at breakneck speed. "The most aggressive expectations are thus promulgated by Mr. Field, and fostered by bombastic articles in the American press known to be immediately under his influence." Whitehouse then added: "Mr. Field was the most active man in the enterprise, and he had so much steam that he could not wait so long as three months." Field countered with a somewhat generous left-handed compliment, and said: "A great responsibility rests upon those who have in any way contributed to the failure of this enterprise; but for my own part, I can safely say, that neither zeal, labour, caution, nor anxiety, was wanting upon the part of Edward Orange Wildman Whitehouse."[21]

Whitehouse did not exaggerate his criticism of Field's haste. When engineers and electricians alike expressed their concerns to Field, he brushed them aside. He refused to listen to any problem that threatened to upset his timetable. It is a fault that drives all promoters, without whom projects such as the laying of the first transoceanic cable might never have been undertaken for decades to come.

Bright dealt with many protests from the managers of the Gutta Percha Company and from Glass, Elliott & Company, all bitter complaints of being hurried. In actuality, it is no wonder the cable failed, being but a prototype whose beta site happened to be beneath 2,000 miles of the North Atlantic. The manufacturers did not want to be implicated in the cable's failure and took an easy ride on the condemnations being mobilized by faultfinders against Field. They might not have been so hasty had they waited another year. In April 1860 the Atlantic Telegraph Company sent Cromwell Varley and a survey ship to Newfoundland to recover a portion of the cable. Soundings showed the seabed to be much rockier and hazardous than they expected. They also recovered five miles of cable and ascertained two irrefutable facts: the gutta-percha had not deteriorated, and the electrical condition of the core had been improved by two years' submersion.

After the cable failed on September 2, Field spent eight months in the United States commiserating over the loss before the juices of rejuvenation began flowing again. In May 1859 he departed for England to pick up the pieces. In America, only Wilson Hunt and Peter Cooper still believed in him. In Great Britain the people had taken the loss in stride. The Atlantic Telegraph Company still had a little money in the bank. Raising more would not be so easy. Yet, the challenge inspired him. The old confidence returned. He had learned from his mistakes. He still held shares in the company. This time there would be no mistakes.

All he needed was more money—and a little more time.

CHAPTER 11

OTHER SCHEMES AND OTHER ROUTES

Much had happened in Great Britain during Field's absence in America. Tal Shaffner, an electrical engineer who Field, Cooper, and Morse all regarded as a rogue freelancer, had laid hundreds of miles of landlines connecting the western states with the east. Knowing New York, Newfoundland, and London Telegraph Company's plans to lay an Atlantic cable, Shaffner said, "I do not say that a galvanic or magnetic electrical current can never be sent from Newfoundland to Ireland: but I do say that, with the present discoveries of science, I do not believe it practical for telegraphic service." That the 1858 cable worked, though only briefly, convinced Shaffner that the "present discoveries of science" showed signs of improved technological advancements.[1]

During the early 1850s Shaffner often communicated with Charles and John Bright. With their help he published *The Telegraph Manual*, which became a useful tool for telegraphers working his landlines. The manual also provided a comprehensive 844-page history of the development of telegraphy. A brief autobiographical note appearing in the back of his *Manual* read:

> Early in 1854, Mr. Shaffner visited New York City, to aid in the reorganization of the Newfoundland Telegraph Company, the secretaryship of which had been offered to him with a salary of twelve thousand dollars per annum. The new company was organized, having as proprietors some ten members, of whom Mr. Shaffner was one. Not satisfied with the administration of the company's affairs, he withdrew from the company forever.[2]

Shaffner never made it clear whether the "Newfoundland Telegraph Company" mentioned in his autobiography was the one started by Frederick Gisborne that failed, or the New York, Newfoundland, and London Telegraph Company formed by Field and his associates. There is no record of Shaffner being connected with either firm, but his short biography refers to "ten members," which coincides with the original number of investors sought by Field and Cooper. Nothing in Field's early correspondence mentions Shaffner, suggesting that in 1854 the two had never met, nor is there anything in the early records of the New York, Newfoundland company's documents stating that Shaffner had been offered $12,000 a year as secretary. Chandler White performed the secretarial duties of the company, and like Field and the others, worked without a salary.[3]

Shaffner's many foreign acquaintances referred to him as a colonel. There is no record of Shaffner having served in the U.S. Army, though it is possible he belonged to a militia organization. In April 1843 he gained admittance to the Maryland bar, and a year later witnessed one of Samuel Morse's demonstrations of the magnetic telegraph. Intrigued by the device, Shaffner educated himself in its use and in 1846 began buying rights to lay telegraphic lines into the south and the west from his base of operations in Louisville, Kentucky. He expanded rapidly, and by 1852 had strung lines to Pittsburgh and New Orleans, with another line running from Louisville west to St. Louis and St. Joseph, Missouri. To connect those cities, he laid submarine cables under the Mississippi, Ohio, and Tennessee rivers. Shaffner eventually received many honors in Europe, but his own short autobiography fails to reveal how he became a colonel.[4]

In 1856 Morse began complaining because renegade operators like Shaffner were connecting to patented lines leased to Field and Cooper's American Telegraph Company. Some used Morse's patents; others merely copied them. Shaffner declared open season on telegraphy and with unparalleled swiftness contracted for lines in advance of competition, swearing to shoot on sight any intruder. That the country needed a homogeneous network under unified management did not concern him. The rights alone would make him rich. On one hand, Field did not like Shaffner's methods of operation and thought of him as a ruthless monopolist. On the other hand, Field and Cooper, by establishing the American Telegraph Company, attempted to do precisely the same.

Shaffner wrote that he had "entered into the Newfoundland enterprise with a view of carrying out *his* ocean telegraph," but after studying advances in submarine cables, he began to search different routes across the Atlantic. Instead of Ireland, he looked to connect Europe through Scotland and Norway. He believed the 1858 Atlantic cable failed because it followed the wrong route, despite being chosen with Maury's scientific guidance.

When in May 1858, Senator David C. Broderick of California approached Shaffner, Henry O'Reilly, and John J. Speed about connecting western states, Shaffner was already giving thought to running his own Atlantic cable and undercutting Field and Cooper's dreams of monopoly.

The idea for the American transcontinental line came from Western Union's president, Hiram Sibley, not Shaffner or Broderick. But Shaffner held a broader view: let Sibley connect America, the greater profits would come from connecting Europe. He went to his map and concluded that the best way to tie the continents together was to run the line from northern Scotland through the Faroe Islands to Iceland, from Iceland to Greenland, and from Greenland across Davis Strait to Byron's Bay, Labrador. He spoke of the route as having "natural stepping-stones which Providence had placed across the ocean in the north."[5]

To validate his theory, Shaffner chartered the small bark *Wyman*, and with his family on board, departed from Boston on August 29, 1859, to make a preliminary survey. He took a few soundings between Labrador and Greenland, but the accuracy of those soundings could not be regarded as reliable because of the methods he used. He landed at Glasgow, Scotland, in November and presented the results of his voyage to the public, using his survey to convince whoever would listen that no insuperable difficulties lay in the way of accomplishing the task. J. Rodney Croskey of London came forward and advanced money to the Danish government for Shaffner's rights to use the Faroes, Iceland, and Greenland for what soon became the North Atlantic Telegraph project.

At first, Bright viewed the scheme with skepticism, but he soon saw its feasibility and attached himself to the enterprise as its technical advisor. Had Field been in London at the time, he might have labeled Bright's association with Shaffner as treasonable, but in 1859 the Atlantic Telegraph Company was no longer a viable operation. Bright, however, had his own consulting engineering business to look after and could not afford to spend his time under the thumb of Cyrus Field.[6]

On May 15, 1860, Lord Palmerston gathered an influential deputation, headed by the Right Honorable Milner Gibson, to hear Shaffner's presentation. The proposal made enough sense to the committee for Palmerston to engage the Admiralty in another survey. In June 1860 Captain Sir Leopold McClintock (also M'Clintock), a Royal Navy officer familiar with navigating the polar seas, sailed from Portsmouth with instructions to survey Shaffner's route. By then, Shaffner had gathered a number of potential financial supporters in England and Denmark.

Shaffner's enthusiasts pooled their resources and bought the steam yacht *Fox*, which had been employed in the successful search for the remains of Sir John Franklin's fatal 1845 Northwest Passage expedition. Shaffner then hired Captain Allen Young of the merchant marine to command *Fox*, mainly because the latter had served under McClintock during the Franklin search and was also familiar with the Arctic. While McClintock made soundings at sea, Shaffner's group intended to locate sites for situating telegraph stations among the steppingstones to Labrador. Dr. John Rae, an intrepid Arctic explorer, volunteered his services and took charge of the overland survey. Having been cultivated by Shaffner as a potential partner, the Danish government added Lieutenant von Zeilau and Arnljot Olafsson to the expedition.

On July 18, before the survey departed from Osborne on the Isle of Wight, Queen Victoria, the Prince Consort, and other members of the royal family honored the enterprise by a visit to *Fox*. The queen expressed lively interest in the expedition, an enterprise that Cyrus Field still knew nothing about.

On July 31 *Bulldog* and *Fox* got underway and set a course for Torshavn (formerly Thorshaven), the principle harbor of Denmark's Faroe Islands. Captain Young spoke for the group on *Fox* when he said, "We were naturally anxious to reach the spot at which our work was to commence, and to ascertain the first foreign station at which the telegraph cable was to be landed." So convincing had Shaffner's presentations been that Young absolutely believed that this would be *the route* for the future Atlantic cable.[7]

Soundings began in 102 fathoms of water southeast of the Faroes, and samples from the bottom contained a combination of sand and shells, a particularly good environment for a well-armored cable. The bottom never changed in composition all the way to the Torshavn. A bay protected the port, provided good anchorage, and never froze, making the area an acceptable site for landing a cable. Finding the region congested with ships, Shaffner conferred with a local seafarer who suggested a small cove down the bay called Sandygerde, where ship anchors were less likely to hook a cable. The Gulf Stream swept around both sides of the island as it journeyed south and east, causing no turbulance among the islands, and the four-knot current carried by the spring tide was never strong enough to disturb a cable.

The ships moved up the Faroes and on the evening of August 5 stopped to investigate Haldervig, where the survey team found an excellent harbor with little traffic and a seabed of mud at thirty-four fathoms. The site presented Shaffner with a second option that Young described as "well adapted for the reception of the cable," being in "a tolerable depth of water, in a perfectly landlocked position." This gave Shaffner a valuable alternative. He could bring a cable into a single point on the island or step it over the islands, thereby grabbing onto a little more land.[8]

On the morning of August 12 *Bulldog* and *Fox* approached Djúpivogur (Benfiord), Iceland, and found the seabed offshore identical to the Faroes but the inner harbor filled with rocks and frequented by small sailing vessels. Shaffner located a better landing site five miles up the fjord at Gautavik where less drift ice entered the harbor. The inhabitants reported that no icebergs had ever entered the fjord, nor during their lifetimes had it frozen. The only difficulties in laying a wire came from frequent coastal fogs that might cause a cable ship to wander off course, but Young assured Shaffner that "fogs and thick weather . . . [could] be overcome by selecting proper seasons, and taking precautions in landing or embarking the telegraph cable." McClintock agreed, confirming in his opinion "that a cable would remain undisturbed at the bottom, the shore end being carried up a fiord."[9]

At Djúpivogur, Dr. Rae went ashore with a survey team and numerous scientists interested in seeing Iceland's interior. On August 15 the group started a 450-mile trek along the coast, skirting fjords and rivers, and avoiding areas having volcanic disturbances. The survey team averaged thirty miles a day and marked out the best route for stringing land wires. Following the advice of some helpful inhabitants at Reykjavik, the survey party located a promising landing site for a telegraph station not far from the capital. Though exposed at times to heavy surf, ships never dropped anchors near the site, thereby eliminating the worrisome problem of snagging the wire.

On August 21 *Fox* entered Reykjavik, where Shaffner and Young went ashore to make inquiries about the coast. The port official suggested trying Hval Fiord, which appeared to have the advantage over any other location in Faxe Bay (now Faxaflói). Young sounded up the fjord to Maria Havn, where he found fourteen fathoms of water and a seabed of mud. There on a sandy beach and in a landlocked place lay a second quiet zone to build a telegraph station. "Faxe Bay never freezes over," McClintock noted, "and I can find no record of drift ice within [the bay] since 1683. Merchant vessels come and go throughout the winter." Shaffner now had a site to land his cable and a choice of two for running it to Greenland.[10]

Delighted with the survey, Shaffner enjoyed a surge of optimism when on August 31 *Bulldog* and *Fox* sailed for Greenland. On October 2, after a very stormy passage, the two steamers reached Frederikshaab on the southwestern coast of the glacier-covered island. Young paused to repair storm damage before steaming south to conduct soundings in Julianshaab Fiord (now Julianehabsfjord), a forty-mile stretch of water reaching deep into Greenland's southern mountains. There they found a small Inuit settlement at Igaliku (also called Gardar) at the site of the Old Nordisker Ruins. From this beautiful arm of the sea *Fox* sounded to the head of the fiord, followed by an overland party led by Dr. Rae. Because of early ice and snow, Rae could not get across southern Greenland to assess the possibility of landing the shore end on the eastern side of the island and stringing a landline to Julianshaab Fiord on the western side. Doing so would have carried the wire over or around more than forty miles of glacier.

Going into Julianshaab Fiord took the exploring party into Einarsfjord and over to Eiriksfjord, where in the year 942 a dispossessed Norwegian named Eirik the Red began the first European settlement in Greenland. Unlike today, the southern portion of the island was indeed green, more temperate, and less hostile. Norse settlers from Iceland scattered their farms throughout the upper reaches of the fjords, and in 1859 the remains of their dwellings were in much better condition than they are now. As the decades passed into centuries, the climate gradually cooled, sending the Norsemen south and onto the North American continent, spreading artifacts from their civilization to Labrador and Newfoundland. The exact southernmost point they reached in America may never be known. In the year 1347 a Viking ship with eighteen Greenlanders deserted their homes and returned by sea to Iceland. Of the Norsemen who settled in Einarsfjord and Eiriksfjord, nothing more was ever heard. Five hundred years later a telegraph promoter named Shaffner stopped at the long deserted site with visions of creating a relay station for the North Atlantic Telegraph Company.

After studying the surveys, Captain Young optimistically declared:

> I am of a decided opinion that *a depth of not less than 150 to 160 fathoms* can be carried from the middle of the fiord abreast the settlement out to sea, with a general muddy bottom. The depth of the water will effectually preclude injury to the cable from the largest icebergs ever seen upon the coast. Although many bergs lay among the coast, we saw none aground in this valley of the fiord. . . . [In] my decided opinion [this route] is favourable to the practicability of the undertaking, and that Julianshaab will, under all circumstances, be well adapted for the reception of the cable. . . . The cable once laid, no drift ice can in any way injure it, if the proper precautions are taken in securing the shore end.[11]

Shaffner could not have been more pleased by the survey, for it corroborated everything he had said about the polar route. Nobody questioned the ability to lay the cable from Greenland to Labrador. If they could get the wire into Julianshaab, they could run it the rest of the way.

Before returning to England, Young mapped out the route and prepared a timetable. He suggested laying the cable from Scotland to the Faroes during the fair weather of June or July, using the last quarter of the moon to avoid the greater tides. He recommended that the next, or perhaps the first, leg of the cable be laid from Iceland *to* the Faroes, rather than the reverse, so a cable-laying vessel could avoid the fogs that prevailed along Iceland's east coast. He suggested laying the Iceland-Faroes cable during the clear-weather days of May and June.

Greenland posed a more difficult problem because nobody knew much about the glacial island's meteorological conditions. The section across the North Atlantic between Iceland and Greenland and below the Denmark Strait blew a tempest at all seasons of the year. Young believed that while the engineers laid the landline across Iceland, the cable ship could wait and pick the best weather before striking out for Julianshaab.

Having been through the Labrador Sea and Davis Strait on past occasions, Captain McClintock agreed that the cable should be laid from Iceland to Greenland during early autumn when drift ice and icebergs were less prevalent, though he warned that on occasion some of the southern fiords remained blocked for as long as two years at a time. He expressed confidence, however, that once the shore end reached land, no drift ice or icebergs could injure it. McClintock described an abundance of difficulties running a cable along Shaffner's route, but he declared them all surmountable. He noted that many vessels visited southern Greenland during the summer and fall and returned to Europe uninjured and fully laden with fish, hides, oil, and bone, implying that the shipmasters made no special effort to protect their ships from ice.

After the expedition returned to England, McClintock sent a full report to Charles Bright. Missing were details on Labrador, mainly because winter weather caused a hasty departure from Greenland. The report included the distances between landing places:[12]

	Miles
From northern Scotland to Faroe Islands	225
From the Faroe Islands to Iceland	280
From Iceland to Greenland, S.W. Harbor	700
From Greenland to Labrador	550
Total distance	1,755

From an electrician's perspective, four short cables were preferable to a single length spanning the entire Atlantic. Except in the 550-mile stretch between Greenland and Labrador and a 700-mile stretch between Iceland and Greenland, the soundings turned up little water more than 500 fathoms deep. Had they surveyed the route with the proper equipment, they would have found depths of 1,700 fathoms between Iceland and Greenland, and depths of 1,800 fathoms between Greenland and Labrador—depths nearly equal to those on the telegraphic plateau.

Objections came from the engineers, who argued that icebergs forming along the coast of Greenland would settle on the cable and crush it. McClintock thought that if the cable stayed toward the center of the inlet icebergs would be avoided. He believed the main problem would come from the unwillingness of a trained staff to work in so inhospitable a region. Aside from those concerns, McClintock favored the route, emphasizing that ice would not become a problem, and by laying a landline across Iceland to Faxe Bay, "you will avoid the only part of the sea where submarine volcanic disturbances [occur]."[13]

On January 28, 1861, the captains of the HMS *Bulldog* and the steam yacht *Fox* made their reports to the Royal Geographic Society before a packed house. McClintock gave his reasons for endorsing the route, adding that the seabed from Scotland to Labrador consisted mainly of ooze. Dr. Wallich, the naturalist on the expedition, reported finding brightly colored starfish living in depths beyond a mile, quashing contemporary beliefs that

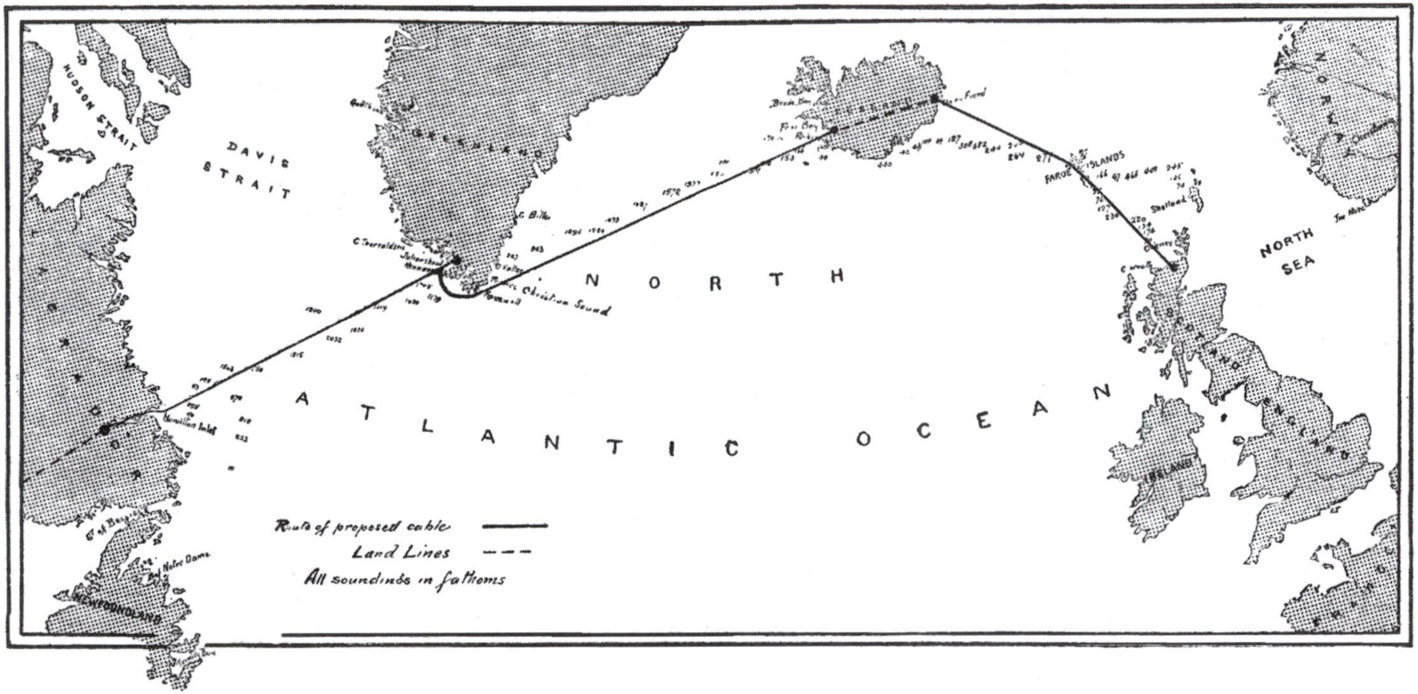

Taliaferro Shaffner's proposed North Atlantic cable route took the cable through Iceland, Greenland, and Labrador. (From Charles Bright, *The Story of the Atlantic Cable*. Digitized by Debra Peffer.)

nothing could survive under such enormous pressure. Dr. Rae gave the particulars of his land survey, showing the best route across Iceland to avoid the island's geysers.

Though the expedition produced an attractive alternative to the 1858 route, discouragement over the failure of the Atlantic Telegraph Company's cable still festered in England. Shaffner tried to raise £500,000 to float the expedition but could not. Some investors feared the ice floes, and those with money refused to risk it on the "Grand North Atlantic Telegraph" project. After so much trouble and expense, and having accomplished nothing to promote his scheme, Shaffner returned to the United States at the outbreak of the Civil War.

Shaffner and Field both missed out on two other Atlantic cable schemes that went nowhere, the first of which wore the name "South Atlantic Telegraph."

Shaffner's "stepping-stone" concept caught the eye of new knots of speculators. The first group suggested running an enormous length of cable from southern Spain to Brazil, looping through the island of St. Vincent to Madeira, and from there to the Canary Islands, Cape Verde, St. Paul's, the penal colony of Fernando de Noronha, and finally to Cape São Roque. Once connected to Brazil, the promoters planned to island-hop across the West Indies and from there to the United States. Lieutenant Maury's survey showed a relatively shallow plateau except near the Island of St. Paul's where the seabed descended to three miles.[14]

Another group consulted Bright on the practicality of a submarine cable running from Portugal to the Azores with an intermediate stop at Bermuda before laying the last leg to South Carolina. Being that these proposals involved troublesome foreign governments, the British rejected them, though in future years both proposals, with minor variations, became realities.

Thus ended the schemes for finding an alternate route across the Atlantic. Only one viable route remained, right across the burial ground of the 1858 cable. With the outbreak of Civil War in America, the effort came to a standstill—everywhere but in the mind and spirit of Cyrus Field and a small cadre of experienced cable layers in England.

— Chapter 12 —

Time-Out for War

On June 8, 1859, Cyrus Field met with the directors of the Atlantic Telegraph Company for the first time in eleven months. They appeared to have been waiting for him, as if no one among them could raise money in Great Britain but an American. He heard no talk of liquidating the company or abandoning the project. During his absence Glass, Elliot & Company had laid more submarine cables; one connecting England to Holland, another of 280 miles connecting the German city of Hanover, and more recently a 368-mile length tying Great Britain to Denmark. Ten more cable expeditions were planned for 1859. The world had not quite reached the stage of cable mania, but interest continued to grow among the more progressive nations of the world.

During the meeting Field persuaded the directors to approve £600,000 for a new expedition across the North Atlantic. They agreed to increase the capital but gave the hard part to Field, the task of raising funds from a disillusioned public. The vastness of the project had grown beyond the resources of the company's small group of investors. Too much private capital had already been risked and lost during two years of failure. The directors believed, and Field agreed, that the time had come for the government to underwrite the next expedition, or at a minimum guarantee the interest on new capital even if the next expedition failed. Field, being the company's eternal optimist, believed that "with such a guarantee, the capital could be raised in London in a day." He had no aspirations about raising money in America, where the temper of the nation still steamed over being swindled by what some called Field's fraudulent hoax.[1]

Reanimated by his friends in London, Field applied to William Ewart Gladstone, Lord Palmerston's chancellor of the exchequer, asking for a guarantee of 8 percent interest for twenty-five years on new capital, regardless of success or failure. England wanted the cable, and the bold request stimulated interest on Gladstone's part. England still hoped to be connected to Canada, and Palmerston understood the importance of improving communications with the United States, which during the 1850s had become an enormous maritime rival.

While Field related to the directors his promising conversation with Gladstone, news reached England that the cable to India, being laid under the auspices of the Red Sea Telegraph Company, parted during the first lap from Suez to Aden. The government had guaranteed the interest on £800,000, considerably more than asked by Field, leaving the British treasury liable for paying stockholders £35,000 a year for twenty years. After hearing the bad news, Field held another conference with Gladstone, who had turned suddenly circumspect about underwriting another cable promotion.

When it became known that the Red Sea cable had not been manufactured to the higher standards established by Bright, Gladstone came back to Field with an equitable offer. The government agreed to guarantee the interest on the capital and also to increase their annual subsidy from £14,000 to £20,000—*providing the cable worked.* Field should have been happy with the agreement, but Gladstone would not give him the unconditional guarantee he needed to raise new capital.

The Red Sea debacle produced another consequence. The Palmerston government wanted no more high-risk cable expeditions initiated until the companies engaged in the work solved the technological problems. On July 1, 1859—ten months after the failure of the Atlantic cable—the Board of Trade formed an eight-man committee of the most eminent scientific and engineering authorities in Great Britain to investigate the science associated with submarine cables and establish a uniform set of standards. The four members representing the Board of Trade consisted of Captain Douglas Galton of the Royal Engineers; Professor Charles Wheatstone, a celebrated electrician who functioned as the board's electrical authority; engineer George Parker Bidder, an inventor and mathematical genius best known for his ability to make lightning calculations in his head; and William Fairbairn, late president of the British Association for the Advancement of Science. Wheatstone held many patents, among them a device for measuring electrical resistance, an invention shared with William Cooke. The other four members came from the Atlantic Telegraph Company. Cromwell Varley, having replaced Wildman Whitehouse, represented the company's electrical interests. Bright appointed Josiah Latimer Clark and Edwin Clark, two electrical engineers with long experience in the business of telegraphing, and George Saward agreed to act as the board's secretary, a role he filled most capably for the Atlantic Telegraph Company. The committee agreed to sit in conference until it perfected solutions.[2]

After failing in 1859, Lionel Gisborne (not Frederick) made one last effort in 1860 to lay a cable across Egypt and down the Red Sea to Karachi, India (now Pakistan), this time making connections to intermediate stations along the way. Because the Turkish government authorized the project, the British felt they had to support it. The irregular seabed, combined with paying out insufficient slack, left sections of the cable suspended between rough underwater ridges. One by one, every section developed faults. No single message ever passed through the entire line. The promoters never engaged especially well-qualified men to lay the cable or provided the necessary materials to make repairs. Once again the British government got the bill—this time £36,000 per annum for twenty years.

The Palmerston government refused to underwrite any major cable-laying effort until the committee reported its findings. During the two years of the committee's investigation, the firms of Glass, Elliot and W. T. Henley laid twelve cables, the shortest being ten miles and the longest 240 miles. They all worked. The poor ratio of success, however, justified caution. More than 11,000 miles of submarine cable had been laid, but only 3,000 miles still transmitted messages.

In 1861 Glass, Elliot & Company, using the initial findings of the Board of Trade to manufacture cable, laid the longest submarine cable in the world—1,535 miles from the island of Malta to Alexandria, Egypt. The cable contained 532,645 pounds of copper and 5,829,930 pounds of iron. Though shorter in length than the Atlantic cable, in every aspect it weighed more.

During the same year, Bright and Latimer Clark attacked cable terminology. Such words as current and resistance meant different things to different people. Without a standardized vocabulary, scientific literature on the new technology would continue to befuddle research groups. The two engineers employed a precise vocabulary for electrical testing—a step that may have prolonged the life of the 1858 Atlantic cable had standard terminology been in place during the Whitehouse-de Sauty effort to make the wire speak.

In 1864 Bright and Clark, having resolved many problems identified by the Board of Trade, applied the latest technology to connect Europe to India by using the Persian Gulf as the cable carrier instead of the Red Sea. The new cable, 1,450 nautical miles long, consisted of multiple improvements. The Gutta Percha Company used a substance known as Chatterton's Compound to glue the insulation to the conductor. Glass, Elliot & Company used a preservative developed by Bright and Clark that prevented the oxidation of galvanized iron wires. To verify the integrity of the cable, they also devised a system for testing with hydraulic pressure equal to conditions at the bottom of the sea. To demonstrate the progressiveness of submarine cable conductor technology between 1861 and 1864, the Persian Gulf cable, though nearly of the same length as the Atlantic cable, used half as much copper for the conductor (292,500 pounds)—as Morse once recommended—and twice as much iron for armoring (9,677,544 pounds), as Bright had recommended.[3]

These two triumphs raised the public's confidence in Great Britain and prepared the way for another attempt at the North Atlantic.

The moratorium on cables stymied Field's efforts to raise capital. He could only sit and wait. A decree by the Atlantic Telegraph Company's directors authorized Field to return to New York and recruit Morse, Henry, Commander Maury, William Everett, and Commander Berryman to act as an advisory committee in America. Field enjoyed some latitude in forming the committee and sent an invitation to Alexander Dallas Bache. Field doubted whether he could get Maury, Henry, Bache, and Berryman in the same room without creating an acrimonious skirmish. He also doubted whether Morse would participate because of his patent feud with the American Telegraph Company. As a consequence, Field never formed a committee.

In December 1859, Field returned to New York to spend Christmas with his family, only to be beset by another calamity. A fire that began in a building next to his factory on 57 Beekman Street consumed his warehouse. Rushing to the site to inspect the damage, Field found the buildings ravaged and his entire inventory destroyed. Though personally devastated by the disaster, he called upon a friendly competitor, Seymour & Company, and made arrangements to share the latter's facilities. Beside the report of the fire in the evening news, Field placed an advertisement announcing that business would continue "without interruption." He had insured the building and contents for $80,000, but discovered that his loss exceeded $120,000. With nothing to keep him engaged in the cable business, he focused his entire attention on rebuilding his business and reestablishing manufacturing operations back on Beekman Street.[4]

The months Field spent at home reacquainted him with escalating factional disturbances between the North and the South. Antinorthern sentiments combined with the upcoming presidential elections to create national instability. Sectional rivalries threw the papermaking industry, along with everything else, into economic chaos. At the Chicago "Wigwam," where the new Republican Party met to nominate a presidential candidate, Field supported Senator Seward of New York, who in 1857 helped push cable concessions through congress. His neighbors, Peter Cooper and David Field, supported Abraham Lincoln—they had become converts after hearing the latter's famous "House Divided" speech at Cooper Union. When Lincoln became the Republican presidential nominee, Field wrote a sympathetic letter to Seward. He recognized the importance of having Seward's friendship when the time came to lay the next cable.

During 1859–1861, the committee formed by the British Board of Trade initiated an immense number of experiments that in 1862 filled a very large volume. The investigation covered the electrical and mechanical properties of copper and gutta-percha; chemical changes in materials when submerged; the effects of temperature and pressure on insulation; the ductile strength of copper, iron, and steel wire; the durability of tarred hemp, used separately and when bonded together; the size and composition of conductor wires; the form and size of cables and their relative strength and flexibility; the voltage best suited for telegraphing across long distances; and the speed at which messages could be sent and received. The groundbreaking study produced the first set of national standards on the science and practice of manufacturing and laying submarine cables. But not until July 13, 1863, did the board specifically state:

> a well-insulated cable, properly protected, of proper suitable gravity, made with care and tested under water throughout its progress with the best known apparatus, and paid into the ocean with the most improved machinery, possesses every prospect of not only being successfully laid in the first instance, but may reasonably be relied upon to continue for many years in an efficient state for the transmission of signals."[5]

By then America had been at war with herself for more than two years.

During the Civil War, Field continued to travel back and forth between New York and London, always looking for ways to revive interest in the cable. The Lincoln administration found little time to listen to cable schemes. With the national debt soaring and thousands of men spilling their blood on American battlefields, the country showed no interest in a transoceanic cable until the *Trent* affair caught their attention.

On November 7, 1861, the British mail steamer *Trent* sailed from Havana, Cuba, with two Confederate commissioners on board, James M. Mason of Virginia and John Slidell of Louisiana, bound respectively for London and Paris to plead for recognition of the South. Captain Charles Wilkes, commanding the USS *San Jacinto*, intercepted *Trent*, fired two shots across her bow, and dispatched a boarding party to remove Mason and Slidell. Wilkes became a national hero to the public and an instantaneous embarrassment to the executive branch of government. Even congress erred. After heaping praise upon Wilkes, they performed a tactical flip-flop when the brilliant feat turned into a flagrant violation of international law.

The illegal seizure resulted in an instant demand by Lord John Russell for an apology and the release of the commissioners. Taking no chances, the British loaded 8,000 troops on Brunel's *Great Eastern* and shipped them to Canada to guard the border. Secretary of State Seward devised a way to cool the heads of a growing number of warmongering Englishmen and avoided an unwanted war with Great Britain. Wilkes, Seward said, acted without orders. The London *Times* summed up the altercation succinctly, writing, "We nearly went to war with America because we had not a telegraph across the Atlantic." Diplomatic exchanges still took four to six weeks to pass back and forth across the ocean.[6]

Field used the *Trent* affair as an opportunity to revitalize interest in the cable. On December 17, 1861, he wrote George Saward, urging, "now is the time for the directors . . . to act with energy and decision, and get whatever guarantee is necessary from the English government to raise the capital to manufacture and lay down . . . a good cable."[7]

Field also knew how to get attention at home. Instead of going directly to President Lincoln, he wrote Major General George B. McClellan, commander in chief of the Union army, urging that the army connect all its forts between Washington and Pensacola, Florida, by submarine telegraph. McClellan agreed, replying, "I most fully concur in the importance of the submarine telegraph proposed by Mr. Field, and earnestly urge that his plans may be adopted and he authorized to have the plans carried into execution."[8]

On New Year's Day, 1862, Field wrote Seward and attached a copy of McClellan's endorsement without confessing how he induced such an enthusiastic response from the general. Instead of explaining his thoughts on connecting Washington to federal forts, Field reverted to the project that had drained his savings for six years. Using McClellan's letter and the *Trent* affair to make his case, Field wrote:

> The importance of the early completion of the Atlantic telegraph can hardly be estimated. What would have been its value to the English and the United States government if it had been in operation on the 30th of November last, on which day Earl Russell was writing to Lord [Richard] Lyons, and you at the same time to Mr. [Charles Francis] Adams, our minister in London?
>
> A few short messages between the two governments and all would have been satisfactorily explained. I have no doubt that the English government has expended more money during the last thirty days in preparation for war with this country than the whole cost of manufacturing and laying a good cable between Newfoundland and Ireland.
>
> Will you pardon me for suggesting to you the propriety of opening correspondence with the English government upon the subject.[9]

Seward replied: "It will afford me pleasure to confer with you on that subject at any time you may present yourself for that purpose."[10]

Armed with Seward's invitation, Field took the next step and wrote Adams, suggesting that he "call the attention of Earl Russell to the matter." Though he had only exchanged letters with Seward, Field took the liberty of adding: "You may say to him that the President entertains the most favorable views of the great enterprise in question, and would be happy to cooperate with the British government" in laying the cable now.[11]

Field, in an effort to promote his own interests, had no authority to advise Adams that the president entertained *any* views on the enterprise. Eight volumes of Lincoln's correspondence edited by Roy P. Basler never mentioned the cable or Cyrus Field. The few conversations Field later held with the president dwelt almost entirely on cable connections between coastal forts. After Lincoln granted an audience, Field spoke so fast that the president, being a deliberative man, could not follow him. When Field tried to switch the conversation to the Atlantic cable, the president asked him to slow down. "Does anybody understand you?" Lincoln asked. Field smiled and said that his telegraph operators usually did. "Then send me a telegram," Lincoln said, "and I'll read it."[12]

Taken aback by the president's remark, Field stepped into the War Department's telegraph office and asked David Homer Bates, the manager, to take a message for the president. Bates experienced the same problem as Lincoln, recalling that Field:

> being of an excitable nature, his words flowed from his lips in a rapid, intermittent stream, while his thoughts outran his spoken words ten to one, so that it was not long before I, not being a shorthand writer, was engulfed, and the result was, judging from my notes, that Field's memorial, like an ocean cable, was discernable only at its two ends. . . . Several weary hours were spent in this way, and when at last some sort of order had been evolved out of seeming chaos and the memorial finally completed and signed, Field shot out of the door and rushed over to Stanton's room, waving the document as it if were a danger-signal, leaving me alone and in a semi-collapse. Drawing long breathes of relief at the removal of the tension, I returned to my regular cipher-work, resolved never again to act as an amanuensis for Cyrus W. Field.[13]

The only time Lincoln spoke of the importance of an Atlantic cable occurred eleven months later, during his annual message to congress on December 8, 1863, in which he said, "I recommend to your favorable consideration the subject of an international telegraph across the Atlantic Ocean, and also of a telegraph between this capital and the national forts along the Atlantic seaboard and the Gulf of Mexico." Of the two proposals, Lincoln expressed far more interest in the latter because he wanted news of the war in preference to telegrams from across the ocean, though both would have been nice.[14]

What stunned Field more than Lincoln's indifference to the Atlantic cable was the president's arrangement with the czar of Russia for the construction of a telegraph through Russian America (Alaska), across the Bering Strait to Siberia, hence to St. Petersburg, thereby connecting San Francisco with every major city in Europe by going around the world the other way.

Field did not know the details and viewed the scheme as just another wild speculation. Lincoln distrusted the British, who were blatantly aiding the Confederacy, and entertained no notions of joining with a potential enemy in a cable project.[15]

Most of Field's visits to Washington took place with Seward or with Secretary of War Edwin M. Stanton. David Bates recalled Field's numerous visits to Stanton's chambers, and he specifically remembered "transcribing from dictation a memorial to the Government, urging the laying of a coast cable." According to Bates, Lincoln never mentioned the Atlantic cable during his hundreds of visits to the telegraph office.[16]

After asking Adams to inform Earl Russell that Lincoln was interested in the cable enterprise, Field returned to London. Like a seasoned promoter, he understood that if Lord Palmerston agreed to back the cable thinking it had the endorsement of Lincoln, then Lincoln might be more willing to participate if he thought the cable had Palmerston's support.

After Field arrived in London on February 27, 1862, he met with Russell, who listened but remained guardedly noncommittal. On March 1, growing impatient for a response, Field again called upon Russell, stating that he asked nothing from either government, "being quite content to risk the sacrifice of the whole amount," but he needed approval to raise new subscriptions. The strained relations in 1862 between the United States and Great Britain did not bode well for Field's new scheme. British blockade-runners and British-built commerce raiders infuriated Lincoln, his cabinet, congress, and northerners in general. Four days later Earl Russell replied that Her Majesty's government "have come to the conclusion that it would be more prudent for the present to defer entering into any fresh agreement on so difficult a subject." After Field failed to get help from Russell, Curtis Lampson, vice chairman of the company, took the proposal directly to Palmerston, who agreed to meet with Field, John Brett, and George Saward.[17]

Palmerston asked some interesting questions, taking Field aback when he said, "I heard the other day that the American Government had a notion of establishing telegraphic communication with Europe through Asia."

Field waved Palmerston's comments aside, asserting that only soundings had been proposed. When Field mentioned "soundings," Palmerston suspected that he knew more than Field, and replied, "My notion from what I heard was, that the Russian line was to be a long line, with a very short sea passage." Field replied, "The sea passage would be about 4,000 miles if carried from island to island, and only sixty miles if taken via the Bering Straits [*sic*]." He explained that the Atlantic cable, being much shorter, ran underwater for only 1,640 nautical miles.

Palmerston appeared to be amused and said, "The Russian land line *was* started, I thought, upon the notion that a submarine cable was precarious, but you would not gain much by it if that be so." Palmerston asked for more information and closed the meeting by saying that "the answer to an application to the Government for a guarantee would be, under ordinary circumstances, that commercial speculations are not contributed to by the Government; it is only in exceptional cases that that is done." Field made one last argument, claiming an exceptional case, wherein "the Government would obtain enormous political advantages from the means of a speedy communication with her own colonies." Palmerston already understood the advantages but would make no commitments with America at war.[18]

Palmerston's suggestion that the Russian line had *actually been started* came as a shock to Field. Neither Lincoln nor Seward had mentioned it, and if true, he wondered why. Getting back to New York became urgent, but if a serious competitor had entered the race to connect the continents, he had to cement his relations while in England. He called upon Glass, Elliot & Company, urging them to undertake the cable project at their own expense by providing the wire, the men, and the ships. The company promised to consider the proposal and respond later. Field continued to press Russell for a favorable answer but received only circumspect replies. One solitary note of encouragement came from Paul Julius von Reuter, the creator of one of the most powerful news agencies in the world. He promised "no less than £5,000" a year for the use of the line.[19]

Spurned by the British a second time, Field returned to New York on April 11, 1862, only to learn that he had also been spurned in the city. Reporters had observed his departure to England, London correspondents reported his arrival, and the same newsmen in New York observed his return. Many New Yorkers used imaginative methods to make themselves wealthy from the war. Field's unexplained trips to London led to speculations that he had invested money in British enterprises supporting the Confederacy. Letters in both the London *Standard* and the New York *Herald* stated that a grand jury had presented a bill of indictment against him for "treasonable proceedings with the public enemy." Field rushed to Washington and found that the press accounts were true. The bill did not identify the "public enemy," and the grand jury would not relinquish the source of the complaint to the public.[20]

On April 14 Field shared his concerns with Edward Bates, the U.S. attorney general. Bates studied the matter and the following day replied: "upon reading the enclosures the affair (as far as it concerns you personally) looks rather like a stupid, practical joke. Could the scheme have been meant as a blow to your business in Europe?" A day later the grand jury dismissed the charges. This did not stop death threats but slowed them down.[21]

Field needed the goodwill of the British and did his best to quell public acrimony. He also needed to be in both places at the same time, especially since the charge of treason may have stained his name in England. Helped by the war, Field & Company paid off most of its debts, eliminating one of his worries, but he had to cash equities to keep his family comfortable while he traveled.

When Bates suggested that someone might have cooked up a scheme to "blow your business in Europe," he might well have expanded the "blow" to include his cable business in the United States. Immediately upon the outbreak of the war, the American Telegraph Company lost nearly half of its lines, those being south of Maryland. The company also lost the entire area from the Ohio River to New Orleans, which immediately became available to their rival, the Western Union Telegraph Company.

In 1861 Hiram Sibley, Western Union's energetic president, had already opened the line to California. The connection made it possible to communicate across the continent. The only link missing was one with Europe. This, in itself, increased Field's anxieties to such a degree that he bombarded the directors in England with a steady flow of letters, warning, "if *we do not get it laid in 1863 it will be our own fault*."[22]

Field was not completely aware of the plans being propagated behind his back. The failure of the 1858 cable encouraged speculations by outsiders. Using Western Union as his base, Sibley became the chief promoter of connecting America with Europe by running a submarine cable under Bering Strait. Sibley's aggressive agent, Perry Collins, obtained a government grant to survey the route. Morse, still squabbling with Cooper and Field over patent rights, hedged his interests by endorsing Sibley's plan. The longer-range plan of the Collins Overland, or Russo-American telegraph, involved the Russian Asiatic telegraph. Sibley intended to use the same link to expand Western Union operations into Central and South America.[23]

As a defensive measure, the American Telegraph Company decided to pay $500,000 in stock for Morse and Kendall's Patent Telegraph Lines. Field and Cooper's company now owned all the important lines on the eastern seaboard but seven lines operated by Smith & Company between New York and Boston. The American Telegraph Company paid Francis O. J. Smith $301,000 just to put him out of business and end a legal battle that had been raging between Smith and Morse for many years. The deal made Morse and Kendall happy—they received $107,000 in stock for patent rights—but gave the American Telegraph Company control of all the lines in the east. On October 12, 1859, Cooper reorganized the company with a right to raise its capitalization to $2,000,000. All that remained to fulfill their monopolistic objectives was to lay the Atlantic cable. At last, the interests of Field, Cooper, and Morse were again in harmony. From this date forward the American Telegraph Company and the Western Union, each with aggressive managers, would energetically push to acquire or absorb every independent telegraph company in North America, including each other.[24]

Lincoln's disinterest in the Atlantic cable had more to do with his immediate interest in the progress of the war. He found uses for the Atlantic cable in ways not originally intended by Field and having nothing to do with the Atlantic Ocean.

In 1862 the War Department purchased fifty miles of Field's 1858 cable. The Military Telegraph Corps laid twenty miles of it across Chesapeake Bay from Cape Charles to Fort Monroe. The section represented the longest submarine telegraph cable in the United States. The wire, either because of inherent defects or the dragging of ship anchors, routinely failed.

The wire went out of service a few days before the Confederate ironclad CSS *Virginia* (formerly the USS *Merrimack*) attacked the Union squadron at Hampton Roads, Virginia, and on March 8, 1862, destroyed the USS *Cumberland*, the USS *Congress*, and ran the USS *Minnesota* onto a shoal. While the *Virginia* rampaged through the Union squadron, army telegraphers made hurried repairs to the line and by evening restored it to working order. That night Major General John E. Wool, commanding the Union district at Fort Monroe, cabled Stanton that the USS *Monitor* had arrived. The famous duel between the *Monitor* and the *Virginia* occurred the following morning and ended in a draw. On March 9 General Wool sent another message to Washington to calm the nerves of Stanton, who had spent the day at the window looking in the direction of the Potomac River, as if momentarily expecting to see the giant enemy ironclad crawling up Pennsylvania Avenue.

In August 1864, after General Grant's Union army skirted Richmond and began the siege of Petersburg, the Military Telegraph Corps laid the rest of the Atlantic cable in the James River, connecting Jamestown Island, near Norfolk, with Fort Powhatan, located below the Union supply center at City Point. The submarine cable proved to be more reliable than the landlines, which Confederates broke as fast as the Yanks repaired it. Thus ended the Atlantic cable's contribution to America's Civil War.

On October 20, 1862, Field returned to London. During his absence he had kept constant pressure on the directors to raise money. In a lengthy letter to Saward he wrote: "I hope that we will . . . have *all* of the stock for a new cable subscribed within one month, and our other arrangements so perfect that I can at an early day return to my family and country."[25]

Field went directly to Glass, Elliot & Company, from whom he had not heard regarding his cable proposal. They agreed to undertake the responsibility but not the full risk and articulated their conditions. For an estimated cost of £675,000, paid weekly to cover the cost of labor and material, they offered to take full responsibility for the cable. They would manufacture the cable to the new standards promulgated by the Board of Trade's committee but insisted that the shore ends be reinforced by heavier wires where ships anchored. When the wire worked to predetermined specifications, Glass, Elliot would receive 20 percent of their cost in shares of the company. They would also subscribe £25,000 in advance to purchase stock and, if President Lincoln wished to participate, they would provide and lay cables connecting Union forts along the eastern coast.[26]

After four years of groping to sustain interest in the Atlantic cable, he now had Glass, Elliot on the hook though not yet caught. The directors had raised a few pounds during his absence, though nothing near the £675,000 needed, but with the assets of Glass, Elliot behind the project, Field believed the money would come. He also had a bargaining chip with the United States government—a competent British firm willing and able to lay the coastal cables Lincoln and Stanton said they wanted.

On December 20 the Atlantic Telegraph Company issued its new prospectus setting forth the valuable rights and subsidies that had been negotiated with Glass, Elliot and invited public subscriptions. The time had come for Field to go home, raise capital in America, and get the work of seven years finally finished—or so he thought.

CHAPTER 13

OF DOLLARS AND POUNDS

On January 1, 1863, Abraham Lincoln issued the Emancipation Proclamation and set a new tone for the country. Three days later Cyrus Field, suffering from another stormy passage, returned home. He found New Yorkers more buoyant than before. In September at Antietam, General McClellan's Union army had pushed General Lee's legions out of Maryland and back into Virginia, and some optimists on Wall Street predicted the war's end.

After spending eight days with his family, Field took the train to Washington to present Glass, Elliot's generous proposal to connect Union forts along the seaboard to the War Department's telegraph office. He also sought financial support from the government to lay the Atlantic cable. Welles and Stanton agreed to study the proposal, and while they did, Field returned to New York.

Frustrated by delays in getting answers from the government, Field wrote George Saward on January 27, grumbling, "The whole country is in such a state of excitement in regard to the war that it is almost impossible to get any one to talk for a single moment about telegraph matters, but you may be sure that I shall do all I can to obtain subscriptions here."[1]

With the threat of invasion from the South removed, and the public in a more victorious mood, Field used the growing national ebullience as a propitious moment to present his case before the New York Chamber of Commerce. On March 4 he spoke to an assembly of the city's leading merchants and brought them up to date on the Atlantic telegraph. Because most of the attendees were in the import-export trade and waited weeks for their quotations to cross the Atlantic, he extolled the cable as a means to command foreign commodities markets. He read the letter from Glass,

Elliot, in which they offered to undertake the laying of the cable on such generous terms, and then he related the British Board of Trade committee's work in resolving the technical problems of the past. At last he made his sales pitch, promising twelve to eighteen words a minute. From a single cable across the Atlantic, working sixteen hours a day for 300 days each year, Field projected annual revenues of $2,065,000 and a profit of 40 percent.

The New York Chamber of Commerce had just passed a resolution condemning Great Britain's support of the South and open hostility toward the North, and now came Field trying to raise money for a mainly British enterprise. He softened the gathering's animosity toward the British by referring to Glass, Elliot's generous cost-plus proposal to lay

> a submarine cable from [Fort] Monroe to Galveston, Texas . . . bring it out in their own ship, lay it down, and only ask payment when it is in perfect working order. If it is not a success, they are willing to lose the whole part of it; a risk sufficient to show their confidence in laying it successfully.[2]

The tactic partly worked. Abiel A. Low, the chamber's president, marshaled his members behind the plan and unanimously passed a resolution, seconded by Peter Cooper, which read: "That, in the opinion of this meeting, a Cable can, in the present state of telegraphic science, be laid between Newfoundland and Ireland with almost absolute certainty of success, and will when laid prove the greatest benefit to the people of the two hemispheres, and also profitable to the shareholders. It is, therefore, recommended to the public to aid the undertaking." Low and Cooper already owned shares in the company, which were now virtually worthless, and by encouraging others to invest they hoped to recover their losses.[3]

While he held the chamber's attention, Field used every trick in the book to raise money, warning that if America ignored the cable out of anger towards Great Britain, investors in England would buy all the stock and control the cable. The argument produced a few small investors who came forward "more from sympathy and admiration of his indomitable spirit than from confidence in the success of the enterprise."[4]

After raising a few dollars at the Chamber of Commerce, Field addressed gatherings at the Board of Brokers and the Corn Exchange, generating interest but not much cash. Having exhausted his resources in New York, he spent the next months logging 1,500 miles between Boston, Philadelphia, Buffalo, Providence, and Albany and described his efforts as "going from door to door." On March 27 he wrote Saward: "I never worked so hard in my life." In a later letter he said, "I have subscriptions from all these places." They added up to only £66,000 ($330,000), one-tenth of the capital required to restart the project.[5]

On May 4, 1863, General Lee's Confederates defeated Major General

Joseph Hooker's huge Union army at Chancellorsville, Virginia, and created a fresh wave of hysteria over the outcome of the war. Subscriptions came to a halt, the dollar tumbled against the British pound, and a new credit crisis loomed on the national horizon. Having heard nothing from Seward or Stanton on the Glass, Elliot proposal, Field suspended domestic fund-raising efforts. He checked Field & Company's books, noted profits of $17,038 during the past six months, and satisfied that the family had enough money in the bank, made arrangements to return to England.[6]

Great Britain needed to be connected with speedy communication to its far-distant colonies as badly as the Union army needed to be connected to its forts, but when Field reached London in early June, he learned that Saward had made no progress raising money. Saward admitted calling

> upon nearly every capitalist and mercantile house of standing in Glasgow and in Liverpool, and some of the directors have gone round with me in London for the same purpose. We have no doubt induced a great many persons to subscribe, but they do so as they would a charity, and in sums of corresponding amount.[7]

In mid-July Field received a startling letter from Field & Company warning that the Confederate army had crossed into Pennsylvania: "Business has been almost entirely suspended for the last week on account of the great excitement arising from the rebel invasion of Pennsylvania. . . . Harrisburg, Baltimore, and Philadelphia are threatened by Lee." Never during his lifetime had Field felt a greater need for the Atlantic telegraph.[8]

He could barely concentrate on business, and feeling too distressed to work, he drove to Reuter's with a friend to get the latest news. The clerk refused to answer his questions, declaring that if he did, he would lose his job. Field promised that if that happened, he would give the man a job with an increase in pay, and asked, "Is the steamer in from America?" and, "What is the price of gold in New York?" The clerk cracked open the door and said, "The steamer is in and gold is 131." Field put his foot between the door and the jamb and refused to remove it until he received every particular. "There has been a three day fight at Gettysburg; Lee has retreated into Virginia, Vicksburg has fallen." Field gave three cheers and spent the rest of the day visiting friends, most of whom came from the North but espoused the southern cause. He enjoyed a few minutes of pleasure reading aloud a bulletin he snatched at Reuter's and raised no subscriptions that day.[9]

On July 25 Field received shocking news from his New York company: "Since our last letter a most fearful riot has broken out here in the city; it still continues, and business is almost entirely suspended."[10]

The New York riots started after Governor Horatio Seymour challenged the constitutional right of the government to enforce the draft. On July 11, when the provost marshal drew the first names for the draft and published them in newspapers, angry mobs began to gather. By July 15 protestors numbered 50,000. They burned a church and orphanage, attacked the office of the New York *Tribune*, terrorized a large part of the city, killed a dozen people, and caused more than $1.5 million in damage. Lincoln sent troops from the Army of the Potomac, and by July 18 the city returned to normal.

Field could only assess the situation at home from what he read in London papers. He received a jolt a day later when he opened a letter from his brother's wife:

> My husband just got back in time to save, by prompt and vigorous action, our property. Our poor servants were terribly alarmed; they were threatened by incendiaries that warned them to leave the premises. . . . Think of one hundred and eighty soldiers sleeping in our stable, the officers being fed in the basement. . . . As the rioters approached our house they were met by a company of soldiers that Dudley had just sent for; their glittering bayonets and steady march soon sent them back before they had time to effect their demoniacal purpose.[11]

A major action took place at Third Avenue and Twenty-first Street, a block away from Field's residence, where Union soldiers killed thirteen rioters, wounded eighteen, and arrested dozens more. Field spent several days at Reuters collecting news from home as it came by ship to Queenstown, but he heard no more of this frightening incident until he returned to New York.

Field remained in London during July and August, still crusading each day to raise funds. The tide of war in America had turned against the South, and Field worked hard to restore harmony between England and the United States. His good friend Gladstone, who held the purse strings of the British government, remained adamant, however, that Jefferson Davis had established a nation.

Field encountered two types of prospects. Those who had money politely avoided him, and those who had influence but no money gave him words of encouragement. Secretary of the Treasury Salmon P. Chase fell in the latter class, writing on August 21: "I trust you are succeeding well in your great scheme of the inter-continental telegraph. It is an enterprise worthy of this day of great things. If I had the wealth of an Astor you should not lack the means of construction." The Astors belonged to the class of superrich who avoided him. Later, after Field returned to New York, he invited Chase to his home, and the secretary politely declined.[12]

Worn by travel, frustrated by the war in America, and irritated because no one on either side of the Atlantic showed much interest in the cable, Field returned to New York. This marked his thirtieth crossing since becoming involved with the cable project. The London directors had either sold or subscribed to themselves shares worth £220,000. Coupled with the capital raised by Field in America, the company now had £286,000 shares subscribed, less than half the funds needed to float the next expedition. With so little interest in the project, Field knew he could not move the expedition ahead in 1864 without more money. On the trip home he made a hard decision—to sell Field & Company and focus all his time and diminishing net worth on the cable.

Arriving home on September 23, Field confronted an awkward situation when asked by the British consul to welcome Vice Admiral Sir Alexander Milne and his North American squadron to New York. With two British-built Confederate commerce raiders—*Alabama* and *Florida*—still destroying American merchant ships on the high seas, a visit from the Royal Navy annoyed most New Yorkers. Field, however, for favors past felt obliged to welcome and entertain the squadron.

Early in October four British ships, led by the HMS *Nile*, arrived off Sandy Hook, New Jersey. Field understood the importance of maintaining good relations with the British. He still had a cable to lay. Treasury secretary Chase did not make Field's chores any easier when he suggested that Milne be asked to help "remove all causes of alienation [between England and America] by full reparation for the injuries inflicted on American commerce by unneutral acts of British subjects." Field hosted a grand reception for the admiral, his wife, and fellow officers in his home. He cautiously mentioned the matter of reparations, making the subject more a suggestion by the government than a concern of his own. When Milne sailed for Washington on October 9, Field advised Chase that the admiral departed with "very pleasing impressions . . . of the country and people," but made no comment on reparations.[13]

After Milne departed, Field sold his stock in Field & Company to two firms in New York. Now free to devote all his time to what had become his life's work, he nonetheless used the remainder of the year to spend with his family. A flurry of letters arrived from George Saward, who wanted him back in England. Work on the cable had ceased for want of money. Field merely replied, "If you have new and formidable difficulties you must make greater exertions." In mid-January he said good-bye to the family and returned to London.[14]

Field had become the driving force for fund-raising, and not much got done in his absence. On February 6, 1864, the London *Telegraphic Journal* duly reported the cable promoter's return, writing: "The Atlantic telegraph project is again attracting attention. Mr. Cyrus W. Field, one of the leading spirits of the undertaking, is again amongst us, full of hope and ready to embark once more in the gigantic enterprise."[15]

During Field's absence, John Bright had crossed paths with fifty-eight-year-old Thomas Brassey, a London financier with his fingers in businesses around the world. Brassey's biographer, Arthur Helps, called him a man whose "ruling passion was the execution of great works of the highest

Without the help of Thomas Brassey, the 1865–1866 cables may not have been laid for another decade. (From Edward Brailsford Bright, *The Life Story of the Late Sir Charles Tilston Bright*. Digitized by Debra Peffer.)

utility with punctuality and thoroughness," but his protagonist had one defect—"a difficulty in saying no, which led to involvement in some disastrous undertakings."

Thomas Brassey had money. He was the largest railway contractor of the century. In 1850 his company employed 80,000 men on four continents and held contracts worth $140 million. The company had built a hundred railroads and had more under construction in places like Queensland, Argentina, and Delhi. Brassey understood the railroad construction business. He knew nothing about transoceanic cables.[16]

In February 1864, when Field met with Brassey, he never forgot the conversation, writing:

> in attempting to enlist him in our cause he put me through such a cross-examination as I had never before experienced. I thought I was in the witness box. He inquired

of me the practicability of the scheme—what it would pay, and everything else connected with it; but before I left him, I had the pleasure of hearing him say that it was a great national enterprise that ought to be carried out, and, he added, I will be one of ten to find the money required for it.[17]

In Thomas Brassey, Field found the Peter Cooper of England, and he went to work to locate nine more men just like him. Using Brassey's name and financial prestige gave Field new credibility, and he pressed forward with renewed energy. He introduced himself to John Pender of Manchester, a parliamentarian soon to be knighted, and asked if he would join Brassey in the enterprise. Field made his pitch while walking with Pender from 28 Pall Mall to the House of Commons. When they parted, Pender agreed to match whatever Brassey subscribed.

As a millionaire industrialist and a director of Brett's Magnetic Telegraph Company, Pender understood the cable business. In April 1864 he used his influence to merge the Gutta Percha Company, which manufactured the conductor, with Glass, Elliot & Company, which produced the armoring, and formed the Telegraph Construction & Maintenance Company, thereby consolidating cable technology under one roof. During the next decades, the new company would produce virtually all of the world's submarine cable.

The merger also brought new talent to the enterprise: Willoughby Smith, Gutta Percha's gifted electrician, John Chatterton, inventor of insulating materials bearing his name, and Henry Clifford, who had helped Canning lay the 1858 cable. Richard Atwood Glass, who had a gift for finding talent, became managing director of the firm, and Brassey and Daniel Gooch became members of the board.[18]

Without Brassey and Pender, Field may never have met Gooch, an engineering genius who at the age of twenty-one had become superintendent of Britain's Great Western Railway and later its chairman. The meeting set the stage for important events yet to come.

In 1842 Gooch and Brunel gave Queen Victoria her first ride on a steam car, taking Her Majesty from Windsor to London. The Queen's Master of the Horse, concerned for her safety, went to the station and examined the locomotive according to the Manual of the Horse. He climbed into the cab in his scarlet livery, white gloves, and wig. When Brunel asked an equerry what this portended, the latter replied, "The Master of the Horse will, of course, drive the locomotive." Brunel and Gooch lured the courtier to the engineer's cab and turned the locomotive loose. As James Dugan noted, "The Master of the Horse arrived in London covered with soot and beating away at his wig which was smoldering from sparks. Although the iron horse never succeeded in unsaddling the Master as a court functionary, he has been permanently discouraged from operating H. M. locomotives." Now twenty-two years later, Gooch had become wealthy. He owned a large

Daniel Gooch, who helped to buy *Great Eastern*, lived most of the rest of his life on the vessel. (From Edward Brailsford Bright, *The Life Story of the Late Sir Charles Tilston Bright*. Digitized by Debra Peffer.)

interest in *Great Eastern* but had never been able to find a way to make her pay.[19]

With men like Brassey, Pender, Gooch, and Glass holding the reins, the Telegraph Construction & Maintenance Company subscribed £315,000, the entire remaining amount of capital required, giving the Atlantic Telegraph Company the £600,000 needed to revive the project. The new company also took an additional £100,000 in bonds to cover contingencies. Field's group had never enjoyed a financial structure so steeped in funds. With Brassey, Pender, and Gooch involved, other contractors concluded that all the cable problems must have been solved and offered to take a portion of their payment in shares. In one sweep of the hand, Englishmen led by Brassey broke the financial deadlock, relieved the weight borne so long by Field, and put the Atlantic cable back on track.

The shore-end cable designed for the 1865–1866 expedition was more heavily armored and insulated than any cable ever produced. (From Charles Bright, *Submarine Telegraphs*. Digitized by Debra Peffer.)

The design and construction of the new cable evolved after two years of testing by Charles Bright and Latimer Clark. The conductor and insulation received a few changes that closely followed the design projected by Bright in 1857—seven stranded copper wires weighing 300 pounds (compared to 107 pounds) with 400 pounds of gutta-percha insulation per nautical mile (compared with 261 pounds). No copper went into the wire having less than 85 percent of the conductivity of pure copper. Machines wound each of the seven strands to .048 inches in diameter, coated the center strand with gutta-percha and Chatterton's Compound, and then wound six outer strands around the center strand. After forming the conductor, machines added more Chatterton's Compound before tightly wrapping the assembly in layers of gutta-percha, thus eliminating air spaces between the conductor and the insulation.

According to William Thomson's law for the working speed of the cable, the seven-wire arrangement provided the most efficiency, depending inversely on the resistance of the conductor as well as the electrostatic capacity of the core. He believed that the transmission speed of the new cable would double per minute the number of words transmitted in 1858.

The conductor wire moved through a four-stage gutta-percha applica-

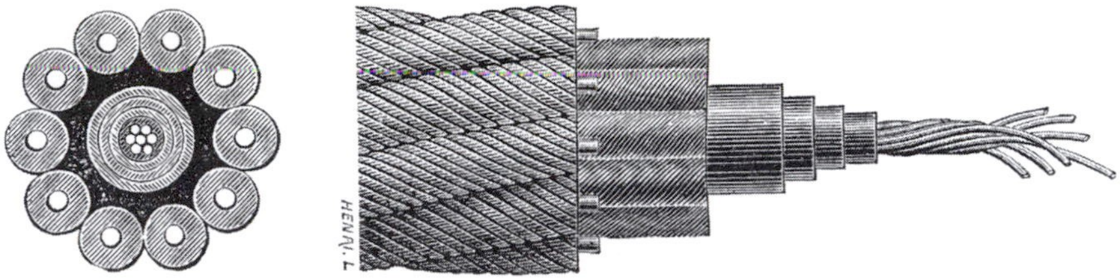

The ocean cable designed by the Board of Trade consisted of the improvements Charles Bright had recommended as far back as the winter of 1858. Seven small stranded copper conductor wires formed the core, covered by four layers of gutta-percha insulation, wrapped in tarred hemp, and protected by ten stranded wires wound in impregnated hemp. (From Charles Bright, *Submarine Telegraphs*. Digitized by Debra Peffer.)

tion. Under pressure, an accurate die deposited a sleeve of pure gutta-percha around the conductor. Topped by Chatterton's Compound, the conductor then went through three more applications of gutta-percha and compound before being wound on reels and immersed at seventy-five degrees Fahrenheit in a continuity-testing tank for twenty-four hours. Because warm water decreased the insulating properties of gutta-percha, Bright set the test bath at twenty degrees higher than the summer temperature of the water in the North Atlantic. Before the workers removed the coils from the tank, electricians subjected the conductor and the insulation to conductivity tests and discarded any section that failed. After testing, inspectors unwound the reels and examined the entire length by hand, rewinding it on large drums for shipment to the armoring factory.

Workers at Glass, Elliot's East Greenwich works submerged the drum in water and retested the coil for continuity. If the checks matched those taken at the conductor plant, the drums went into coldwater storage tanks and remained there until called for by the armoring line.

Armoring accomplished two purposes. It added additional protection to the insulation, but it also improved the mechanical strength of the core by surrounding it with heavy wire, thereby preventing the conductor wires and the insulation from stretching beyond their limit of elasticity. After the 1857 and 1858 cables broke, Bright knew the spirally wound wires that provided the outer armor had to be strengthened. By using a heavier wire tightly wound around the core, the new cable weighed 3,575 pounds per nautical mile compared with 2,000 pounds per nautical mile in 1858.

Coils fed onto the East Greenwich production line received a thick padding of catechu-treated jute yarn to prevent the gutta-percha insulation from being damaged during the iron-sheathing process. The section moved directly into the armoring machine, and as quickly as the cable received its ten-wire spiral wrapping, workers coiled the finished product in large vats

Sketch of the 1857 cable. When compared to the 1865–1866 cable, the conductor did not change but everything else did. (From Charles Bright, *The Story of the Atlantic Cable*. Digitized by Debra Peffer.)

of water and again tested the entire length for continuity. The iron used in the wire had the strength of steel without the springiness, and to protect the iron from rusting, machines covered it with a jacket of tarred Manila yarn. The new design, though heavier, reduced the specific gravity of the cable and rendered it more capable of supporting its own weight on the seabed.

The heavier construction enabled the cable to bear eight tons of tension, or about eleven miles of its own extension in seawater. Since the telegraphic plateau never exceeded two and a half miles in depth, there was no reason for the cable to break. Though nearly twice as heavy in weight, the cable was still only 1.1 inches in diameter compared with five-eighths inches in 1858. In the air it weighed 3,575 pounds per nautical mile, but only 1,400 pounds in the water. Only the shore end was heavier, having an additional outer sheathing of twelve strands, each strand containing three stout galvanized iron wires of .284 inches, bringing the weight to twenty tons per mile.

The Atlantic Telegraph Company ordered 2,300 nautical miles of cable, though the surface distance from Ireland to Newfoundland was only 1,640 nautical miles. Some of the surplus would be needed for paying-out slack in deep water. Field took no chances of running out of cable. This expedition had to succeed.

With Gooch involved in the enterprise, Field's company leapt the next hurdle as if by magic. With the Union still at war, Field knew the pointlessness of asking Secretary Welles for naval vessels to carry cable. He also doubted whether the Admiralty would provide four cable-carrying ships—two could not carry the load. Gooch provided the solution: *Great Eastern* would carry *all* the cable. "They seem to have been made for one another," Gooch said. She would lay the cable for nothing, but if the expedition proved successful, the owners of the ship wanted £50,000 of company stock. Perhaps Field remembered the conversation with Brunel in 1856 when the latter took him to his shipyard at Millwall, swept his arm towards the enormous vessel, and said, "Here's the ship to lay your cable, Mr. Field."[20]

The *Great Eastern*'s time had finally come, but not in the summer of 1864—not quite yet.

— CHAPTER 14 —

"THE SHIP TO LAY YOUR CABLE"

Some called *Great Eastern* the "Eighth Wonder of the World." She evolved slowly, plank by plank, plate by plate, on the Isle of Dogs, misnamed for the dingy Millwall quarter of greater London's dockyards where the smell of sewage and garbage lingered in a vaporous stench above the polluted Thames River. Isambard Kingdom Brunel designed her to carry 4,000 passengers—twice as many as the RMS *Queen Mary*, launched seventy-seven years later. Two thousand workers scurried about a colossal hulk five times the size of the largest vessel ever built, including Noah's Ark. Using Biblical measurements in cubits, Sir Isaac Newton calculated the Ark's dimensions at 515 feet long and 86 feet wide, giving her a displacement of 18,231 tons. At 693 feet long and 120 feet wide, Brunel's creation displaced 22,500 tons. A half century later her breadth could not have squeezed through the new Panama Canal. Though he called his leviathan *Great Eastern*, he may as well have called her the "White Elephant" because she never achieved her commercial purpose. No vessel matched her in size until 1906, when the RMS *Lusitania*, another enormous passenger ship, slid down the ways and eleven years later came to a disastrous end when sunk by a German submarine during World War I.

Brunel designed *Great Eastern* to carry six masts and five funnels, more than any ship has ever carried since. Her two steam engines generated more than 10,000 horsepower, "enough to run all the cotton mills in Manchester." Her bunkers held 15,000 tons of coal and fed ten boilers. A huge engine powered the fifty-eight-foot paddle wheels, which at full speed rotated once every 3.5 seconds. Another enormous engine drove her twenty-four-foot screw. Brunel missed an opportunity to advance the science of propeller technology by designing a flat rather than a curved blade for the

Teams of men struggle to get ready for the launching of *Great Eastern*. Pictured to the left in a tall beaver hat is Isambard Kingdom Brunel, the ship's designer. (From *Illustrated London News*. Digitized by Debra Peffer.)

screw. Two screw propellers would have powered the vessel better than the arrangement Brunel chose, but the enormous size of power plants in the 1850s made it impossible for him to mount two engines side by side. Nevertheless, *Great Eastern* could almost circumnavigate the globe without refueling. For auxiliary power she carried 6,500 square yards of sail, eclipsing in canvas that worn by some of the great clipper ships of the day. And if that were not enough, Brunel strung a pair of hundred-foot utility steamers from her sides. Fully laden, *Great Eastern* outweighed the combined tonnage of the 197 British ships that fought and defeated the Spanish Armada in 1588.[1]

Brunel richly illuminated the ship with gaslights. He cooled or warmed her with a unique ventilation system. He designed her to be longer than the largest ocean trough ever measured by the Admiralty, making her steady enough in rough sea to eliminate seasickness. The inner cabins contained staterooms three times the size of any ship afloat. The elegance of her grand ballroom eclipsed some of the finest banquet halls in London and New York.

When on November 3, 1857, the time finally came for her launching, musicians were already playing "The Leviathan March" and "The Leviathan Galop." Neither tune quite described *Great Eastern*'s stubborn descent into the Thames. She had taken four years to build at a cost of

£600,000 ($3,000,000), the same sum that Field needed for his 1865 cable. When in 1856 Brunel took Field to see the vessel, she still needed fifteen months of work before she could be launched. Too big to be built in drydock, she gradually took shape on the soft riverbank where the Thames made two sharp reversals in its journey to the sea. John Scott Russell, who built the ship, laid her parallel to the river because nowhere on the Isle of Dogs could a vessel 700 feet long be built stern-first because the Thames was only 1,000 feet wide. For three years Londoners watched as the behemoth grew to a height of fifty-eight feet, overshadowing the riverside dwellings huddled about her. When the time finally came to launch her, she had become the "crystal palace of the sea," the subject of dozens of renderings by artists, poets, and composers, and the most fascinating architectural structure of the day.

In 1857 *Great Eastern* represented the heaviest object that man had ever attempted to move. She lay on two timber cradles that rested on 120 iron rollers placed across 160 railway rails which in turn were supported by a two-foot-thick foundation of concrete laid atop 2,000 timber piles driven thirty feet through mud to the gravel base of the Thames. From these cradles 12,000 inert tons needed to slide 330 feet on a slope of one foot to every twelve to reach the high tide mark of the river. Brunel estimated the force required to get her to the water and used a combination of hydraulic rams to push her, steam tugs on the river to pull her, gigantic steam winches on shore to lower her down the ways, and huge windlasses to check her descent if she slid too fast. The London *Times* warned the masses who paid to witness the christening: "The launch is likely to be a long and tedious affair, which will probably occupy eight to ten hours."[2]

Brunel did not know that the directors had sold thousands of tickets to spectators and built grandstands to accommodate them. The *Times* estimated the crowd at 100,000, noting among the sightseers diplomats, counts, and dukes from continental Europe. As a crowd with umbrellas began gathering for the misty noon launching, Brunel ducked under the ship to supervise the slicking of the ways with grease. When he climbed to the rostrum to direct the launching, he spied Chairman Henry Thomas Hope's daughter ready to swing the champagne bottle. The directors intended to call the ship the *Leviathan*. Brunel had always called her *Great Eastern*, and because he designed her, the name stuck. Prior to the launching Hope suggested other names, to which Brunel curtly replied, "You can call it Tom Thumb if you like." Miss Hope smashed the champagne bottle against the ship's bow. A whooping cheer echoed through Millwall and across the Thames. Brunel had no handheld radio to coordinate the pushing and pulling required to jockey the great immovable object down the ways, and the noise of the crowd drowned out his efforts to communicate with the riggers. James Dugan, in *The Great Iron Ship* described the launch:

The crankshaft for *Great Eastern's* massive paddle wheels weighed forty tons and was the largest forging in the world. Isambard Kingdom Brunel looks on from the left. (From *Illustrated London News*. Digitized by Debra Peffer.)

"She moves!" they yelled. "She moves!" The stern slid three inches. Brunel waved his red flag for the hydraulic rams to push. There was a scraping squeal, the earth shook, and the *Great Eastern* started to slide. Among the thousands who simply stood and sighed was the gang on the sixty-ton stern checking drum. The ship took up the slack of their chain and sent the windlass spinning in reverse. The huge handlebars caught a dozen workers and threw them above the heads of the crowd. Spectators and workers ran in panic, except for Brunel and the foreman of the forward drum crew, Ned Hepworth . . . who applied his brake. The ship stopped with a horrible complaint of iron. The crews of the river barges lost their heads and leaped into the river.[3]

At the first sign of trouble, the barge crews fled, along with a mass of spectators holding seats near the launching gear. Brunel tried to restore order and finally got men back on the winches and steam rams. *Great Eastern* made deep groaning noises but would not budge. Gears stripped from the bow winch. Chains parted, sending six-inch links hurtling like shrapnel into the grandstand. Then rain began to pour, and Brunel brought the launch to an end. He retired from the scene, berated by hoots, hisses, and catcalls from a crowd now wet and dirty from flying mud. Some joker suggested making "big ships in big holes and let the water in when the ships are finished, instead of trying to make the ships travel on railroads."[4]

Brunel postponed the launch until December's spring tide. He told the directors he wanted no more spectators at the site. He broke so much chain that he had to borrow from the Admiralty. During the last days before the tide he moved the ship seventeen feet before the cylinder on a ten-inch ram broke. He replaced the ram with two more and slid the vessel another fourteen feet. A hundred sightseers watched with interest from scaffolding bridging two housetops. The contraption collapsed, toppling all of them to the ground. Horse-drawn ambulances rushed the injured to the local hospital.

Working frantically in readiness for the tide, Brunel nudged her another thirty feet. Two more rams exploded. He drove piles on the opposite shore, stretching chains across the river to pull her, but the ship would not move. The December tide came and went. While preparing for the next spring tide, Brunel borrowed every heavy-duty ram in the country, banking twenty-one rams together into a combined force of 6,000 tons—half the deadweight of the ship—and moved the vessel three inches before the rams began to burst. The circus continued until January 31, 1858. With no spectators in sight—they had all given her up as wedded to the land—*Great Eastern* slipped into the water. In a last act of defiance she fouled several barges on her trip across the river. Brunel untangled the mess by scuttling the barges. The ship's launching took its toll on fifty-one-year-old Brunel. He now walked with a limp, lost most of his thick brown hair, and looked frail.

Building and launching her cost $4,000,000, a third more than originally subscribed and nearly double the original estimate. To finish her added another $600,000. The shipwrights who built her explained that the overrun had little to do with labor and material costs. They claimed a riveter had been sealed alive in one of the hull cells, and his screams could not be heard above the hammering. His ghost jinxed the ship, they said, and bad luck would be her future.

The stockholders tended to agree she would never pay, but nobody wanted her, not even the Royal Navy. Cost overruns drove the shipyard owner into bankruptcy. The stockholders lost their total investment and wanted out, so Brunel decided to buy his own creation. He formed the Great Ship Company, raised $1,750,000, and bought the ship for $800,000.

Captain William Harrison took command of her, and a few months later while sailing a gig to shore, a strong gust capsized the boat and drowned *Great Eastern*'s first captain. During her shakedown cruise an explosion demolished the grand saloon, knocked down the forward smokestack, killed five of the crew, and scalded fifteen more. Any other ship would have sunk.

Having suffered a paralyzing stroke, though clear of mind, the news devastated Brunel. He became the next victim of the disaster and on September 15, 1859, died. The public blamed *Great Eastern*, but Brunel had never been a man to delegate. When financial and construction problems struck during the building of the Thames Tunnel, Brunel worked ninety-six hours without sleep. During the construction of the Great Western Railway he had never slept more than four hours. His nerve-wracking labors with *Great Eastern* added a final jolt to his health. The string of tragedies surprised no one. Those who worked on the ship and believed in ghosts expected more of the same during the coming months.[5]

After Brunel died the surviving directors anticipated enormous profits by turning her into the greatest luxury liner afloat. They added a grand saloon, plush sofas, teak chairs, marble tables, skylights, and a magnificent superstructure rising five stories above the hull. Operating costs eventually disillusioned the stockholders. The directors resigned, but not Daniel Gooch. He took over the reins determined to make the great ship pay. The "Mighty Home on the Deep" had not yet carried her first passenger, so in 1860 Gooch and the new directorate hired Captain John Vine Hall and opened bookings for her maiden voyage to New York. Everybody in the United States wanted to see her, but curiously enough, not many people wanted to travel on her. The directors sent a fast steamer to New York to get Michael Murphy, known on both sides of the Atlantic as the best Sandy Hook pilot in the business. Gooch believed that nobody could get *Great Eastern* safely up to Manhattan but Murphy. When she failed to sail on time because of a drunken crew, those who bought tickets disembarked and booked passage on a Cunarder.[6]

On June 17, 1860, the great ship departed from Southampton with only thirty-five paying passengers, no cargo, and 418 crewmembers. Passengers got lost on the ship, but only three persons became seasick. Gooch and two directors joined the voyage. As Murphy rounded the tip of Long Island for Flushing Bay, he struck an uncharted rock (today's Great Eastern Rock) and ripped an eighty-three-foot gash in her bottom. The vessel's double hull saved her, and only through a recent development in underwater repair was she able to be mended.

When *Great Eastern* finally passed up the Hudson River, Gooch remembered the stirring reception: thousands of New Yorkers cheering from the wharves, waving and yelling from housetops, and filling "every spot where a human being could stand and get sight of the ship."[7]

Murphy took her up the North River to 45th Street, and to the amazement of the crowd, spun her around in midriver, almost within her own length, by reversing one of the paddle wheels. Then he conned her slowly downstream to her berth between West 11th and 12th streets. He misjudged the distance. The bow struck the crowded wharf head on, causing it to buckle, and the paddle wheel chewed five feet off the wharf before Murphy got her under control. The crowd screamed and ran, trampling over each other to get out of the way. One eyewitness declared: "The *Great Eastern* tried to cut New York in two."[8]

Field wanted to see the mammoth vessel that Brunel once predicted

Great Eastern takes to the sea from Southampton and with only thirty-five paying passengers and heads for New York. (From *Illustrated London News*. Digitized by Debra Peffer.)

would be the ship to lay his cable. He bought ten-dollar tickets for his family and friends for a two-day round-trip excursion to Cape May. The guests found the ship filthy, the food sickening, the waiters intoxicated, and nothing to drink but bad champagne. With only 300 beds available, 1,700 passengers went without sleep and spent the night in the gambling casino. Gooch gave up his lavish stateroom and sought solace on the bridge. Others curled up on the open deck and suffered from eruptions of soot spewing from the ship's five volcanic funnels. Towards morning a light rain streaked faces powdered with soot to the ashen gray of walking dead. Stewards made the rounds, selling washbasins for a dollar, a clean towel for another dollar, or a soiled towel for a little less, depending upon its degree of dirtiness. The passengers had eaten all the food during the night, but for another dollar or two a waiter could produce a cup of coffee. For good reason, *Great Eastern* never became a respectable luxury ship. When the liner returned to New York, Gooch found "the newspapers were full of abuse," and lamented, "I was very glad when it was over."[9]

During the two-day excursion, however, Field roamed the ship. He inspected the engine room and hold, developed an impression of her enormous size, and made a mental note that if she ever became available, here indeed was the ship to lay his cable.

Instead of a passenger liner, the "Wonder of the Seas" made its American debut as a floating exhibition hall. During four weeks at New York she sold 143,764 tickets without moving from the wharf. After that, interest flagged and Murphy moved her to ports along the eastern seaboard. When summer ended, Murphy returned to New York and resumed his duties as a pilot. During the homeward voyage, Captain Hall collapsed with a nervous breakdown. Gooch had grown tired of Murphy and Hall running into things and hired Captain James Walker, a trusty veteran from the Cunard Line. After Walker got the vessel to Queenstown, he wanted no more to do with her.

Wherever *Great Eastern* went she lost money. By the beginning of 1864 her debt exceeded $500,000. Two accidents costing $650,000 added to the directors' woes. She racked up more losses during her brief lifetime than the Atlantic Telegraph Company, which had deposited theirs on the ocean's bottom. Gooch and Brassey, being the bondholders, took her over. During the closing weeks of 1863, the directors studied their options: to sell the vessel or scuttle her, because every day she remained afloat she cost the company money. As Gooch's syndicate pondered her disposition, Cyrus Field knocked on the door of Thomas Brassey's mansion in search of funds.[10]

Field had met Gooch in 1860 when he took his family on the unpleasant overnight junket to Cape May, but he may not have been aware of Gooch's close association with Brassey. Being heavily invested in the ship, Gooch was besieged by creditors. The company put the leviathan up for auction, but the owners retained the right to withdraw the ship if no one bid £100,000. A voice that the ushers could not locate said, "Fifty thousand," after which no one raised another pound. Gooch withdrew the ship and closed the auction, announcing that "*Great Eastern* will be offered at a peremptory sale without reserve" in three weeks.[11]

In the meantime, Gooch renewed his acquaintance with Field. Together with Brassey they wooed John Pender, another of *Great Eastern*'s directors, who agreed to join them in a bid of £80,000 for the ship. They had found a greater purpose for her, not as a passenger ship but as the transporter of the Atlantic cable. Gooch took his secretary and checkbook to the next auction and bought *Great Eastern* for £25,000. Brassey put up half the money pooled for the auction, not because he needed the ship or ever intended to use her. "He was in the habit of studying . . . every novel project in the engineering world," said Arthur Helps, "and their development was largely due to his liberal pecuniary aid."[12]

By the strange irony of coincidence, two unsuccessful companies came together in a single enterprise. Field's two companies had lost more than $3,000,000 stretching cables across the Atlantic, and the *Great Eastern* lost more than $5,000,000 betraying three companies that had tried to make her pay as a luxury liner. She had killed scores of men during her construction, and because of the labors she imposed on everyone, she also killed her creator. She became a hazard in every port and burned money almost as fast as she burned coal. Only Field would attempt to put two failures together to make a success.

When March came, Field tried to go home, but the directors begged him to stay. There was little he could do. When the Telegraph Construction & Maintenance Company asked for eight months to manufacture the cable, Field agreed not to press them. *Great Eastern* had no crew, but this was Gooch's problem. When Gooch could not find a man to captain the ship, Field went to see Samuel Cunard about releasing James Anderson, providing the veteran skipper agreed to take the job. Field knew Anderson well, having taken many voyages on ships he commanded, and considered him among the best in the business. Anderson wanted to try his hand with *Great Eastern* and to Field's offer replied: "I have been afraid at times that you may have thought me lukewarm upon the subject of commanding the *Great Eastern*, and am desirous that you understand that I have restrained my enthusiasm because I have not thought it likely I should be chosen."[13]

In May, Field convinced the directors to let him go home, arguing that *Great Eastern*'s great depth made it necessary to find a new landing site for the cable. At Trinity Bay he met Captain Orlebar, commanding the British survey steamer *Margaretta Stevenson*, who had been waiting for him. Together they spent several days plying the coast. Twenty miles closer to the sea than Bull's Arm Bay, they found a deep and sheltered cove with the comforting name of Heart's Content. Field could not resist. He gave the tiny fishing village his blessing, fixed it on his map, and went home.

Gooch moved *Great Eastern* to Sheerness to fit her with three huge iron tanks for storing the cable. Because the uptake of one of the ship's five boiler rooms passed through the main hold, he shut down a pair of boilers and removed the funnel. To balance the weight, one tank went into the forehold, another the afterhold, and the third amidships. Each of the tanks measured twenty feet, six inches deep and varied in width from seventy-five feet to fifty-two feet in diameter. The smaller tank forward held 693 nautical miles of cable, the other two tanks each had the capacity for carrying 898 miles of cable. After being tested and declared watertight, millwrights set the tanks on three-inch concrete foundations. Underneath the three holds hundreds of nine-inch square timbers tied to the keelson supported the load.[14]

In February 1865, Gooch discovered that *Great Eastern* could not get close enough to Glass, Elliot to load the cable. The Admiralty detailed the lighters *Amethyst* and *Iris* to transport the wire from the factory to the ship. Coiling began on *Great Eastern* at the rate of twenty miles a day and continued until June 22.

Canning and Clifford of the Telegraph Construction & Maintenance Company designed entirely new paying-out machinery. John Penn & Son

Great Eastern's crew receives cable from lighters and begins coiling it by hand into fifty-two-foot diameter tanks installed in the hold. (From William H. Russell, *The Atlantic Telegraph, 1865*. Digitized by Debra Peffer.)

of Greenwich built the new contraption—a more elaborate machine than the designs used on *Agamemnon* and *Niagara*—and fitted it to *Great Eastern*'s afterdeck. A cable-conveying device began at the forehold, where six wrought iron V-sheaves fed the coil through a trough fixed with small guiding wheels to the paying-out station. The six large wheels of the paying-out machine contained small friction wheels with brake straps weighted by levers. As the cable wound its way through the sheaves, it passed through a long vat of cold water guided by wheels that fed the wire onto a drum.

Two Appold brakes, also operating in water, maintained a carefully regulated tension on the cable. The engineers used a dynamometer similar to the 1858 design and located it between the stern wheel, which fed the cable into the sea, and two intermediate wheels. The instrument measured tension on the cable and could change it by adding or removing weights to the brake. A man stood by the dynamometer to monitor the tension-indicating needle. As long as the dynamometer stayed within the prescribed range, no adjustments were required.

From the braking mechanism the cable flowed onto a large stern wheel designed with a bell-mouthed shield to guide and protect the cable as it paid into the ocean. The new apparatus, from front to back, worked so smoothly and with so little friction that a weight of only 200 pounds could draw the cable from the hold and feed it into the sea.[15]

Unlike the earlier 1857 and 1858 expeditions, the company made provisions for cable emergencies. *Great Eastern* carried buoys and five miles of heavy wire rope wound on reels. If the cable had to be cut, mechanics could clamp it to the wire rope, fix an anchor to one end and a buoy to the other, and if necessary, cast it overboard and retrieve it later. In the ship's bow, engineers added tackle and machinery for picking up the cable if it broke.

Work refitting *Great Eastern* proceeded slowly. The expedition had been postponed until the summer of 1865, and the delay worked to everyone's benefit.

Field returned to America in May 1864 and found the nation still engulfed in the Civil War. He looked for something to occupy his time. He had the money and the ship, and by the spring of 1865 he would have the cable. After a brief visit with his family, he traveled through the Maritime Provinces and the northern states consolidating the lines connecting the New York, Newfoundland company with his base in Manhattan.

The war had become one of attrition. General Grant's spring campaign of 1864 took the Army of the Potomac to the gates of Petersburg but no farther. General Benjamin F. Butler bottled up his Army of the James at Bermuda Hundred, Virginia. On September 2, 1864, Major General William T. Sherman's army rolled into Atlanta, Georgia, and on November 16 began its "March to the Sea."

Field tried to constrain himself while waiting, but on October 24 he wrote George Saward: "I can hardly keep the business of the Atlantic Telegraph Company out of my mind for a single minute."[16]

To keep occupied, Field hosted a number of dinners. To one held on October 19 he invited Major General John A. Dix, commanding the Department of the East, and Lord Lyons, the British minister. The two men were enjoying a pleasant chat when a telegram from Vermont arrived for the general. Confederates operating in Canada had crossed the border, taken possession of St. Albans, robbed local banks of $200,000, set several buildings on fire, killed a man, and terrorized the region.

Dix excused himself from the table, went into Field's study, and told the household telegrapher to send a message to the commanding officer in Burlington, Vermont, with instructions to relieve St. Albans, capture the invaders, and if necessary, pursue them into Canada and kill them. When Dix rejoined the dinner party he took his host aside and told him what had happened. Field instantly smelled a Confederate plot to draw Great Britain into the war by creating another *Trent* affair. He pulled Dix and Lord Lyons into a separate room where he forced them to discuss the incident. Dix rescinded his order to Burlington and the three men returned to the dinner table as if nothing had happened. No American troops crossed the border, Lyons urged the Canadians to look into the matter, and Field probably avoided another round of diplomatic headaches between the United States and Great Britain.[17]

After General Sherman captured Atlanta and Grant commenced the siege of Petersburg, Abraham Lincoln won reelection for a second term. With the war winding down, Field visited Washington in early 1865 to petition Lincoln and Welles for two ships to join the cable layers. The British had committed *Terrible* and *Sphinx* to the expedition and Field believed the government would want to be represented in the enterprise. Lincoln left the decision up to Welles, who flatly refused to provide escorts. Welles might be accused of lack of foresight, but he had good reasons at the time for making no alliances with the British. The Palmerston government had allowed four commerce raiders to get to sea and turned a blind eye when colonies gave them succor. Also, English merchants had supplied the Confederacy with $10,000,000 in arms and munitions against cotton certificates.[18]

On March 8, 1865, Field booked passage on the steamer *China* and returned to London. It would be Captain Anderson's last trip on a Cunard liner before taking command of *Great Eastern*. The two men spent hours discussing the work ahead. By the time *China* reached her mooring berth at Liverpool, Anderson knew all about the cranky problems of the "Wonder of the Seas." He put his action plan together, leaving nothing to chance, and a few days later wrote Field:

> The essentials, as far as I am concerned, would be to *see for myself all* the ground tackling *clear* and efficient, the steering gear . . . in good order; the sails necessary to steady the ship in a chance breeze; [and] the *compasses* and their *adjustment*. . . .
>
> I should be ready to get around me such a staff of men that I might hope to rely on at least a portion of them. . . . I would not, of course, incur the expense of employing a large crew at present, but I would select a good nucleus, and have the ship's work and discipline well in hand in good season.[19]

Confident that he had picked the right man to command *Great Eastern*, and satisfied that the details of preparation were in competent hands, Field departed for Cairo as a representative of the New York Chamber of Commerce to inspect the Suez Canal. He found himself among eighty-five delegates representing fourteen countries. He spoke of the cable in laudatory terms to all of them.

While in Egypt, the Civil War ended, and John Wilkes Booth assassinated President Lincoln. The news of the president's death came to Field as a shock. During his last conversation at the White House he knew the president wanted to heal the wounds of the country and reestablish good relations with England. On May 1, when Field returned to London, he met publicly with Charles Francis Adams and a group of Americans, and said,

On May 24, 1865, the Prince of Wales and his retinue of friends and associates look into the after tank on *Great Eastern* as the crew coils cable. (From William H. Russell, *The Atlantic Telegraph, 1865*. Digitized by Debra Peffer.)

"If Mr. Lincoln could speak today he would urge upon everyone to do all he could to allay the passions . . . excited in America; and I hope all will comply with what I believe would be his wish."[20]

On May 24 the Prince of Wales, accompanied by many distinguished guests, visited *Great Eastern* to inspect the creature modified to lay the cable. The entourage arrived early, ate a hearty breakfast in the dining room, and spent the day inspecting the ship. Anderson's crew had cleaned her up and she looked in fine trim. Pender and Glass took the group into the electrician's room where His Royal Highness sent a message through 1,395 nautical miles of wire, which, in the course of several seconds, registered at the receiving end: "I wish success to the Atlantic cable." The other 900 miles of cable had not been loaded, being either at the armoring works or en route to the ship on lighters. The two small vessels had been shuttling back and forth for eight weeks carrying 140-mile sections to the ship's side. The visitors watched as a small steam engine drew the cable off a lighter and mile by mile into the mammoth hold.[21]

Five days later a tinkling bell at Glass, Elliot announced that the last mile of cable had just spun off the armoring machines. For eight long months the machines had never stopped whirling, wrapping hemp and wire around the core. After spinning out 2,300 nautical miles of cable, the machines suddenly fell silent. The directors all came to witness the event. They con-

A lighter pulls alongside *Great Eastern* to unload her cable from the Glass, Elliot works. (From William H. Russell, *The Atlantic Telegraph, 1865*. Digitized by Debra Peffer.)

gratulated each other, shook hands with the employees, gave a dignified cheer, and proceeded westward to Ship Tavern, where they had arranged a princely supper for themselves. During the usual round of toasts, John Pender, the company's chairman, raised his glass and robustly said: "[To] Cyrus W. Field, Esquire—may his energy and perseverance in behalf of the Atlantic Telegraph Company be rewarded by the permanent success of the cable."[22]

On Wednesday, June 14, the *Amethyst* completed her final trip to *Great Eastern*, bringing the last 245 miles of cable from the armoring works. She stood by, waiting in line for the *Iris* to be emptied. Field came on board with his brother Henry. Despite much activity below, the 700-foot deck of the giant ship looked deserted with nothing in sight but the paying-out machinery aft. They walked about the ship, looked everywhere, and saw no sign of the cable.

> We walked up and down on the deck of the *Great Eastern* without seeing this gigantic [cord] which is to bind together the Old and the New World; and it is only on having the place pointed out to us that we find where the cable lies and by what process it is brought on board.

They peered into the dimly lit hold and saw men coiling the cable into a tank, chanting:

Three fishers went sailing away to the West,
Away to the West as the sun went down.

"The sounds rose up from the dark, deep cavern with startling effect," Henry Field recalled, "producing an indescribable impression. We proceeded on; but the song of the sailors who are taking charge of the Atlantic telegraph cable is haunting us like a dream."[23]

Unlike his brother, Henry Field had never seen the massive ship. She no longer looked like the elegant luxury liner envisioned by her builders, but he could still see the vestiges of her former magnificence.

> Our guide conducts us all over the big ship, through miles of galleries, passages, staircases, and promenades; through gorgeous saloons, full of mirrors, marbles, paintings, and upholstery, made "regardless of expense;" and through buildings crowded with glittering steam apparatus of gigantic dimensions, where the latent power of coal and water creates the force which propels this monster vessel over the seas. In vain our attention is directed to all these sights; we do not admire them; our imagination is used up.[24]

On June 22 the last coil slithered through the steam donkey and came to rest in the hold. The electricians connected the end and tested all 2,300 miles of cable. The signal looped through three holds and into the receiving instruments seconds later. Chief electrician de Sauty gave a whoop and shook hands with Willoughby Smith. The occasion did not signal the end, but the beginning. From this minute forward, until the cable was connected from Ireland to Newfoundland, the wires would never rest.

De Sauty telegraphed a brief message to the bridge. The cablemen were ready to sail.

— Chapter 15 —

So Close and Yet So Far

More than a year had passed since the directors made the decision to lay the cable in a continuous length from one ship instead of two. No ship but *Great Eastern* could carry the weight. On June 24, 1865, she steamed from the Medway carrying 7,000 tons of cable, 2,000 tons of water-filled iron tanks, and 7,000 tons of coal. She stopped at the Nore and took on board another 1,500 tons of coal, bringing her deadweight to 21,000 tons—five times the displacement of the USS *Niagara*. Fully loaded, she drew twenty-eight and a half feet forward and thirty-four and a half feet aft.[1]

The great ship carried 500 sailors, technicians, and mechanics. Farther down the deck stood a motherly cow, 10 bullocks, 20 pigs, 114 sheep, and a poultry-yard filled with 29 geese, 14 turkeys, and 500 hens. Into the larder went 28 bullocks, 4 calves, 22 sheep, 4 pigs, 300 fowl, 18,000 eggs, and hundreds of barrels of meat, vegetables, and fruit. "Such a freight," one observer noted, "had not been seen . . . since Noah's Ark was stranded on Mount Ararat."[2]

Had the Telegraph Construction & Maintenance Company, the sole managers of the expedition, accepted all the applications from the public begging to join the voyage, *Great Eastern* may have booked for the first time since her creation a full passenger list. But the expedition was not of pleasure but of business. Even the directors were barred unless they served a purpose. Daniel Gooch made the trip because his syndicate owned the ship. No director of the Atlantic Telegraph Company joined the expedition but Cyrus Field, who had business in Newfoundland.

Because of the scientific value of the expedition, the company allowed six young electrical and mechanical engineers on board to assist in the testing room and the engineer's department. Then, when every journal in

London demanded a seat, the company excluded all but London *Times* correspondent William H. Russell, who was allowed to bring along a few artists. Russell was probably almost as well known in America as in England. He invented the term "war correspondent" by his dispatches from the Crimean War and the Sepoy Mutiny. During the American Civil War his famous battle accounts earned him the sobriquet "Bull-Run Russell," and without his comprehensive account of *Great Eastern*'s first cable-laying campaign, much of the history of the expedition would have slipped into oblivion. A most deserving journalist, he would later be knighted.[3]

Because of the Telegraph Construction & Maintenance Company's financial stake in the enterprise, the firm supplied its own officers to manage the expedition, the captain and crew to sail the ship, engineers to lay the cable, and electricians to test it. Even such eminent electrical engineers as William Thomson and Cromwell Varley, both members of the Atlantic Telegraph Company, were not permitted to interfere or to give advice unless "asked for in writing." Thomson brought four electricians. They were to do nothing until the cable was connected at both ends, after which they were to pass messages between Newfoundland and Ireland to verify the system's performance to predetermined standards.[4]

De Sauty headed the electrical staff, using two well-qualified electrical engineers to split shifts: Willoughby Smith and H.A.C. Saunders. Four assistants, two instrument clerks, and a mechanic completed the electrical department. De Sauty's staff had been running tests on the cable since the first links came off the stranding machines. The technicians understood their roles—to demonstrate that this cable was "many times more perfect" than cables of the past. For every 1,000 impulses sent through the cable, 999 came out the other end.[5]

Canning headed the mechanical staff, ably supported by Henry Clifford. In 1858 both men had performed similar roles on *Agamemnon*. During the intervening years they laid cables in the Mediterranean, the Persian Gulf, and the North Sea. With them came ten engineers and mechanics to run the paying-out machine.[6]

Captain Anderson organized the enterprise along the lines of a naval expedition, and that is how he intended to run it. Everyone on board had a specific task, the exception being Cyrus Field, who had nothing to do. Anderson expected every man to be at his place, and when off duty, to go below decks and keep out of the way of operating personnel. He had the good sense to borrow from the Admiralty Staff Commander Moriarty, a veteran navigator from *Agamemnon*'s 1858 expedition.

At noon on Saturday, July 15, the voices of 200 sailors filled the air as they bent their backs to raise the ship's seven-ton Trotman anchor. Each link of the chain weighed seventy pounds. For a while it seemed that the Thames would not let go of the ship, but after fifteen minutes of hard labor, the

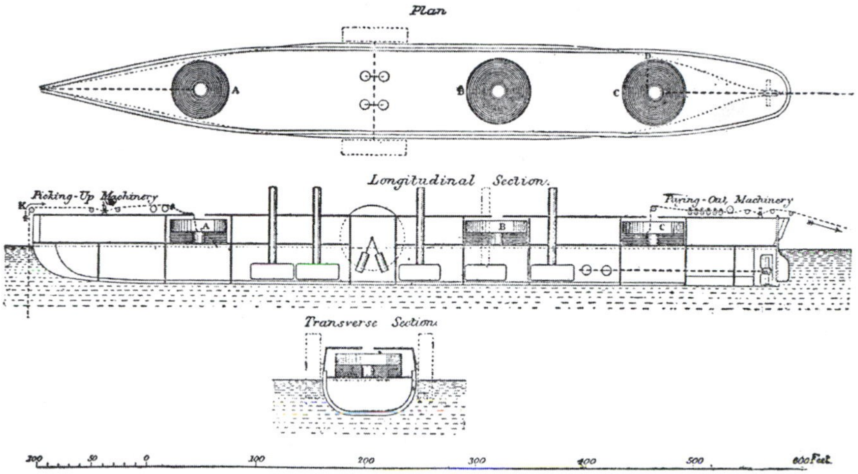

Cross-section of *Great Eastern* showing the stowage of her cable. (From Charles Bright, *The Story of the Atlantic Cable*. Digitized by Debra Peffer.)

muddy bottom released its grip on the anchor. A signal gun fired, and the voyage began.

The steamer HMS *Porcupine*, that had guided *Niagara* up Trinity Bay in 1858, led *Great Eastern* out of the Nore and into the English Channel. The men of the cable crew peered at the cliffs of Dover as the ship passed down the Channel, glided past the Isle of Wight, and quickened her pace as she moved down to Falmouth. There on July 17 she rendezvoused with the steamer *Caroline*, which carried the shore end. With a brisk headwind blowing and 540 tons of cable in her hold, *Caroline* struggled to keep up with the powerful *Great Eastern*. "It did seem extraordinary," said Willoughby Smith, "that one could sit at ease at the stern of the *Great Eastern*, while a man on the bridge of the *Caroline* held his position with great difficulty, firmly grasping the rail." Anderson pulled alongside *Caroline*, passed a hawser to the steamer, and took her in tow.[7]

Despite strong westerlies, *Great Eastern* plunged along at six knots, carving a path through the crests with barely a shudder. The little *Caroline*, pitching and rolling heavily in the seas, broke the towrope and ran for Valentia on her own. "It was an awful sight," said Gooch, "to see how she laboured [and] how the seas washed over her."[8]

Anderson passed inside the Skelligs, stood in close to the lighthouse, and sent a boat ashore to communicate with local port authorities. From the bridge he could see the HMS *Terrible* standing off Valentia. Gooch believed that her commander, Captain Charles Napier, "did not have his heart in the work." Nearby lay the HMS *Sphinx*, Captain John Hamilton, who Gooch merely described as "a very nice fellow." Anderson fired a gun to announce his arrival, steamed for Bantry Bay, and on the morning of July 19 anchored in seventeen fathoms. "The rush of Irish on board when we dropped our anchor was an entertaining scene," said Gooch, "bringing with them milk, eggs, poultry &c for sale, and our decks soon looked like a market—but it was not a cheap one."[9]

Canning had changed the site for landing the shore end from Knightstown to a wild spot in Valentia's Foilhummerum Bay, where waves rolled in from the Atlantic and crashed against huge overhanging cliffs of shale furrowed by watercourses. High on the cliff sat an old moss-covered tower surrounded by traces of a moat built during the time of Cromwell. Safe from the pounding waves of the Atlantic and deep inside the bay lay a section of sandy beach at the base of the cliffs, a perfect bed for the shore end. The sweep of the waves ran parallel to the cable, not athwart it, and once laid the wire would rest in safety. Among the cliffs stood a few rickety cabins, built by natives, half-fishermen and half-husbandmen, that eked out a frugal living by whatever means they could.

Across the field from the cliff stood a wood building slathered with pitch and tar, the company's new telegraph station. The plainness belied what lay inside: Thomson's mirror-speaking instruments, connecting wires for the cable, banks of batteries, magnets, Werner von Siemen's electronic instruments, and all the latest innovations in telegraphy. A hallway led from one end to the other, with comfortable rooms for living and sleeping on the right and left, and at the far end the telegrapher's instrument room. Outside, wires strung on poles ran across the island to the station built in 1857 near Knightstown.[10]

On the plateau between the station and the cliff hundreds of country people craned their necks each day for a glimpse at *Great Eastern*. When word of her arrival circulated, hundreds came by land and sea, and soon the cliffs were covered with tents and canopies made from old sail. Those who came ashore from the cable ships to spot the area for landing the cable could smell burning peat fires, a reek of raw whiskey, and an appetizing aroma from frying bacon. Nearby they heard the sound of the fiddler and the piper, and they stopped momentarily to watch lasses lift their skirts and dance the jig. The whole area, from the blue bay to the bare brown cliffs, became dotted with red, scarlet, and green shawls worn gypsylike by women and girls. Yachts came around from Cork, and fishermen paddled into the bay in canvas coracles.

Anderson never brought *Great Eastern* to Foilhummerum Bay. She stayed in a deep anchorage off Bantry, leaving the shore-end duties to *Caroline*, the steamer *Hawk*, the steam yacht *Princess Alexandra*, and the tender *Advice*. Disappointed by not being able to see the great ship, sightseers straggled over to Knightstown for a look at *Terrible* and *Sphinx*, but all they could see were thin ribbons of distant smoke rising from the ships' funnels. Sir Peter Fitzgerald, Knight of Kerry, came to town to welcome

Electricians at the telegraph station on Valentia Island connect the shore-end to their instruments. (From *London Illustrated News*. Digitized by Debra Peffer.)

the cable crew, but nobody from Her Majesty's ships came ashore. The good and hospitable knight grumbled, rebuking the officers in command of the ships for being so thoughtless, and moved his party to Foilhummerum Bay.

On July 19 work parties ashore began cutting a ditch from the base of the cliff to the beach. A few sightseers having nothing to do lent a hand, and the work went quickly. They helped to carry down the earth-end, already connected to the telegraph station. The work crew passed it through a culvert of masonry and deposited it in a cut made as far into the bay as the state of the tide permitted. Three days later *Caroline* began dispensing the shore end onto a pontoon bridge of longboats and twenty-five yawls belonging to local fishermen. As the boats reached the shallows, sightseers on the cliffs tumbled down to the beach to lend a hand, and amid shouts and cheers they lugged the shore-end up the cliff and across the field to the telegraph station. Out of breath and drenched with sweat, they passed it to the electricians.

Sir Peter Fitzgerald, who had established his mobile headquarters with Sir Robert Peel at the back door, spoke to the gathering outside the instrument room. After saying "it may seem almost presumptuous in me to open my mouth on this occasion," he did so with great gustoes of praise. "I do not think we should be quite silent when such an undertaking has been inaugurated," he declared, and, when nobody could be found to deliver a prayer, Sir Peter raised his hand and said, "Glory to God in the highest, on earth peace, good will toward men."

Sir Robert embellished the ceremony with a few words, declaring, "We are about to lay down, at the very bottom of the mighty Atlantic, which beats against your shores with everlasting pulsations, this silver-toned zone, to join the United Kingdom with America." His metaphoric remarks drew a few blank looks from the country folk. "Now, gentlemen," Sir Robert continued,

> probably one of the first messages that will be sent by this cable will be a communication from the Sovereign of this great country to the great ruler of the mighty continent at the other side of the Atlantic. I will ask you to give three cheers for her Majesty the Queen.

When the cheering stopped, Sir Robert concluded his toast with: "I give you, with hearty good will, health and happiness to the ruler of the United States, President [Andrew] Johnson." Thirty minutes later the men of *Caroline* departed from the "silver-toned zone" and returned to their ship.[11]

At 2:00 P.M. *Caroline*, towed by *Hawk* and attended by *Princess Alexandra* and *Advice*, began paying out the shore-end along a marked channel. At 10:30 that night *Caroline* arrived at a buoy anchored in seventy-five fathoms of water twenty-six miles west of Valentia. The ship's operator wired Foilhummerum that *Caroline* was in position to transfer the shore-end to *Great Eastern*. A dispatch went to Anderson in Bantry Bay, and at 3:00 P.M. the following day the electricians on the great ship began splicing the landward end to the main cable in the after tank. Sir Robert, Sir Peter, and a bevy of gentlemen and ladies insisted upon going aboard *Great Eastern* for one last celebration. With the swell running too high for gangway ladders, Anderson's sailors hoisted the party to the deck in boatswains' chairs.

Field used the occasion to send a letter home to his wife, writing: "You may expect us at Heart's Content about the 5th of August. I am in good health and spirits, and all is going well."[12]

At 7:15 P.M., July 23, the splice frame slipped into the sea. De Sauty, the chief electrician, verified signals with the Foilhummerum station and said he was ready. *Great Eastern*'s paddle wheels rumbled into motion, and the ship moved west. Jack-tar knew that sailing on Sunday meant good luck, even though a reputed ghost roamed the ship. According to Henry Field, sailors liked hearing "the last sound from shore be the blessed Sabbath bells," as land passed out of sight. No sacred chimes came from shore, but the tranquil summer evening gave everyone hope.[13]

Tars from *Terrible* and *Sphinx* climbed the shrouds and from the tops

Great Eastern takes the cable from *Caroline* (far right) and begins laying the 1865 cable from Valentia to Newfoundland. (From William H. Russell, *The Atlantic Telegraph, 1865*. Digitized by Debra Peffer.)

gave a hearty cheer. Parting salutes rumbled back and forth as the departing tenders set a course for Queenstown. "Bull Run" Russell captured the moment, writing, "Their colours were hauled down, and as the sun set a broad stream of golden light was thrown across the smooth billows towards their bows as if to indicate . . . the path marked out by the hand of Heaven." After so many appeals to the Lord since the 1857 expedition, one might believe that by now those prayers had been heard.[14]

As *Great Eastern* gathered momentum, mechanics on the paying-out machinery eased the brake, and the apparatus rumbled to life. Drums rotated and sheaves turned, pulling cable from the after tank and spinning it through a clockwork maze until feeding the thin, black wire in a graceful curve over the stern wheel.

The electrician's testing room—a darkened chamber holding the connecting ends of the conductor—occupied a cabin between the captain's stateroom and the entrance to the grand saloon. Outside the door hung a brass gong, only to be struck if signals stopped. A single large table held the delicate sending, receiving, and resistance-testing instruments. After splicing the shore-end, a series of continuous electrical tests began flowing through 2,300 miles of cable.

The testing cycle on *Great Eastern* contained twenty-nine specifically sequenced actions lasting exactly one hour. Electricians repeated the series

The new paying-out machinery designed for *Great Eastern* at work in the mid-Atlantic. (From William H. Russell, *The Atlantic Telegraph, 1865*. Digitized by Debra Peffer.)

every hour of every day. At the same hour, Foilhummerum ran a thirty-four-point test cycle, which the land-based electricians also repeated every hour of each day.

Once underway, Captain Anderson gradually increased the speed from three to six knots. The cable snaked through the mechanism, passed over the stern, and vanished mile after mile into the sea. Canning chose to lay the cable on the dates Commander Maury recommended nine years before. Anderson wanted to take advantage of the light westerly winds, for in going against the wind *Great Eastern* was as steady as a rock. "Every expectation was realized," said Henry Field. "To the Big Ship the ocean was an inland lake. . . . At midnight [we] went to sleep, to dream of an easy triumph."[15]

Henry O'Neil discovered a printing press on the ship and began publishing "The Atlantic Telegraph," a newspaper that soon became the expedition's primary source of humor. It provided a distraction that relieved the anxieties felt by all. O'Neil gathered material from those on board, incorporating news from Valentia, stock quotations, cartoons, and bad poetry written at Cyrus Field's expense. Soon everyone on board looked forward to the next issue, complaining that the shipboard publication, written in longhand, came "far too seldom."[16]

At 3:15 A.M., July 24, after eighty-four miles of cable had been paid out, the testing room received its first shock when the light on Thomson's reflecting mirror skittered off the scale and vanished, signaling a fault. Electricians sounded the gong, and the entire staff hurried to the testing room, which "looked like a sick-chamber where some royal patient lay trembling between life and death." Anderson slowed the ship while de Sauty attempted to restore the signal. After several minutes he looked up, shook his head, and said the line, though it still passed a small amount of current, could not be revived. Anderson fired a gun to alert *Terrible* and *Sphinx* and ordered fires started for the boilers that delivered steam to the donkey engine that operated the picking-up machinery in the bow.[17]

From the log kept in the testing room, which tracked resistance, five electricians began calculating the distance of the fault from the ship. At first, none of the calculations agreed. After much debate they concluded that the trouble could not be more than ten miles astern. Mechanics lashed onto the cable hanging off the stern and carried it around to the side of the ship. They shackled the cable to wire rope, cut it, and let it fly with its shackling into the sea. At 400 fathoms wire rope stopped running off the reel, and Anderson conned the ship's head around. Mechanics rewound the reel, brought the cable end back on board, and hauled it forward, which was no easy matter because the ship was an eighth of a mile long with boats, paddle boxes, hawse pipes, and deck utilities in the way. Hours passed. After much trouble, as the recovery exercise had not been tried before, the mechanics looped the wire rope holding the cable through the picking-up mechanism.

The apparatus refused to work, and mechanics shifted the steam supply to one of the ship's main boilers. Several hours passed before the drums and wheels of the picking-up machine began turning. The cable came grudgingly over the bow at the rate of a mile an hour. The weather held, being fine but cloudy, and as the picking-up process proceeded, the signals between the ship and shore inexplicably improved.

As the cable came on board, mechanics cut sections for individual testing and found nothing wrong. Finally at 9:00 A.M., July 25, after more than ten miles of cable had been retrieved, inspectors found a two-inch piece of wire the same thickness as the armoring imbedded in the insulation and touching the core. Slightly bent in the middle, one end looked blunt and jagged; the other end sharp and bright. The sharp end looked like it had been carefully cut with a pair of snips and forced into the insulation, but no one could tell how the pin got into the tank. After exhausting all possibilities, Canning and de Sauty concluded that a piece of wire must have fallen among the coils and been squeezed into the insulation as the cable passed through the paying-out machine, thereby "opening a minute passage through which the electricity, like a jet of blood from a pierced artery, went streaming into the sea."[18]

Mechanics made the splice and lowered the cable back into the sea. After a twelve-hour delay the paying-out machinery spun into motion, and once again *Great Eastern* resumed her course. About a half mile of wire had looped through the sheaves when another fault shut down communication with shore. Once again Anderson idled the engines and waited for Canning to decide what to do. Faces became downcast, and the old salts that comprised the crew resurrected the story of how the legendary ghost had jinxed the ship and everything on her.

De Sauty could not believe the fault lay in the cable. For more than an hour he examined the leads to the instruments, thinking that somehow they had gone to ground. Others blamed the splice. An anxious group formed outside the testing room, from time to time popping their heads inside to get a status report. Cyrus Field, whose confidence and equanimity seldom faltered, looked visibly shaken. As one observer noted, "Who could bear up against a life of picking-up?" Gooch registered a private concern in his diary, worrying that such news could cause an instant drop in the value of the company's stock.[19]

Late afternoon, mechanics cut the cable between the two tanks to see if the fault occurred on board. Tests confirmed their worst fears. The continuity of the cable on board was perfect. Finding nothing wrong they had no alternative but to repeat the laborious process of cutting the cable, shackling it to wire rope, reversing the direction of the ship, and retrieving the cable from the bow. As they prepared to make the cut, the index light on the reflecting instrument reappeared like a beacon of hope. Electricians began their regular tests with shore and announced everything in perfect working order. De Sauty emerged from the testing room to confer with Thomson, and Canning went forward to stop work on preparing the picking-up machine.

At 4:15 P.M., after losing thirty-seven hours over a small piece of wire, *Great Eastern* resumed her voyage to Heart's Content. The alterations of hope and fear having subsided, men not on duty converged on the saloon and spent an animated evening in scientific discussions. When Field went to the deck to get a breath of fresh air, he noticed that the wind and the waves had risen. He walked aft to the paying-out machine and spoke to the mechanic on duty, who said the headwind had slowed the vessel to five knots. *Great Eastern* barely registered a tremor, so he went to bed with the assurance that all was well.

In the morning a strong northwest wind brought haze and heavy seas. *Terrible* thumped through the troughs, burying her bows in foam with dogged determination while *Great Eastern* plowed through the waves as steady as a steamer on the Thames.

Sphinx shouldered the heavier burden. Having reached the 150-mile mark she had the difficult task of taking soundings in rough weather. Somewhere along this stretch the seabed rose to 200 fathoms before falling off gradually to 700 fathoms and then descending rapidly to 1,750 fathoms. The change affected the paying-out process. More slack had to be delivered when reaching the slope.

Towards noon the sea and wind increased. As *Great Eastern* approached the underwater slope, *Sphinx* sent down her topgallant masts, then her topmasts. She could no longer make headway and fell farther astern. The weather thickened, bringing a mist. At 1:45 P.M. *Terrible* signaled that *Sphinx* could no longer keep up, but with the cable flowing smoothly through the running gear, Canning told the captain to keep the ship on course. By late afternoon *Sphinx* fell hull down on the horizon.

As each hour passed, it became increasingly important to know the depth of the water, but neither *Great Eastern* nor *Terrible* carried sounding equipment. Having passed the 200-mile point, Canning noticed increases in tension on the dynamometer; a certain sign that the cable had not settled on the bottom and was hanging like a clothesline above the seabed. Transmissions to shore improved, another indication that the cable had descended into deeper water. Canning eased the brake, allowing slack to flow until the dynamometer stabilized again. As evening descended *Terrible* drew closer abeam, still fighting the swells with both sail and steam, but *Sphinx* had vanished.

On July 27 the day broke bright on a sparkling whitecapped sea bounding under a clear blue sky. Having run 320 miles from Valentia, *Great Eastern* began approaching a section of ocean where the seabed rose from 2,100 fathoms to 1,529 fathoms, and the problem became one of paying out too much slack rather than too little. At the same time, coils in the after tank were almost depleted, and the cable had to be switched to the forward tank. To prepare for the switch, Canning needed soundings but could not get them. The rest of the crew knew nothing about the problem. They were planning what journeys to take in America and looking for advice on where to hunt big game in Newfoundland.

William H. Russell caught the flow of optimism, writing: "The sound of the piano, a tribute to our own contentment, rose from the saloon, and now and then the notes of a violin became entwined in the melodious labyrinth through which the amateur professors wandered with uncertain fingers. The artists sketched vigorously." A more curious search party shuffled about in the bowels of the ship. "None of them," wrote Russell, "found out the hiding place of the ghost who haunts the ship; but they discovered crypts under the tanks, and meandered . . . about the shafts and boilers" without ever finding the "disembodied essence of a poor plate-riveter, who disappeared in some aperture of the nascent ship, never to be seen of mortal eye again . . . [though] he is heard at all hours, with ghostly hammer, tap-tap-tapping on the iron walls of his prison."[20]

July 28 came and went without seeing *Sphinx*, leaving a flank exposed to a midocean accident. Anderson signaled *Terrible* to take the point, and the British warship steamed ahead, posting herself off *Great Eastern*'s starboard quarter. The cablemen agreed, "There was a sense of companionship in seeing her near us."[21]

In the morning electricians and engineers held a brief meeting in the saloon and reported, "Everything has gone on most admirably during the night." Varley and Thomson, who could do nothing except when asked, confirmed the reports, adding that the wire exceeded the specified standards. Anderson increased the speed of the ship, and the coils whipped through the sheaves. He took a reading at noon and reported the distance from Valentia at 634 miles: the distance to Heart's Content, 1,028 nautical miles. Field looked at his bathymetrical map and noted that the ship had passed over the ocean's 2,400-fathom valley and for the next several hundred miles had nothing ahead but the smooth telegraphic plateau.

The mini-celebration lasted an hour. At 1:10 P.M. the gong sounded. Electricians had been watching the mirror-reflecting instrument for several minutes, hoping for an aberration to cure itself. Anderson ordered the engines slowed. Five minutes later the ship drifted to a stop. Field rushed to the testing room and looked inside. Varley turned to him and said, "Dead earth." Electricians worked the wire for two hours but received no impulses from shore. They finally asked Thomson for an opinion. The latter looked at the data and said the fault was not far from the ship.

De Sauty ordered the cable cut to test the coils in the tanks. He found them perfect. Anderson already had the forward steam donkey running for the picking-up machinery. Clifford's engineers stood by, ready to cut and shackle the cable at the paying-out machine, but he waited for a decision from Canning. The great depth of the water added another problem. Perhaps it would be better if the ship backed rather than come about, but Anderson said she would not steer sternforemost. The engineers paused to reconsider the problem. The piano ceased playing, glum faces gathered outside the testing room, and a passing sailor mumbled that he would never see Newfoundland. Field voiced his own ever optimistic view, saying, "I have often known cables to stop working for two hours, no one knows why, and then begin again. Most likely it's some mistake on shore."[22]

During the discussions the cable continued to trickle through the paying-out machine as the ship drifted, adding more weight and work to the picking-up process. The longer Canning waited, the greater became the problem. Everyone waited for his decision. The cable had to be shackled and cut, carried forward, and secured to the picking-up machine, and with the strain of the cable fluctuating between 800 and 2,000 pounds with the rise and fall of the ship, the question became whether all these mechanical functions could be accomplished before the cable broke.

Canning finally ordered the cable cut, and mechanics, with every chain and stopper at their fingertips, severed the stern end, shackled it to the wire rope, and heaved it into the ocean. Then began the orderly tumult of sailors and men with stoppers and guy ropes slung along the bulwarks and through the shrouds passing the cable the full length of the ship to the picking-up machine. Canning had trained them well. They clambered forward along the ship's beam, over the boats, round the paddle boxes, hauling at hawsers and slipping bights, holding on and letting go stoppers, while Anderson, standing on the bridge, tried to con every movement of the ship to keep the precious cord from fouling or trailing under the ship.

In 2,000 fathoms, the cable dragged along the bottom, fiercely tugged by the drifting ship. If the cable or a shackle parted, it would be the end. At length Anderson brought the ship's head around so Clifford's mechanics could get the wire rope into the picking-up machinery. The mechanism began rumbling, and the wire rope came over the bow, slowly bringing the cable to the surface, then up the bow and into the pick-up drums. Into the foggy night, drenched by drizzle, the two eccentric steam engines puffed and snorted, pulling the cable out of the deep at a mile an hour. In the dim light of lanterns mechanics stood by the machinery, looking for breaks in the cable. They ran their hands carefully along the armor, feeling for anything sharp. A few gooey specimens that looked like worms fell to the deck. The dynamometer on the picking-up machine read 3,000 pounds. Too high, Field thought, as he tapped the gage. He trekked back and forth between the saloon, the testing room, and the bow, but the men shook their heads, said nothing, and kept working.

At 10:00 P.M. one of the workmen hollered that he had found the fault, but because of so little light no one took time to examine it. They cut the cable, spliced it to the coil in the hold, and resumed communications with Foilhummerum. Nineteen hours had been lost, and Anderson did not get underway again until Sunday morning, July 30. Even then things went poorly. As the crew began to pass the cable from the bow aft, the wire inexplicably flew off the drum. Several fathoms became entangled in the wheels and jammed the machinery. The accident required two new splices, adding another three hours' delay.

Still nobody looked at the recovered cable, which lay in a tangle on the hurricane deck. Mechanics and electricians, fatigued almost senseless by the past twenty-four hours, went to bed. *Sphinx* had not been seen for two days, and Anderson thought she might have passed in the night. The weather turned cold, thick, and hazy—like typical summer iceberg weather—and a chilly breeze set in from the north. With the cable again running splendidly through the paying-out machine, Field and his associates spent the day warming in the saloon, hopeful that their tribulations were over.

At 1:00 A.M., July 31, Field noticed the ship had stopped, so he climbed out of bed to investigate. He found the mechanics and the crew at the forward tank making preparations to transfer the cable to the after tank. Spying de Sauty among the group, he asked if the fault had been found in the recovered cable. De Sauty replied that he would have his electricians examine it at daybreak.

In the morning Canning cut the damaged cable into sections and hauled

Mechanics make a splice at sea after cutting the cable to look for a fault. (From William H. Russell, *The Atlantic Telegraph, 1865*. Digitized by Debra Peffer.)

them to the testing room. The electricians hooked their instruments to the ends and tested each length until they found the fault. Clifford took the defective section to his cabin and began untwisting the strands of iron and hemp. He had barely unwound a foot of armoring when there, before everyone's eyes, shined another bright piece of iron wire, looking like it had been nipped at one end to form the point of a pin. Its outer end did not project above the armor, giving the appearance of having been driven intentionally into the conductor. "Now here," said Clifford, "was demonstration of villainous design." "No man who saw it," wrote Russell, "could doubt that the wire had been driven in by a skillful hand." Therefore, the group concluded, the same malefactors must have caused the first fault, and further investigation revealed that both accidents occurred when the same workers were in the tank.[23]

Canning remembered that acts of sabotage had happened before on the England-Holland line when in 1858 it was laid across the North Sea. A man was afterward arrested for driving a nail into the cable. He later admitted being hired to do it by a rival company to affect prices on the London stock exchange. The Atlantic Telegraph Company had such a rival: the Western Union, who sought to lay their line through Alaska and Siberia. But Canning trusted his men. He knew almost every one of them because they had worked for him before.

The plot thickened after Canning heard rumors that one of the cablemen had expressed gratification after the first fault occurred, but nobody could point him out. Field and other travelers on board who had nothing to do came forward and offered to supervise the tanks. Canning summoned the cablemen to the bow, showed them the coil and the wire, and after each of them examined it, he asked what they thought. Without hesitation, they said, "it must have been done by design," and admitted "there was a traitor among them." They spoke forcibly of lynching the offender without having any idea who to hang from the yardarm. The men engaged in the tank at the time received transfers to other duties, and volunteer watchmen led by Field created their own roster and established two-hour shifts.[24]

Extra supervision seemed to work. On August 1 *Great Eastern* passed the halfway mark, having logged 948 nautical miles from Valentia with only 717 remaining to Heart's Content. Anderson accelerated to seven knots, and the cable flew through the machinery without a spasm. De Sauty reported the conductor working "almost beyond belief," adding, "when in the middle of the ocean, the communication was so perfect that they could tell at Valentia every time the *Great Eastern* rolled." Henry Field spoke for his brother when he said, "With such omens of success, who could [not] but feel confident?"[25]

Canning knew the contour of the seabed would begin to change and he needed soundings, but *Sphinx* had long ago vanished. *Terrible* still chugged along two miles off the starboard quarter and maintained her given station. During the noontime meal Anderson confirmed that barring further mishaps, the ship should make landfall Friday night, August 4, or early Saturday morning. In another day or two the ship would be over the Grand Banks and out of deep water. Canning took the captain at his word and put a crew to work transferring the shore-end from the main tank to the after tank.

Early morning, August 2, while Field stood watch on the tank, he heard a grating noise. Someone shouted, "There goes a piece of wire!" At first, because of the noise, Field did not hear the words distinctly and failed to get the message to the mechanic on the paying-out machine. The fault whipped through the sheaves and into the sea. Minutes later the electrician sending messages to Foilhummerum saw the light quiver and wander on the scale. This time the current varied, not indicating a "dead earth" but certainly a problem. De Sauty banged on the brass gong and informed the bridge. Anderson slowed the engines, but because the seas were running high with a good breeze out of the northwest, the ship began to drift. Both Thomson and Varley believed that once the cable dropped into the deep, pressure would restore the insulation, but Canning wanted no chances taken and ordered the cable shackled, cut, and transferred forward to the picking-up machinery.

As mechanics began cutting the cable near the tank, one of the workmen discovered a piece of wire projecting from the cable—a piece with one end sharp and the other end broken, just like the wires that had caused the earlier faults. The discovery turned everyone's thoughts. Perhaps the cable carried its own deadly form of mischief. The brittle piece of charcoal iron had pierced the hemp of the coil in the tank but had not reached the conductor. Though some of the cablemen still spoke of sabotage, Canning and Clifford now concluded that the problem came from Glass, Elliot's plant and not from any malfeasance on the part of the cable crew.

The arduous work of bringing the cable to the bow began, but because of wind, waves, and drift, the ship's head would not come around. The wire rope holding the cable end continued to pay out. Anderson finally brought the ship about and the slow process of picking up the cable commenced at the rate of one mile every one hundred minutes. After one of the eccentric engines on the picking-up machinery went out of alignment, a man with a handspike stood by to knock it into place. Next the steam supply failed, and the picking-up process came to a halt for repairs. Minutes later the cable caught on the iron rim of a hawsepipe and began to chafe against the bow. *Great Eastern* could not go astern without snapping the cable, and being unable to go forward without overrunning the cable, she lost steerage.

At this critical point the wind changed direction, drifting the ship over the cable. In desperation, the crew brought a buoy to the bow with a shackle and swivel and tied it to the cable below the hawsepipe. The strain on the cable became immense, but the cord held, and the cablemen got a loop over a V-grooved wheel on the capstan. As the crew eased the worn portion of the cable on board, the dynamometer jumped above 6,000 pounds, the highest mark on the dial. The chain shackle and wire rope suddenly climbed up and out of the groove, rode momentarily on the rim, and then slammed down with a crash on a small wheel, giving the cable a tremendous jolt. Moments later, as the wire rope started through the machinery, it suddenly parted, flew through the stoppers, and with one bound leaped through the air and splashed into the sea.

Moriarty, the staff commander, had just reached the companionway to make his daily report on the ship's progress. He intended to say that *Great Eastern* had come 1,062 miles from Valentia with only 607 miles to go. He took one look at the grim figures standing by the paying-out machine and another look at the end of the tortured cable lying on the deck. "I fear," he said, "we will not feel much interest now in knowing how far we are from Heart's Content." He turned politely and started back to the bridge to report the disaster to the captain.[26]

Many of the men, unaware of the difficulties at the picking-up machine and even less aware of the change in ship's drift, were casually enjoying the noontime meal when the disaster occurred. Canning suddenly appeared in the saloon, "and in a manner which caused everyone to start in his seat, said, 'It is all over! It is gone!' then hastened to his cabin." Moments later

Field entered from the companionway, his cheek blanched, his lips quivering, and said blandly, "The cable has parted and has gone overboard."[27]

Canning and his engineers blamed the ship's bow for running over the cable and cutting it, but Gooch said, "there was no part sharp enough to have such an effect." He blamed it on Canning's men, writing, "It was a mistake to use a chain stopper [on the cable], and all the sailors and nautical part of our crew said no one but a land lubber would have done so." Gooch must have made a point because Canning shifted to rope stoppers and never used chain again.[28]

At Foilhummerum the electricians knew nothing about problems with stoppers. They waited patiently at their instruments for a resumption of signals, but none came. Some wondered if *Great Eastern* struck an iceberg and took the cable to the bottom. The tars on board blamed it on the ghost that made scratching noises on the hull, and according to some sources, also made occasional appearances on gloomy nights. But on board the ship, a decision had to be made, and Canning made it.

And so the work began.

— Chapter 16 —

Acts of Desperation

Disasters never stopped men of purpose, and *Great Eastern* had its share of both. Field pulled his staff together to draft a new prospectus. Canning had lost two cables in the 1850s, but he had not lost one since. Captain Anderson felt partly responsible because when the wind shifted and drove *Great Eastern* over the cable, he lost his steerage and could do nothing to reduce the tension on the cable.

Canning brought grappling devices on board—not that he ever expected to use them. He had grappled cables before, and there were men on board who had fished them up from 700 fathoms in the Mediterranean. But the Atlantic cable lay more than two miles deep: nobody knew exactly how deep. Canning believed his chances of success were a million to one, but with $3 million at stake, he had to try. The missing *Sphinx* added another troublesome factor to the effort. She carried the only depth-sounding gear and had not been seen for six days.

Captain Moriarty's noon readings marked the ship's position within a half mile of where the cable broke, and Anderson had logged the coordinates. The ship was within a mile or two when Canning went to Anderson with his desperate scheme to grapple.

On August 4, 1865, while Canning's mechanics rigged a five-pronged grapple to five miles of wire rope, Anderson came about, steamed fourteen miles to windward, and bearing slightly to the east, shut down the engines. Using a light, moderating breeze out of the west, he ordered the boatswain to pipe out the canvas to control the drift of the vessel. With *Terrible* standing nearby, the largest sailing ship ever afloat eased gently toward a spot that would lay the vessel perpendicular to the cable.

Canning's two 300-pound grapples contained five flukes, sharply curved

Preparing grapples and readying buoys in an effort to fish for the cable in midocean. (Charles Bright, *The Story of the Atlantic Cable*. Digitized by Debra Peffer.)

and tapered with a toothlike tip. The cable crew fastened one of the grapples to a wire rope capable of holding ten tons. A shackle and swivel tied each 100-fathom section of rope together. At 3:30 P.M., August 2, the grapple splashed into the deep, and the greatest fishing expedition ever cast upon the waters began on the bottom of the North Atlantic.

Time passed slowly. Electricians shut down the testing room and lounged in the saloon or napped in their cabins. Life all but stopped on the great drifting ship. Wind ruffled the sails, now and then a yard slapped against the mast, and the only sound on deck came from the bow where the picking-up machine grated and squealed as shackles and swivels bumped through sheaves. In subdued silence, mixed with human doubts and human hope, the grapnel line spun off whirring wheels as it descended into the ocean.

The groaning apparatus became smoking hot, and mechanics doused the wheels with water that crackled and hissed and threw off puffs of steam. Two hours later the dynamometer needle moved, indicating the grapple struck bottom. Men at the wheels, counting shackles as they passed through the machinery, reported two and a half miles off the reel. Canning ordered more slack, and another hundred fathoms went into the sea. No one could hope to grapple a cable at such depth, but Canning said that with a little luck he could do it. The naysayers stood apart, convinced that the grapple would snag on a rock and be ripped from the wire. If by some miracle prongs hooked the cable, most believed that the flimsy wire would surely break. Whoever heard of grappling anything at 15,000 feet?

Exactly where the cable lay surpassed the reach of human knowledge. Darkness descended, the dynamometer holding steady at 5,500 pounds. At 10:00 P.M. it suddenly jumped to 8,000 pounds, held long enough to swing the ship's head slightly into the wind, and then slid back to 5,500 pounds. The grapple had snagged something and then let go, but what?

During the early hours, August 3, *Great Eastern* continued her slow drift, still guided by sail. Engineers waited to be called, softly airing their doubts. To pass time they recalculated the length of line needed to hook the cable. Then they calculated the force required to bring nearly three miles of wire rope, grapple, and cable back to the surface. They believed the task hopeless but said nothing to discourage Canning, who already felt devastated by the disaster.

At 6:00 A.M. *Great Eastern* swayed slightly, her head turning into the wind. The dynamometer jumped to 7,000 pounds and held. Mechanics on the picking-up machine shouted, "We have caught it! We have caught it!" The good news flowed from one end of the ship to the other. Men scrambled to the bow. Despite the fearful reading on the dynamometer, Clifford assured everyone that the tension on the cable would be much less.

Forty minutes passed while Anderson conned the ship's bow up to the grapnel line. The picking-up machinery, taxed to the limit dispensing the wire, now gave loud snorts as mechanics kicked in the retrieving gear. After a few revolutions of the drums, the dynamometer registered 8,500 pounds. To ease the strain, Anderson held the ship directly over the cable. A half hour passed, and the shackle and swivel marking the first 100 fathoms came on board and lay heaped on the hurricane deck. A crowd gathered near the bow, ignoring the risk of being in harm's way should the wire break. At 7:55 A.M. the second length came on board, the strain on the line holding steady between 6,500 and 7,500 pounds.

At 8:10, with 400 fathoms of wire retrieved, the machinery's spur wheel broke and drove the tension on the dynamometer above 9,000 pounds.

The wire rope parted, whipped across the deck, lacerated the face of one observer, and laid the jaw open of another. More than two miles of wire rope would have joined the cable on the seabed if stoppers applied by the brakeman had not caught the shackle and saved the grappling equipment.

With the picking-up machinery temporarily out of commission, the cable crew transferred the rope-retrieving operation to the capstan. By noon a half mile of wire rope lay heaped on board, and prospects of recovering the cable looked brighter. Spirits rose, and once again talk of triumphantly entering Heart's Content began to resonate among the onlookers.

"Bull Run" Russell stood among the cablemen as the wire rope came over the bow. He was there when:

> The whole of our speculations were abruptly terminated at 2:50 o'clock, P.M. As the shackle and swivel of the eleventh length of rope, which would have made a mile onboard, were passing the machinery, the head of the swivel pin was wrung off by the strain, and the 1,400 fathoms of line, with grapnel attached, rushed down again to the bottom of the Atlantic, carrying with it the bight of the cable. The shock was bitter and sharp.[1]

Engineers had calculated that the wire rope might part, or the cable might break on the bight, but no one believed the stout iron swivels would separate.

Almost on cue, a fog hovering above the ship settled thickly around her, adding to the general gloominess of the setting. Canning and Clifford, however, did not relent. They put two teams of men to work: one to bend another 2,500 fathoms of wire rope to a grapnel, the other to rig a large buoy to mark the spot where the rope parted.

Anderson blew the ship's fog whistles to signal *Terrible* of his change in position and steamed slowly to the windward, firing a gun at twenty-minute intervals. Nothing could be seen in the fog-shrouded darkness. After steaming fourteen miles to a favorable position, Anderson cut the engines and allowed the ship to drift. The cablemen let go another grapple, and the second blind grope began.

At daylight on August 4 *Great Eastern* drifted through the fog. Few slept that night, kept awake by the constant shrieking of fog whistles and the booming of cannon. To get a reading of the depth, the mechanics rigged sounding tackle from all the spare line and heaved it overboard with a heavy lead sinker. At 2,300 fathoms the weight touched bottom. While retrieving the line, it broke, adding another two miles of cord to the ocean bed.

Late morning the fog lifted, and an officer from *Terrible* came on board to ask what the cable crew intended to do. Canning said he planned to remain in the mid-Atlantic and grapple the cable as long as he had material to do it. At noon the orb of the sun penetrated the murk, and Moriarty

The cablemen lower a buoy over the side to mark the position where the cable had been hooked and lost. (From William H. Russell, *The Atlantic Telegraph, 1865.* Digitized by Debra Peffer.)

took a reading. He shook his head and reported the ship forty-six miles east of the spot where the cable parted. Canning reeled in his grapnel and waited for Anderson to steam back to the fishing zone.

Meanwhile, mechanics built a strong timber raft eight feet square to serve as a permanent buoy to mark the place where the grapnel broke. For line they used damaged cable, and for weight they added a heavy mushroom anchor. On the raft they mounted a large red buoy, topped by a black ball and a red flag on a short staff. Anderson returned to 51°28'W and 38°42'30"E, and Clifford dropped Buoy No. 1 into the ocean.[2]

Electricians inspecting the cable in the tanks reported that the charcoal iron wires used as armoring were the source of all the calamities. They found loose pieces of wire embedded in the hemp wrapping as well as broken pieces wedged between the armor. Canning discovered that the iron wires were of different mechanical properties. While most strands wound around the cable properly, one was brittle and broke when bent. How many broken ends already existed in the submerged cable became a matter of much concern, though only a few had penetrated to the conductor.

On August 5 Anderson attempted to get the ship into position for another drift, but the mast-high fog hanging above the ship became so thick that Moriarty could not get a reading. *Terrible* came in view midafternoon and reported the buoy three miles ahead. Anderson steamed to the buoy and then stood north six miles, hoping to catch a favorable breeze for drifting. The wind failed, the fog thickened, and Canning did not lower the grapnel.

Anderson posted *Terrible* near the buoy, but when the fog settled, both ships lost their bearings and the buoy. While waiting for better weather, Canning continued to search for ways to get the cable on board if they nursed it to the surface. The task seemed insurmountable because tension would increase as the cable neared the surface. He needed to grip the cable in several places to distribute the tension, but *Great Eastern* carried no such equipment. Canning suggested going to Newfoundland to borrow tackling gear, but Moriarty, who had recently come off *Agamemnon*, said that commercial and naval vessels carried no such equipment. Others recommended an immediate return to England to get a complete outfit for grappling, but the rapidly advancing storm season quashed that suggestion.

On August 7 the fog cleared enough for Anderson to spot *Terrible* lying to six miles away. She had found the buoy. With the wind out of the north, Anderson conned *Great Eastern* into position for lowering the grapnel.

The windward breeze held, and a little before noon the cablemen began fishing in 2,300 fathoms of water. At 6:00 P.M. the grapple hooked the cable, turning the ship's head. Anderson gave the engines a little steam to hold her in position while cablemen started the wheels of the repaired picking-up machine, which now incorporated the use of the capstan. The closer the cable came to the surface, the higher the tension rose on the dynamometer. At midnight the cablemen reported 300 fathoms on board. Throughout the night Anderson stood on the bridge, responding to whistles to go forward or to turn astern, maneuvering the ship ever so slightly back and forth to reduce the strain on the cable. For the first time in five days, moonlight flooded the sea, and as each 100-fathom section of rope wound through the capstan, the old feeling of ultimate success revived the cablemen.

On August 8, at 7:30 in the morning, one mile of wire rope lay drying on deck. The dynamometer drifted upwards, registering 8,000 pounds. The cablemen tried to find a way to reduce the tension, but the needle on the dynamometer continued to rise. Shortly after 8:00 A.M. another shackle and swivel came over the bow, passed through the machinery, and started winding through the capstan. After three wraps the swivel pin broke. The rope flew around the capstan, whirled through the machinery and stops, and with irresistible force whipped across the deck and into the sea. Before the end splashed overboard, it slashed right and left at the heads of the cablemen, sending them sprawling to the deck. "This was very disheartening work," wrote Gooch, "and I felt certain our tackle was not strong enough to lift [the cable] to the surface."[3]

Mechanics dropped a buoy overboard and watched another lead sinker

A boat crew from *Great Eastern* attempt to recover a marker buoy that holds the secret to the lost 1865 cable. (From *London Illustrated News*. Digitized by Debra Peffer.)

carry 2,500 fathoms of cable to the bottom. Canning identified the second buoy by using a flag with two red stripes and a center stripe of white painted with the words "Telegraph, No. 3." The new marker took position thirteen miles east of Buoy No. 1, leaving an area in between for Buoy No. 2, should one be needed.

With 1,900 fathoms of wire rope on board, and about 500 fathoms of hemp available, Canning prepared to make one last swipe along the seabed before returning to Sheerness. Both *Terrible* and *Great Eastern* had burned much of their coal, and the weather showed signs of thickening. Captain Napier sent a boat to *Great Eastern* to tell Anderson and Canning that after three days he would have to go to St. John's for fuel. *Terrible*'s boat returned to the ship just in time. At 2:00 P.M. the wind worked into a gale that for the first time caused *Great Eastern* to roll, making it impossible to fish for cable.

On August 9 the wind switched to the south, blowing hard and spitting veils of heavy rain. At noon *Terrible* came in sight, signaling, "Did you see buoy?" Anderson replied in the negative. Napier then asked whether Canning intended to grapple again and received an affirmative reply.

Anderson and Moriarty went nowhere without their sextants, hoping to get a quick reading if the sun peaked through the clouds. They doubted whether the buoys had survived the storm. Blacksmiths broke out their forges, making stronger pins for the swivels. Mechanics crafted new casings for the capstan. Rope makers spliced together a new grapnel line made of wire rope and hemp. Late in the afternoon lookouts spotted a buoy. Finding the small black ball with its tiny red flag on the broad Atlantic was indeed a magnificent feat of blind navigation. *Terrible* came abeam, asking by signals what Anderson intended to do. Canning did not have his grapple ready, so Anderson replied, "Lay to until morning."

Throughout the night forge fires blazed on *Great Eastern*. For those on *Terrible*'s deck, the big ship glowed in ghostly incandescent hues of red and orange pasted against a black wall of sea. A light breeze carried the sounds of hammers driving hot pins through shackles and swivels and the muffled voices of men laboring late into the night forging new sheathing for the damaged capstan.

For the first time in many days, August 10 broke clear and sunny. A brisk gale early in the morning blew *Great Eastern* seven miles off course. At 10:30 A.M. the cablemen tossed the newly forged grapple over the side and waited as 2,450 fathoms of wire rope and hawser descended into the deep. When the wind switched to the east, Anderson idled his engines and ordered fore-and-aft sails, adding more canvas in increments until he had the ship running at drift speed under her fore and main topsails. The ship passed between the two buoys, and after drifting another two miles, Anderson knew that the ship had passed over the cable.

At 4:30 P.M. mechanics began retrieving the wire rope. It came over the bow with sections unraveling. The cablemen blamed it on bad swivels and agreed that the tortured wire could never have caught the cable or brought it up to the surface. One of the flukes had caught on the shank chain. From deposits of gray ooze on the rope, Canning concluded that the depth of the water was only 1,950 fathoms, not 2,500 fathoms. This gave him some encouragement. The cablemen cut away damaged sections of the rope, shortened the line to 2,300 fathoms, and fastened a new grapnel with a shorter shank to the wire. The following morning the cablemen paid out the line and commenced another drift near the buoy. Three hours later the dynamometer jumped to 6,500 pounds, rose to 7,500 pounds, and steadied. Everyone knew they had hooked the cable.

As each section came on board, the anxiety felt by men like Canning, Clifford, Field, Anderson, and Gooch told in their expressions. Nobody dared to mention Heart's Content. Some could not bear to watch and curbed their anxiety by going to the saloon. "None liked to go forward," said Russell, "where every jar of the machinery, every shackle that passed the drum, every clank, made hearts leap into their mouths." By dinnertime,

500 fathoms of wire lay coiled on the deck. "At 6:30 I left the saloon," said Russell,

> and walked up and down the deck, under the shelter of the paddle-box, glancing forward now and then to the bow, to look at the busy crowd of engineers, sailors, and cablemen gathered round the rope coming in over the drums . . . listening to the warning shouts as the shackles came inboard, and hurtled through the machinery till they floundered on the hurricane deck.[4]

Russell turned away and started back to the saloon when he heard the whistle sound on the bridge. He stopped a sailor running aft, who said, "There's a heavy strain on now, sir." The whistle blew again, and about the time Russell reached the hurricane deck, he heard someone shout, "Stop it!" and then "Look out!" Then came silence. "I knew at once it was all over," said Russell. "The machinery stood still in the bows, and for a moment every man was fixed, as if turned to stone. . . . Our last bolt was sped."

Canning rushed forward, shouting, "Is any one hurt?" The cablemen simply lowered their heads, and said, "It is gone." Nearly a mile of wire rope lay on the deck. Russell spoke for everyone when he lamented, "The battle was over." The watch officer methodically entered in his log: "Latitude 51° 24' Longitude 38° 59': end of cable down North 50 West 1¾ mile."[5]

Anderson sent word to the chief engineer to get up steam. He signaled *Terrible* to proceed to St. John's. Before the two ships parted, Field sent a message to his family with Captain Napier, asking that it be cabled from Newfoundland. He had hoped to go home to celebrate, but now he must stay with the ship and return to London.

Captain Anderson turned the head of the massive ship eastward. Signal lights from *Terrible* flashed, "Farewell." Anderson replied, "Good-bye, thank you." Then each steamed away in the grim solitude of the intervening darkness.[6]

For ten days operators at Foilhummerum watched a dead line. The daily progress reports from ship to shore to the British press had long ago stopped.

Professor Airy, Astronomer Royal at the Greenwich observatory, attributed the interruption to "a magnetic storm of singular violence," which began on August 2; the day the cable broke. For thirty-six hours the magnetic storm affected every telegraphic station in the kingdom. Lines running between Valentia and Killarney became useless. Pseudoscientists speculated that the storm somehow disarranged the conductivity of the cable. The electrical disturbances came and went and still no news from *Great Eastern.*[7]

A chorus of voices, rising across the British Isles, croaked, "I told you so." But it was not in the nature of such men as Field, Canning, Gooch, and Anderson to give up. As Henry Field noted, "Yet who shall put bounds on human courage?" And *Great Eastern*, though despairing but not yet defeated, still flew her battle flag.[8]

Chapter 17

An Elephant Stretching a Cobweb

The disappearance of *Great Eastern* caused much consternation in England as the hours of silence grew into days and weeks. Experts who called her top-heavy suggested she had capsized in a mighty swell, and those unable to understand the meaning of a magnetic storm thought perhaps some supernatural influence from outer space had afflicted her iron hull. Those who scorned the big ship ever since she stumbled into the Thames said she "had never been strong enough, that she had fagged in the middle, or had hogged," which happens when a ship breaks her back and the stern and bow fall away.[1]

On August 17, 1865, when *Great Eastern* appeared off Mizen Head, a reporter came on board and said, "We did not know what to make of you. Many think you went down."[2]

From Ireland, Russell sent his narrative of the expedition to the London *Times* before *Great Eastern* sailed for the Nore. What impressed the public was not another failed attempt to lay the cable but the energy, skill, and resolution displayed by the crew in successfully grappling the wire from a seabed two miles deep. They were equally amazed to learn that buoys anchored with telegraph cable had been set at such depths and rode out a gale. As a fringe benefit, the ship recovered some of her lost respect and people took an interest in her again. The cablemen told everyone of her magnificent performance. "In the hour of her deepest failure," wrote James Dugan, "the big ship was a heroine. And Cyrus Field was a hero. He had eclipsed Biblical Job, who had endured seven years of misery. Field had survived eight years [actually eleven] of knockouts, and still had some time to go." Dugan may have been overly generous in his praise of Field. During those years, nobody worked harder to perfect a science than Charles Bright, William Thomson, Samuel Canning, and dozens of others.[3]

On August 8, six days after communication between ship and shore ceased, the directors of the Atlantic Telegraph Company nonetheless met without knowing what had happened during the expedition. Their purpose: to raise £137,200 in fresh capital *to lay a second Atlantic cable.* James Stuart-Wortley, chairman of the company, told the skeptics that the telegraph transmitted perfect signals at 2,400 fathoms, and that the signals improved "every yard they went." Wortley could not explain to detractors why the cable stopped transmitting.[4]

When Cyrus Field disembarked from *Great Eastern*, he held a new prospectus written in the grand saloon on the day that everyone lost hope. For five days he had polished it with his committee of experts. When he appeared before the board to recommend that funds be raised for a new expedition, he expected another hard sell. Instead, he found little need to present his twelve carefully constructed points of argument. On October 12 the Atlantic Telegraph Company abandoned their plans to raise £137,200 for a second cable and voted instead to issue 120,000 shares of preferred stock and raise £600,000 at 12 percent to mount another expedition. This raised the total capitalization of the company to £2,000,000 ($10,000,000), part of which lay on the bottom of the Atlantic. Without waiting for subscriptions to sell, the directors engaged the Telegraph Construction & Maintenance Company to provide new cable and lay it during the summer of 1866.

Canning made it clear to Richard Glass that he wanted no more trouble from the armoring process. Had the external coating not been injured, no faults would have occurred, and had there been no faults, the cable would be working.

The Telegraph Construction & Maintenance Company offered to lay the cable for £500,000, making their compensation contingent upon success. When successful, they wanted £100,000 paid to them in company stock. Gooch suggested fishing for the broken end of the 1865 cable, thereby providing the company with two cables instead of one from the same expedition. The directors agreed, thereby avoiding the cost of laying a second completely new cable. If the capital required could not be raised, the Telegraph Construction & Maintenance Company offered "to take it all themselves—to lay the line at their own risk, and to be paid only in the capital of the company." The directors accepted the proposal and work began to produce another 2,500 miles of cable. In this hopeful state of affairs, Field returned to New York.[5]

On the passage home Field encountered an old acquaintance, who wrote: "We heard Mr. Field was a passenger. We felt the deepest sympathy for him, and to our surprise he was the life of the ship and the most cheerful on board. He said: 'We have learned a great deal, and next summer we shall lay the cable without doubt.' " No one could expect Cyrus Field to say anything less.[6]

After arriving home, Field reminded Cooper that the Newfoundland cable, manufactured to old specifications, had been submerged for ten years. He suggested replacing it with the new design. Cooper agreed, and Field sandwiched ninety miles of extra wire in with the transatlantic cable.

Four weeks later Field received a letter from Captain Anderson who, after describing a litany of problems, closed with: "I am sorry you are not here. Somehow no one seems to push when you are absent."[7]

The letter upset him. He had come home to be with his family and attend the marriage of his daughter Isabella to William Francis Judson of Philadelphia. He also wanted to be home for the holidays, but the more he thought about Anderson's letter, the more he worried that the cable would not be ready by the summer of 1866. Perry Collins, acting on behalf of Hiram Sibley's powerful Western Union, had already started work on the landline through Alaska. After ten years of toil and trouble, and the near exhaustion of his wealth, Field could not afford to lose the game to a pair of upstarts.

With this in mind, he wrote George Saward: "Unless I have more favorable news from London in regard to the Atlantic telegraph, it is my intention to sail for Liverpool . . . on the 13th of December."[8] When no favorable report came, Field packed his bags, kissed the family good-bye, wished them Merry Christmas, and arrived in London on Christmas Eve—just in time to learn that subscriptions had been returned to investors because the issue of new preferred shares required the approval of Parliament. Because the company had been organized with parliamentary consent, the attorney general declared that it could not raise capital in preference shares without additional consent. Because Parliament would not meet until February, work stopped on the cable.[9]

Field went directly to Gooch, Glass, and Brassey. Gooch promised to make *Great Eastern* available for the 1866 expedition. He suggested a way to get around the parliamentary problem: form another company. He was not a man to throw money at speculative ventures. Having been on *Great Eastern* with Field and Canning, he trusted them. As a first subscription, he offered £20,000.[10]

Brassey added his endorsement, and said, "Mr. Field, don't be discouraged; go down to the company and tell them to go ahead, and whatever the cost, I will bear one-tenth of the whole." The commitment came at a difficult time for Brassey. A number of financial disasters in the railroad construction industry threatened to bankrupt the company, yet Brassey, who had no reason to be in the cable business, committed £60,000 to the pot and continued to make financial commitments to the enterprise.[11]

Field took Brassey's commitment to the directors of the Atlantic Telegraph Company and explained the deal. Field and ten others each subscribed £10,000 and together with Gooch and Brassey formed on March 1, 1866, the Anglo-American Telegraph Company. The Telegraph Construction & Maintenance Company added another £100,000 to the enterprise, and in fourteen days Field pooled £600,000. The subscriptions were all committed before the new company issued its prospectus or offered shares to the public. Field now had his fingers in four telegraph companies, all organized around the same purpose.

If the 1866 expedition succeeded and both cables operated successfully, the big winner would not be the new Anglo-American Telegraph Company but the Telegraph Construction & Maintenance Company. The latter would collect £737,140 ($3,685,700) and hold a significant stock position in the submarine cable industry. As Charles Bright observed, "In fact, it was . . . even more of a contractor's enterprise than that of 1865."[12]

The stranding machines at the Gutta Percha works began spinning, and cable streamed off production lines at the rate of twenty miles a day. Had 2,300 nautical miles been required, the cable could not have been made in time. Canning calculated the length of the coils still in *Great Eastern* and said that 1,660 miles would be enough. With the unexpended cable from the last expedition, the total length available when the new expedition started would be 2,730 miles, of which 1,960 miles were allotted to the new line and 697 miles to the 1865 line, leaving 113 miles as a reserve.

While production machinery at the Gutta Percha works hummed, Hiram Sibley came to London and spoke with Field. "I would give $50,000," he said, "to know if you are ever going to succeed. I hope you will; but I would like to know for certain before we spend any more in Russia." Field would have been willing to pay $50,000 to have the answer.[13]

Having reanimated the cable project, Field made arrangements to return to New York. Before sailing, he received a letter from John Bright, who did not like President Lincoln's successor, Andrew Johnson. In one of the nineteenth century's most misunderstood political battles between congress and the executive branch, Johnson faced a constitutional crisis that most Americans blamed on an unpopular president instead of radicals in congress. The press fueled the fight with daily editorials. No wonder John Bright, in writing Field, said,

> I am anxious to know what is doing in Washington, but I have lost faith in the President. . . . His language shows that his temper is not calm enough for dangerous times. In this he falls immeasurably below Mr. Lincoln. But if I despair of the President, I shall have faith in the people.[14]

What Bright expected Field to do about the political wrangling in America is unclear, but in 1863 Lincoln made arrangements with the Emperor of Russia to string a telegraph line from the Pacific coast to the Baltic Sea.

In 1864 Lincoln and Congress both endorsed the Western Union's efforts to lay the connecting line under Bering Strait. Johnson, however, looked to the "entire success of the Atlantic telegraph" as "the opening of an era in the progress of civilization." Neither president, however, seemed to be particularly committed to either project except as a "worth mentioning" item in their annual addresses to congress.[15]

Field sailed from Liverpool on April 7, 1866, and arrived in New York twelve days later. He immediately arranged to return to England the beginning of June to be on hand for the summer expedition. He knew the New York visit would be brief, but he worried about Peter Cooper's consolidation of the American Telegraph Company with Western Union, which by June would bring all the lines in the United States together. Cooper favored the merger, but the unification of the two companies put Field at cross-purposes because of Western Union's promotion of the Russian-American line. Cooper did not much care because his money was in the American Telegraph Company.

For Field, laying the Atlantic cable became a dire emergency. Once again he became a man in a hurry. He tried to restrain himself, aware that past impatience had only led to failures. At times he could barely contain himself. Collins was indeed rushing the Western Union's overland route to Europe in grim competition with Field's interests. Already 300 miles of wire had been strung across British Columbia to Alaska, another 350 in Siberia, and Russians were pushing 7,000 miles of wire eastward from St. Petersburg. Western Union's submarine cable waited near the Amur River for a ship to lay it. The entire multimillion dollar enterprise was poised to fill the void created by Field's next anticipated failure.

In 1866 cable engineers introduced changes in armoring. Instead of using black charcoal iron, which turned brittle, the new cable contained strong, brightly galvanized wires with greater strength and ductility. By eliminating pitch on the hemp, the new cable avoided the troublesome problem of stickiness. The wires would stretch and bear an extra half ton of strain, yet weigh 400 pounds less per mile than the 1865 cable. Shore-end sections also changed. Instead of the entire thirty miles being of heavy construction, the armoring gradually lightened as it entered deeper water.

Canning and Clifford strengthened and improved the paying-out machinery, coupling a seventy horsepower steam engine to the after gear to make the drums reversible so cable could be picked up from the stern instead of the bow, thereby enabling the ship to back. Clifford also added six wheels between the tanks and the brake to serve as secondary brakes before the cable reached the paying-out machinery. To protect ropes and cable if the ship backed, Canning fitted an improved iron cage around the propeller. For auxiliary purposes the ship still carried picking-up machinery forward with improved spur wheels and pinion gearing. Canning chartered two 1,800-ton steamers, *Medway* and *Albany*, to accompany the expedition and fitted them with picking-up apparatus and grappling equipment.

For recovering the 1865 cable, Canning added twenty miles of wire rope, seven and a half inches in diameter, having a test strength of thirty tons. Henry Field called it "the largest fishing line used since the days of Noah." Brown, Lenox & Company provided grapnels of various designs, one type fashioned with spring-loaded prongs to keep the cable from escaping from the line when snatched off the bottom.[16]

Working with Thomson and de Sauty, Willoughby Smith devised a method for continuously monitoring insulation readings while concurrently measuring copper resistance during the exchange of signals with Valentia. On previous expeditions, tests on insulation lapsed up to thirty-five minutes. No longer could a fault be paid overboard without instant detection. Smith also added condensers to receivers, which nearly doubled the working speed. He overhauled the testing room on *Great Eastern* and added a bank of new monitoring instruments perfected by Varley and Thomson.[17]

Electricians at Valentia, having for many months run regular tests on the cable laid in 1865, reported the condition of the insulation and conductor on the year-old line perfect. Likewise, electricians running periodic tests on the 1,070 nautical miles of cable still on *Great Eastern* reported it faultless.

During the months *Great Eastern* waited off Sheerness, Captain Anderson and Robert Halpin, his chief officer, worked day and night to get the ship in perfect trim. She had become a floating island to the creatures of the sea. Mussels and barnacles to a thickness of two feet clung to her hull, creating a rich bed for the growth of long streamers of seaweed. Giving the big ship a combing and rubdown was no easy task, but Anderson devised a simple device to get under her and gave her bottom a good raking and scrubbing. He had her boilers thoroughly cleaned and repaired and made adjustments so that the paddle wheels could be uncoupled and independently changed from going ahead to backing or turning.

As fast as the cable could be manufactured and tested, Anderson's crew hauled it on board and coiled it in the tanks. As the sailing date drew near, *Great Eastern* took on board her stores and coal. With 2,700 nautical miles of cable weighing more than 15,000 tons coiled in three huge tanks, she had never been so heavily laden. Anderson delayed filling her bunkers, fearing that she could not pass through the Medway, so he arranged to take on a third of her coal at Berehaven on the southwest coast of Ireland.

Field returned to England three weeks before the July 1 sailing date. He became a little miffed when the directors suggested he remain in London in case any problems occurred. Field could do nothing in London, but he might be able to settle issues that occurred at sea, so he ignored the directors' suggestion and went with the ship.

The Admiralty augmented the new wire squadron with HMS *Terrible* and HMS *Racoon*. Canning loaded the 1,578-ton steamer *William Cory*, also known as "Dirty Billy," with the shore-end for Valentia. *William Cory*, built in 1857 to lay cables, carried three tanks with a capacity of 17,916 cubic feet. Another British warship waited at Newfoundland to help land the shore-end at Heart's Content. Two escorts chartered by the company—*Albany* and *Medway*—made up the balance of the squadron. *Medway* carried two extra cables: one to replace the old Gulf of St. Lawrence line and the other the shore-end for Heart's Content. Once again, the all-British expedition carried only two Americans—Cyrus Field and his brother Henry.[18]

Cablemen on the expedition were the same as the previous year with a few exceptions. Willoughby Smith of the Gutta Percha works replaced de Sauty as the ship's chief electrician. Varley ran the telegraph station at Valentia Island with Charles Bright's partner, Latimer Clark. Richard Collett and J. C. Laws joined the expedition to take charge at the Newfoundland end. Anderson captained the ship and Moriarty served as staff commander. Thomson made the trip as consulting engineer, and Cyrus Field joined Gooch and a few other stockholders strictly as "onlookers and watchers of their individual interests." Had Field stopped to reflect, and perhaps he did, many of the cablemen who once devoted their energies to the enterprise now lay dead, among them Isambard Brunel, Lieutenant Berryman, Captain Hudson of *Niagara*, and England's own cable pioneer, John Brett.[19]

Daniel Gooch admitted to his diary that he did not feel the same confidence as the previous year. "By what a slender thread our success hung, how little might destroy all our hopes." Then he added, switching hats to that of a purser, and said, "This large party makes beds scarce."[20]

Canning, however, left no stone unturned. He organized full itineraries for each ship, the responsibilities of each person, and covered every foreseeable contingency with instructions. He issued procedures for ship to shore communications, conductivity testing, and missed nothing of importance. Every man in the squadron understood his assignment.[21]

On June 30, 1866, *Great Eastern* steamed from the Thames, followed by *Medway* and *Albany*, and set a course for Berehaven to load coal. She scraped a few barnacles off her bottom as she passed through the Nore. On July 4, when off the southern coast of Ireland, Gooch complained, "One great mistake made is allowing the ship to be so overrun with people, who do no good, and if they do no harm cost a great deal [of] money to feed." Captain Anderson acknowledged the American Declaration of Independence by raising the Stars and Stripes. Speeches followed in the saloon, and Field submitted to hours of lampooning. So many boats converged on *Great Eastern* that Anderson ordered out the firehose to drive them off.[22]

William Cory rounded the southwestern tip of Ireland and on July 7 began landing the shore-end in Foilhummerum Bay. The section weighed

Great Eastern, followed by the HMS *Albany* off the port beam, begins to lay the 1866 cable. (From *London Illustrated News*. Digitized by Debra Peffer.)

eight tons to the mile, was by far the strongest cable ever made, and "as stiff as an iron bar." Forty fishermen's boats, mustered in a line, provided a long pontoonlike affair to transfer the cable to shore. Hand over hand, strong Irishmen hauled the heavy wire ashore.[23]

The Knight of Kerry did not come to host another ceremony. Jack-tar suggested that the knight's absence might improve the expedition's chronic run of bad luck. A London reporter observed the absence of any dignitaries and wrote: "Speech-making, hurrahing, public congratulations, and vaunts of confidence were, as it seemed, avoided as if on purpose. There was something far more touching in the quiet and reverent solemnity of the spectators yesterday than in the slightly boisterous joviality of the peasantry last year."[24]

Henry Field broke the silence by delivering a prayer. With a preacher's knack to conjure words for any occasion, Henry paraphrased from the Gospel of Luke, and said, "Thus stripped and bare this new-born child of the sea was wrapped in swaddling-clothes, covered up with many coatings of gutta-percha, and hempen rope, the whole bound round and round with heavy bands, and the splicing was complete."[25]

Varley made the connection and declared the wire perfect. *William Cory* put to sea and unlimbered the shore-end until she had laid all thirty miles. On July 13, in a drenching downpour, she passed the wire to *Great Eastern*. John Temple made the splice, and the big ship started on her way, paying out cable at three knots an hour, led by *Terrible* and flanked by *Medway* and *Albany*.[26]

The squadron took a slightly different track, running about twenty-seven miles north of the 1865 cable. After a few hours Anderson accelerated to five knots, and the cable flowed through the machinery in a steady stream. On this trip the problems occurred in the tanks. On two occasions coils caught in the bundled cable and hurled miles of kinks too close to the brake drum for comfort. In each instance Anderson had to stop the ship before knotted coils jammed the drums. With a heavy sea, falling rain, and an impenetrable darkness, "Anderson did what I should not have believed possible," said Gooch.

> He managed in such a night to keep the stern of that ship in . . . one position for the three hours it required to disentangle the cable. He could only judge of the strain on the cable by watching the small phosphorescent light in the water where the cable entered it.[27]

Neither mishap proved fatal, but Canning took no more chances. He recruited Field and a few volunteers to keep watch on the tanks. He made them wear a canvas dress that looked much like a modern-day surgical uniform. Designed with no pockets where saboteur's implements could be hidden, the gown hooked in the back and flowed to the floor. As the cable spilled out of the tanks, men wrapped their hands loosely around the armoring to feel for protruding pins.[28]

Gooch found little to do to occupy his attention. The expedition became boring but the tension never ended. "I now hear the rumble of the cable over my head," he wrote from his cabin, "and am constantly listening to it. This stretch of the nerves day after day is hard work, and the mind has no change; morning, noon, and night it is all the same—cable, cable, cable."[29]

Canning sent daily messages from the ship to the Foilhummerum station, which Varley relayed to the London papers:

> Valentia, July 12th
>
> Canning to Glass.—Latitude 51° N., longitude 17° 29' W. Cable paid out, 283 miles: distance run, 263. Insulation and continuity perfect. Weather fine. All going on well. Seaman fell overboard on *Terrible*; was picked up; life saved.[30]

> Noon, July 16th
>
> Canning to Glass.—Latitude 52° N.; longitude 20° 36' W. Cable paid out, 420 miles; distance run, 378 miles. Weather fine. All on board well.[31]

Noon, July 22nd

> Field to Glass.—The *Great Eastern* has passed the place where the cable was lost last year and all is going well.[32]

When *Great Eastern* reached the point where the 1865 cable broke, *Terrible*, using Canning's coordinates, went in search of the buoys but found nothing.

Noon (ship's time), July 23rd

> Canning to Glass.—Latitude 50° 16' N., longitude, 42° 16' W. Cable paid out, 1345.24 miles; distance run, 1196.9 miles. Insulation and continuity perfect. Insulation improved 30 per cent since starting.[33]

Monday, July 23rd

> Field to Glass.—Please obtain the latest news from Egypt, China, India, and distant places for us to forward to the United States on our arrival at Heart's Content.[34]

On Tuesday, July 24, with Western Union still on his mind, Field sent a message to Glass at Valentia: "We are within four hundred miles of Heart's Content, and expect to be there on Friday. When shall the Atlantic telegraph be open for public business?" Field got the answer he wanted. "If you land the cable on Friday," Glass replied, "I see no reason why it should not be open on Saturday." Field breathed a sigh of relief.[35]

On July 26 the seabed rose as *Great Eastern* entered the Grand Banks. Gulls swooped about the ship, squawking for attention. An iceberg floated in the distance, barely perceptible. A thick fogbank marked the area where the warm Gulf Stream collided with the Labrador Current. The four ships lost sight of each other. Fog whistles shrieked at one another and at times sounded dangerously close. Anderson had timed his departure to reach Newfoundland during the full moon, but he seldom caught sight of the disk in the fog.

At 4:25 A.M., July 27, the ship stood off Trinity Bay, and Anderson slowed, feeling his way inside. At daylight the fog miraculously lifted and the sun burst bright over the bay. Ahead stood *Albany*, waiting to guide the big ship into the harbor. She sounded the entrance and rounded the point.

Fisherfolk looked up from their work and those who owned spyglasses brought them down to the water's edge. Minutes passed, and then the enormous hull of *Great Eastern* began edging into the bay, followed by *Terrible*. "They are coming!" echoed the sound of voices along shore. Hundreds of Newfoundlanders climbed into their boats and headed for Heart's Content. Anderson saw them approaching and ordered *Great Eastern*'s anchor dropped directly off the telegraph station. The great ship, slowing to a single knot, still remained connected by a long, thin umbilical cord stretching back to Ireland.

Two British ships, *Niger* and *Margaretta Stevenson* from the North American station, greeted the cable fleet with an exchange of salutes. Such a ruckus had not been heard in Trinity Bay since 1858. Dangling from homes alongshore fluttered the Stars and Stripes and the Union Jack. Boats shoved off to carry the cable from *Great Eastern* to *Medway*. Field added a next-to-last entry in his diary: "We sent the end of the cable to the *Medway* to be spliced. I left the *Great Eastern* in a small boat at 8:15 A.M., and landed at Heart's Content at 9 o'clock."[36]

The cablemen knew their jobs and the work went swiftly. Willoughby Smith sent a short message to Valentia, reporting that the shore-end had been landed and the splice made at 8:43 A.M. Messages of congratulation passed swiftly between Ireland and Newfoundland. The insulation and the continuity remained perfect. Smith reported the speed of communication vastly improved after amputating the surplus cable.

Gooch followed the cablemen dragging the shore-end to the wooden telegraph station at Heart's Content. Never had he seen such wild excitement. "The old cable hands," he wrote,

> seemed as though they could eat the end; one man actually put it in his mouth and sucked it. They held it up and danced around it, cheering at the top of their voices. It was a strange sight—nay, a sight that filled our eyes with tears. Yes, I felt not less than they did. I did cheer, but I could better have silently cried.[37]

Field found more reason to shed tears than Gooch. Some turn of events always seemed to ruin his celebration. The local superintendent of the New York, Newfoundland telegraph line reported that the Gulf of St. Lawrence cable just failed. *Medway* carried ninety miles of new cable to replace the old line, but this would take time Field could not afford to lose. He never stopped worrying about Western Union's trans-Siberian line and went into St. John's for help. He hired the steamer *Bloodhound* and sent her around to Cabot Strait to fish up the old cable and make temporary repairs. To bridge the delay he also chartered a steamer to carry messages from Cape Race to Nova Scotia. The repair work took two days, delaying his messages to New York. When on July 29 the Associated Press received his two-day-old message, which read, "All well. Thank God, the cable is laid, and is in perfect working order," someone might have asked—if so, why did messages take so long?[38]

When the news reached the press, Secretary of State Seward sent his compliments, and Queen Victoria exchanged congratulations with President Johnson. This time the messages took seven minutes to travel between Newfoundland and Ireland, compared with sixteen hours in 1858. Field

A hundred voices raise in a tumultuous cheer as Heart's Content electricians report the cable is working. (*London Illustrated News*. Digitized by Debra Peffer.)

received a flood of congratulations: most read like those received eight long years ago.

On the day the cable spoke, it carried messages at a speed of 7.36 words per minute. The world read closing quotations on Wall Street, prices on the Brussels grain market, and that Congress had finally readmitted President Johnson's state of Tennessee to the Union. When there was no traffic on the cable, each station called the other every fifteen minutes, using the code "NN," which meant "Nothing for you at present."[39]

Dancing and celebrating kept Gooch awake that night while visions of pound and dollar signs flowed before his eyes. In the morning he wrote, "Yesterday we had fifty messages, paying us, I suppose not less than twelve thousand pounds." Gooch was already a rich man, made richer by the success of the cable, but his full reward, as with all the others, was yet to be fulfilled. Field summed it up in a message to his wife: "We leave in about a week to recover the cable of last year."[40]

On August 2 *Great Eastern* began coaling. She had burned more than 7,000 tons of fuel crossing the Atlantic. Steamers had ferried six coal barges carrying 8,000 tons of coal across the Atlantic; one of the barges went down at sea. While waiting for coal to be transferred to the big ship, Canning sent *Terrible* and *Albany* ahead to find the 1865 cable. Both ships carried grappling tackle and planned to make a few passes on their own. If they hooked onto something, they carried buoys to mark it.

Field waited impatiently on *Great Eastern* while she loaded coal. He and Anderson had become great friends, and they visited daily. One night Anderson thought the time had come to inform Mary Field of her husband's future plans. "Mr. Field is not one bit quieter than he was in London," wrote Anderson. "He wants a third cable laid, and two complete lines from here to New York, before he will be satisfied. The success of this one will make the others comparatively easy, but I am not sure if he will even then take the repose both you and he deserve."[41]

During the week, Field showed a different side of his personality. He took Willoughby Smith aside, and said, "When this is over, I'm going to retire to my own farm in the Berkshires, with plenty of cows and chickens, and receive my dividends in eggs and fresh milk." Smith knew Field was joking.[42]

At noon, August 9, *Great Eastern* weighed anchor and three days later, accompanied by *Medway*, joined *Terrible* and *Albany* 607 miles east of Trinity Bay. The two buoys anchored in 1865 had long disappeared, but the sailors' uncanny intuition for knowing the sea's secrets, helped by astronomical observations, led them directly to the area where the cable had parted. They caught the wire once, but like a great slippery eel it wiggled off during a storm. Captain J. E. Commerill of *Terrible* staked out the position with a row of buoys, and when *Great Eastern* hove in sight, Canning knew where to cast his hook.

Canning refined grappling to a science. Once the grapple touched the seabed, mechanics operating the machinery would pay out exactly 200 additional fathoms of wire. Mechanics monitoring the dynamometer would watch for a sudden increase in tension. As each minute passed, they would record the tension and note any variation from the mean. Depending upon the length of the line and the speed of the drift, an increase of a quarter of a ton would normally indicate that the cable had been hooked. Canning did not want the grapple raised until the dynamometer climbed to two tons, just enough to turn the head of the ship. At this point the grappling crew would start to retrieve the cable, and Captain Anderson would back the ship to reduce the tension—no easy task for a vessel the size of *Great Eastern*.[43]

Canning planned to have three ships drag simultaneously near the end of where he believed the cable had parted. He posted *Medway* to the westward, keeping her handy for a special purpose. If the cable could be brought to the surface, he wanted *Medway* to cut it, thereby reducing weight and resistance as it neared the surface.

On August 13 *Great Eastern* made her first drag, caught nothing, and tried again farther to the eastward. Two days later the grapple hooked the cable and brought it up about 100 fathoms. Because of approaching darkness, Canning wanted to buoy it until morning. The buoy rope slipped

The HMS *Medway*, working in conjunction with *Great Eastern*, fishes for the 1865 cable. (*London Illustrated News*. Digitized by Debra Peffer.)

overboard and two and a half miles of wire rope joined the cable on the bottom.

On August 17, working still farther to the eastward, the cablemen paid out 2,400 fathoms of wire rope and at 4:30 A.M. hooked the cable again. Six and a half hours later the long lost cable, covered with slime, emerged from the sea. It swung briefly ten feet above the surface, and before *Medway* could get into position to make a cut, parted. Seventeen months later, while addressing a banquet gathering in London, Field recalled the incident and laconically quipped, "our men began to cheer so wildly that it [the cable] seemed to be frightened, and suddenly broke away and went down into the sea."[44]

Two days later the crew hooked the cable again, ran the wire a mile through the picking-up machine before a severe storm whipped up the sea and suspended operations for several days.

On August 27 *Albany*, working to the westward, hooked the cable, brought it on board, and reported that it came up with only 6,000 pounds tension. Smith brought the wire to *Great Eastern* and gave it a test, only to confirm what he suspected: *Albany* had recovered a broken end three miles long. Captain Temple of *Albany* collapsed from a combination of fatigue and frustration and had to be brought to *Great Eastern* to recover. Captain Commerill of *Terrible* reported his fuel low and his men on half rations. He begged permission to return to Newfoundland for fresh supplies. Canning let the ship go, and the men of *Great Eastern* gathered on deck to watch as another casualty of this befuddling ocean war limped westward.

Great Eastern shifted another eighty miles to the east and found shallower water. Canning expressed concern because after twenty-nine attempts to hook the cable, his store of wire rope and grapples was running low. On August 31 he lowered the grapnel for the thirtieth time and at 4:50 A.M. the following morning caught the cable. The sea had calmed, and Anderson experienced no difficulty maneuvering the ship as the retrieving apparatus began spitting coils onto the after deck. "So delicately did she answer her helm, and coil in the film of threadlike cable, that she put one in mind of an elephant taking up a straw in its proboscis."[45]

At 900 fathoms from the surface, the tension on the dynamometer climbed to 8,000 pounds, so Canning ordered the grappling rope buoyed. Anderson took *Great Eastern* three miles west of the buoy and grappled the cable again. *Medway* went another two miles west and did the same. Canning waited until *Medway* raised the cable to 300 fathoms before ordering her to break it. As soon as the cable parted the tension eased by half, and mechanics began picking up the two-mile length.

At 1:00 A.M. on September 2 the ooze-covered cable made its expected appearance near the surface. Cradled in ropes, two veteran cablemen descended over the side. They unhooked the slimy creature from the grapnel, secured it with a five-inch halyard, and gently lifted it on board. Willoughby Smith and his brother Oliver took the muddy end into the test room.

Field, Gooch, and Thomson watched as electricians cut the shield and insulation to the conducting core and connected it to the instruments. The continuity responded perfectly. "Suddenly Willoughby Smith's hat is off," recalled John Deane, "and the British hurrah bursts from his lips, echoed by all on board with a volley of cheers." Smith sent a short message to Valentia, where James Graves, superintendent of the Foilhummerum station, and two telegraphers named May and Crocker had been watching for weeks for impulses to flicker on the reflecting instrument connected to the comatose cable. "Ship to shore; I have much pleasure in speaking to you through the 1865 cable. Just going to make a splice." Graves, May, and Crocker gave a whoop and telegraphed the good news to London and New York.[46]

Mechanics spliced the 1865 end to the cable in the hold, and *Great*

Cablemen are lowered over the side of *Great Eastern* to clamp onto the 1865 cable and bring it on board for testing. (From *London Illustrated News*. Digitized by Debra Peffer.)

Eastern headed back to Trinity Bay. Field wrote a 5,500-mile message to his wife that went from *Great Eastern* to Ireland, from Ireland to Newfoundland, across Cabot Strait to Nova Scotia, and from there to Mary Field, who was in Newburg, New York: "The cable of 1865 was recovered early this morning, and we are now in perfect telegraphic communication with Valentia, and on our way back to Heart's Content, where we expect to arrive next Saturday. God be praised."[47]

At Valentia, Latimer Clark tried an experiment on the unbroken 3,700 nautical miles of cable between Foilhummerum and Heart's Content. Using nothing more than a silver thimble borrowed from Miss Fitzgerald, the

Knight of Kerry's daughter, he poured into it a little sulfuric acid with a fragment of zinc weighing a grain or two. "By this primitive agency," wrote Charles Bright, "he succeeded in conveying signals twice through the breadth of the Atlantic Ocean in little more than a second of time after making contact." Historian James D. Reid mentioned another experiment made by Professor Gould. Using "a battery composed of a gun cap, a drop of ocean water, and a small strip of zinc," Gould sent "intelligible signals from continent to continent." Wildman Whitehouse with his 2,000-volt powerhouse missed the experiment, having passed on to his heavenly reward.[48]

Eighteen months later, while speaking in London, Field recalled his emotions on the day *Great Eastern* recovered the 1865 cable. He entered the electrician's room to watch the test to determine whether the cable was dead or alive. Finding the current strong, he asked Foilhummerum whether the 1866 cable was still working and whether the cable across Cabot Strait had been repaired. Six alpha characters came back: "Both OK." Field could no longer contain himself. "I left the room, I went to my cabin, I locked the door; I could no longer restrain my tears—crying like a child, and full of gratitude to God that I had been permitted to live to witness the recovery of the cable we had lost from the *Great Eastern* just thirteen months previous."[49]

On September 2 at 7:01 P.M., *Great Eastern* began paying out 680 miles of cable as she steamed towards Heart's Content. Six days later when only thirteen miles from Trinity Bay, tests showed a fault in the cable. Field's heart probably sustained a few palpitations until the electricians announced the fault on board. The cablemen inspected the coils and found a broken wire embedded in the insulation of the year-old cable. The mechanics cut away the fault, spliced the cable, dropped it into the sea, and at 11:00 A.M. on September 8 stood off Heart's Content. The crew from *Medway* set to work laying the shore-end. At nightfall, electricians announced two lines open for business across the Atlantic.

Without *Great Eastern*—the ship designed to carry 4,000 passengers, not 3,800 nautical miles of wire—the Atlantic cables might never have been laid in the 1860s. The two lines settled comfortably in an average depth of 1,900 fathoms (11,400 feet). This remarkable feat laid the groundwork for a multitude of transoceanic cables that followed in the decades ahead. Without the great ship, Cyrus Field may have gone to his grave a beaten man. William Howard Russell called Brunel's leviathan "an elephant stretching a cobweb," and indeed she did.[50]

Chapter 18

The Summing Up

After a brief celebration, Cyrus Field bid good-bye to his friends on *Great Eastern* and joined *Medway*. After making thirty-eight voyages back and forth across the Atlantic he deserved to go home, but a new cable still needed to be laid across Cabot Strait, and in mid-September 1866 he intended to see it done. After that, if he never laid another cable during his lifetime, he had done enough and more than most men of his time.

As Field disembarked from *Great Eastern*, Captain Anderson shook his hand. They had become great friends. Anderson called to his crew, "Give him three cheers!" The hurrahs continued, echoing across the bay as a boat took Field ashore. He looked back as the big ship gathered headway and headed for sea. She had become a part of him, but now *Great Eastern* had her own mission, and men like Canning, Gooch, and the Telegraph Construction & Maintenance Company knew exactly what to do with her.[1]

A few days later *Medway* began stretching a new cable from Cape Ray to the Aspy Bay telegraph station in Nova Scotia. The connection took longer than Field expected, lasting late into September. Finally, after eleven years of ceaseless toil, he bid farewell to his British friends on *Medway* and went home to his family.

A 16,000-statute-mile land wire could never compete with a 2,000-mile submarine cable, but word of *Great Eastern*'s success traveled slowly to Siberia. There several battalions of Yakutsk peasants, led by six Russo-American working parties, were engaged in erecting 20,000 poles to build the easternmost section of a line that would run from Kazan, Russia, to the Amur River, which emptied into the Sea of Okhotsk. During the spring of 1867, 600 Siberian ponies began distributing poles between the Amur and Bering Strait.

A landline had previously been constructed from Moscow to St. Petersburg, and from Moscow to Niznij-Novgorod in southern Russia. The projectors hoped to complete the Amur River section in 1867 and have the entire line to St. Petersburg in operation by 1870. They also planned to run lines south from Kazan to connect with the Anglo-Indian Line at Teheran and Baghdad. When considering its great length, the project made as much sense to millions of doubtful people as the Atlantic cable.

Since 1856, Major Perry McDonough Collins of California had been the commercial agent for the U.S. government in the Amur River area. On May 23, 1863, he obtained from Russia an authorization to build a line through its territory on both sides of the Pacific, which included Russian America (Alaska). The czar granted Collins exclusive rights to the 5,000-mile line for thirty-three years. Collins obtained from England similar rights for a connecting line through British Columbia. In time, Collins hoped to extend the line to Peking and beyond. The overall plan called for two submarine cables, one across Bering Strait, which was only thirty-nine miles wide and about sixty feet deep, and another across Anadyr Bay.

In 1867, 387 miles of submarine cable—made by The Telegraph Construction & Maintenance Company—waited at Anadyr to be laid. A nagging concern existed about submerging a cable in the ice-blocked shallows of Bering Strait, and as an option, the company considered laying the cable across the Aleutian Islands, twelve in number, but doing so would require another 1,900 miles of cable.[2]

Collins also needed rights to cross federal lands owned by the government, and to obtain those concessions he went directly to Field's friend, Secretary of State Seward. On April 12, 1864, Seward petitioned Congress on Collins' behalf and on July 1, 1864, the legislature granted Collins the rights he requested, along with a grant of $50,000 for a "survey of the northern waters, coasts, and islands of the Pacific Ocean and Behring's [*sic*] Strait."[3]

Hiram Sibley, the aggressive president of the Western Union, had in 1861 connected the eastern United States with San Francisco, and by 1864 operated lines to Olympia, Washington, and Victoria, British Columbia. Collins promulgated an agreement with Sibley, and the immense project passed into the control of Sibley's powerful Western Union. In exchange for his rights, Collins received from Sibley one-tenth of the stock issued for what became the Western Union Extension of the overland intercontinental line. Colonel Charles S. Bulkley sailed to Sitka, capital of Russian America, as engineer-in-chief in charge of laying the landline through British Columbia to Bering Strait.[4]

Even Morse, who was still connected with the American Telegraph Company, encouraged Collins to pursue the scheme. Although the long line would mainly benefit the Western Union, he would collect royalties from the company for the use of his patents.[5]

Meanwhile, George Kennan acted as quartermaster for the Siberian Division, which was building the extension between the Amur River and Bering Strait. The pole-cutting camps were hard at work when in May 1867, Captain Hamilton, skipper of the New Bedford whaling bark *Seabreeze*, pulled into a bay and noticed a gang of men waving from shore. He thought they had been shipwrecked and sent a boat ashore. Upon hearing a ship had arrived, Kennan rode to the beach on a Siberian pony and was rowed to the ship. When Hamilton asked what the men were doing, Kennan said they were building a telegraph line.

"A telegraph line," Captain Hamilton snorted. "Well if that ain't the craziest thing I ever heard of! Who's going to telegraph from here?"

Kennan explained the project and then asked about the Atlantic cable.

"Oh, yes," the captain replied, "the cable is laid all right."

With a lump in his throat, Kennan asked, "Does it work?"

"Works like a snatch tackle," Hamilton replied. "The Frisco papers are publishing every morning the London news of the day before. I've got a lot of them on board I'll give you."

Nine months had passed and nobody had informed Kennan of *Great Eastern*'s unexpected success—or perhaps they had been waiting for the Atlantic cable to fail. He read the dreaded news from a stack of papers that dated back to September 1866. Not only had the cable been laid, the 1865 cable had been grappled and repaired, giving the American Telegraph Company not one but two working lines. With twenty-four steamers and sailing vessels engaged on the Siberian line, Kennan wondered why no one had notified him to stop work.[6]

On both sides of the Pacific, work ceased. In British Columbia crews dropped their tools and quit. In Kennan's corner of Siberia, Collins' company opened the greatest flea market in Asia, selling off miles of wire and supplies. Pickaxes and long-handled shovels went fast: in Siberia there were always the dead to bury. Small glass insulators sold as teacups. Buyers of salt pork and dried apples received free candles and a bar or two of soap. Articles flooded the country for hundreds of miles around, most of them "of no more use to the poor natives than iceboats and mouse-traps to the Quaregs of the Sahara desert!" Russia eventually completed the project of connecting Moscow with eastern Siberia, but not for the reasons intended by Collins. Western Union stockholders lost $3 million.[7]

Hiram Sibley soon recovered. In June 1866, using his Western Union network as the centerpiece, he absorbed the American Telegraph system and monopolized the domestic business. In the end, revenues from the Atlantic cable partly compensated the Western Union for the financial blow it suffered by abandoning the Russian-American line. The same fiasco produced another fringe benefit. Because of Collins' survey north to Bering

The years promoting the Atlantic cable aged Cyrus Field, but did little to slow him down. (Courtesy of the Library of Congress. Digitized by Debra Peffer.)

Strait and Colonel Bulkley's wiring of Russian America, the government learned a great deal about the enormous lands north of British Columbia. On July 27, 1868, prompted by a proposal from the secretary of state, the United States bought "Seward's Icebox" for $7.2 million and renamed it Alaska.

Now forty-seven years of age, Field had sold his business and spent most of his wealth on the cable. In 1866 he no longer owned shares in four cable companies. For every share he had owned in the American Telegraph Company, he now owned three in Western Union. When he returned to New York, the sign on the American Telegraph Company offices at 145 Broadway also read Western Union. He still owned shares in the Anglo-American Telegraph Company, which had absorbed the rights of the Atlantic Telegraph Company. For the next several months he would have little time to think about it. The banquets began and never seemed to end. Once again he became the toast of New York and the pride of the nation.

In Great Britain the success of the expedition launched four knighthoods, Sir Captain James Anderson, Professor Sir William Thomson (later Lord Kelvin), Sir Samuel Canning, and Sir Richard Glass. The queen also extended baronetcies to Sir Daniel Gooch and Sir Curtis Lampson. The stress nearly cost Glass, the managing director of the Telegraph Construction & Maintenance Company, his life. When *Great Eastern* returned to England, Glass collapsed from exhaustion and lay in bed for weeks. Cyrus Field received no such royal emoluments from the queen, though she particularly mentioned her regrets at being unable to so honor him because of his American citizenship. The Englishman on the street, however, gave him the sobriquet "Lord Cable," and the informal title spread from the British press to America. On March 2, 1867, Congress belatedly presented him with a large gold medal in a mother-of-pearl box. England, France, Italy, New York City, and the state of Wisconsin had already struck medals and bestowed honorary endowments.[8]

During the eleven-year cable-laying saga, Peter Cooper never faltered in his support of Field, but as the years passed he concentrated his energies more on the American Telegraph Company and other domestic enterprises. When in 1866 the cable suddenly became a two-continent reality, it caught Cooper by surprise. During an interview, a magazine reporter asked him who he thought was the greatest living American. Cooper went to the wall of his office, laid his finger on a portrait of Field, and said, "If any of the foremost men of our time had died, their places would have been filled, but Field did what no other man could do; he saved the scheme and brought victory out of despair."[9]

After the celebrations ended, Field discovered that he still had debts dating back to the panic of 1860. He sold $200,000 of his stock to pay off old Field & Company notes, expecting to recover all of it in dividends from his cable stock. The Atlantic cable, however, quickly became a contentious instrument. The line proved to be incapable of transmitting more than fifteen words a minute compared with 400 words a minute over landlines. Rates on the cable jumped to ten dollars a word, and because of frequent trouble, messages could not always be sent.

Occasional outbursts of acrimony between operators at Heart's Content and Foilhummerum Bay did not help matters. If one station sent a message and did not get an immediate reply, an angry note usually followed. "Attention at your station disgraceful. See it altered. Four messages delayed seventeen minutes before call answered and further twelve minutes before clerk commenced to receive. Send name of clerk on duty." Foilhummerum replied: "George and Mackey were on duty, the former attending fire in kitchen, latter calls of nature in field."[10]

The cable-laying effort cost Field his personal fortune. At times he found himself financially embarrassed, and to everyone but his family he tried to hide it. "Not a luxury was allowed," his daughter Isabella said, "and during those years any wish that might be expressed could only be gratified 'when the cable is laid.' " He heard his family, which included a wife, four daughters, and two sons, often moan, "Oh, if that old cable was only at the bottom of the ocean," to which he would reply, "That is just where I wish it to be." The family hated the cable. Six months passed before Field received a cable dividend, and for the first time in many years the family could afford a few luxuries.[11]

Field's strength lay in his ability to persuade others to follow his lead, and his weakness lay in his overexuberant optimism to completely believe without reservation in whatever he sought to accomplish. He took enormous chances with his wealth in an enterprise he knew virtually nothing about. Neither his upbringing nor his papermaking business prepared him for the technological ramifications involved in the greatest maritime speculation of the century. Despite having no knowledge of electricity and little of engineering, he learned quickly enough to supply the stimulus needed to consummate the nineteenth century's most difficult project.

In 1873 Field convinced the Anglo-American Telegraph Company to take over the 30,000 shares of the New York, Newfoundland, and London Telegraph Company at ninety dollars a share. Much of Field's holdings had been whittled down over the years to pay debts and expenses, and he left no record of his net worth. After nearly twenty years, the first company established and financed by Field and Cooper to lay the Atlantic cable now belonged in its entirety to the British. Cooper, however, had held his shares and pocketed $522,000.[12]

Cyrus Field never got out of the cable business, and he never stopped traveling between New York and London, having established homes in both countries. The Anglo-American Telegraph Company, having absorbed the Atlantic Telegraph Company, now bought their sole European competitor, the French Société du Câble Trans-Atlantique Français, thereby creating a monopoly for the North Atlantic cable business. Great Britain became the cable technology center of the world, and Field continued to act as the intermediary between worldly projects and the interests of the Telegraph Construction & Maintenance Company. He knew how to raise money and promote seemingly impossible enterprises, such as the enormous Pacific cable project—a 6,515-nautical-mile proposal connecting San Francisco with Shanghai through Hawaii, Midway Island, and Yokohama. Spanning the Pacific, however, had to wait until the early twentieth century.

Both Atlantic cables failed in November 1870 after four years of cranky service. Without *Great Eastern*, communication with Europe could have ceased for many years. But in 1869 *Great Eastern*, now commanded by Captain Robert Halpin, had laid a 3,000-mile line between Brest and St. Pierre in the Gulf of St. Lawrence, and the French wire picked up the volume until the original cables were restored. Because of rapid advances in submarine cable technology, a new line laid in 1873 between Ireland and Newfoundland lasted more than a century.

In 1870 *Great Eastern* did what every other ship had failed to do during the previous decade—she laid the cable linking England to India. A year later she ran a cable from Australia to Singapore, and in 1874 she laid the first cable connecting Europe to Brazil, using as stepping stones the islands of St. Vincent and Madeira. Before she ended her career, *Great Eastern* laid five Atlantic cables. By 1900 thirteen cables spanned the North Atlantic, but one or two were usually out of order.[13]

As Arthur C. Clarke observed, "Few things are duller than the record of steady and uninterrupted progress; when the telegraph fleet anchored in Heart's Content on July 27, 1866, the adventurous, pioneering days were over, and with them the excitement they engendered."[14]

During the next hundred years, only three major improvements occurred in submarine cable systems. They had nothing to do with the design of the cable and everything to do with transmitting and receiving equipment. Samuel Morse and Joseph Henry started the industry with a simple mechanism operated by a telegraph clerk tapping out a message with dots and dashes. At the other end of the line another clerk watched a needle or a spot of light dancing back and forth on one of Thomson's mirror-reflecting instruments.

During the early days of manual operation a clerk had to take down the message at every station and resend it to the next station. A message from Newfoundland to New York took as many as six repetitions with six chances for transposition. The expanding network desperately needed a device to automatically receive and transmit the message in its original form. Imagine a transmission from London to New York quoting the price of gold at $125 and having it misprinted in the final message at $152 or $215.

The early "regenerators" attempted to amplify incoming signals, but after passing through the second or third relay station the message became corrupted by distortions on the wire and dots and dashes all looked alike. The problem continued through World War I. Not until 1920 was a device designed that could automatically regenerate an impulse coming through the line, decide whether it was a dot or a dash, and then make a fresh dot or dash. By then dots and dashes had become a generic term for Dits and Dās or Flicks and Flāshes (Boy Scouts codes), pluses and minuses (dashes being positive current, dots being the negative impulse), or in terms of a needle, right being positive and left being negative. Messages passed from New York to Singapore could go through more than a dozen regenerators before reaching their destination. It printed out on a paper tape and was glued to a cablegram form and delivered to the addressee by a messenger.

When *Great Eastern* retrieved the 1865 cable and took it into Heart's Content to establish a second connection with Europe, everyone involved became excited because the system would have one line for sending and another line for receiving. One of the most important developments in telegraphic communication occurred at almost the same time—the system of duplexing—an important technique that enabled a line to carry signals simultaneously in both directions and double the working capacity of the circuit. The trick lay in a little device that separated impulses coming in from impulses going out while at the same time allowing both to flow without interruption. On telephones, two people speaking at the same time cannot hear what the other is saying, but the same signals, if carried on a telegraphic duplex system, would transmit as clear messages.

Next came multiplex working, a system far more complex and remarkable than the regenerator because it permitted several messages to go in the same direction at the same time. A single cable could carry eight messages with four going out and four coming in simultaneously. The system depended upon rapidly operating switch gears capable of using the line for a split second to send and another split second to receive, and so on back and forth. Using such techniques, it became possible by the 1930s to send 400 words per minute over the most ancient lines.

The invention of the telephone eventually changed the role of telegraphic cables and created a new technology. The immediate success of the 1956 Transatlantic Telephone Cable started a new cable-laying flurry. With the sudden advent of transistors and the demise of vacuum tubes, the new cable became obsolete before the first commercial call crossed the line. By the end of the decade a single transistor requiring no more power than a flashlight battery could replace more than 300 vacuum tubes.

Cable transmission of telephone calls led to another invention—the Time-Assignment Speech Interpolator (TASI). Every conversation between two people contained pauses. The TASI swift-acting device filled the smallest pauses by instantly switching to another conversation, making a telephone cable like two-way automobile traffic going in opposite directions in the same lane without colliding with each other—a physical impossibility.

Commander Maury would have been pleased with another change. Long ago he told Field that the 1857 Atlantic cable should be made lighter, not heavier. One hundred years later the British Post Office, which inherited the government's cable responsibilities, discovered that the only strength a cable needed was a solid steel wire at the center and a tube of strong plastic (which had replaced gutta-percha) for external protection. The new lightweight cable put no strain on paying-out machinery, settled comfortably into the soft and quiet bed of the sea, never twisted or kinked, and paid out like line spinning freely off a fishing reel.

Before the use of satellites, telephones depended entirely upon copper lines to carry voice impulses. The first Atlantic cable charged five dollars a word and sometimes more. Later cables carried 2,000 words a minute. Today a commercial phone call can be made to the United Kingdom for ten cents a minute.

More recently the same impulses can be sent at the speed of light through fiber-optic systems. On January 8, 2001, Bill Scanlon wrote: "There's gold

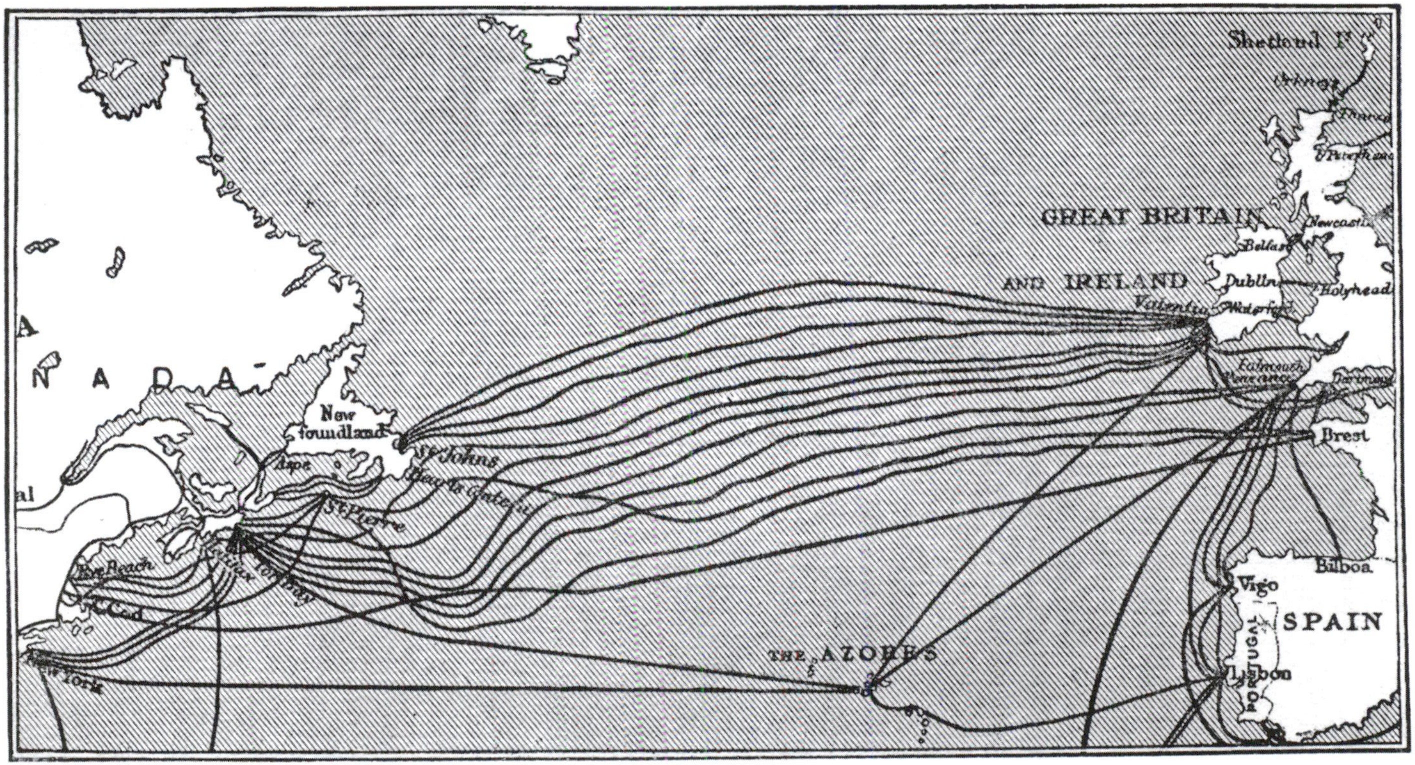

Map showing the spread of North Atlantic cables systems by the year 1903. (From Charles Bright, *The Story of the Atlantic Cable*. Digitized by Debra Peffer.)

under them there oceans. The submarine optical market is expected to grow 40 percent a year—to $37 billion by 2004—as carriers scramble to lay cable across the oceans to connect the continents with ever-faster optic fiber."[15]

The terminology has changed to such an extent that men like Cyrus Field might have been frightened away by the wheeling and dealing promoters of Global Crossing Limited who spoke of "erbium-doped amplifiers driving wave division multiplexed fiber-optic lines" capable of handling forty gigabits of data per second. They called their proposition AC-1, meaning Atlantic Crossing 1—8,000 miles of cable between the United States and Europe. Gary Winnick, Global Crossing's chairman, might have benefited from a study of the mid-nineteenth century cable business before raising more than $20 billion for his big mistake.[16]

One might also wonder how Lord Palmerston and President Buchanan would have reacted to such a pitch. Abraham Lincoln would have shaken his head at such gibberish and asked, as he once did, to send the proposal on a telegram. Andrew Johnson would have been too busy defending his impeachment to have given it much thought. Nor would anyone of that day have considered the feasibility of wireless telegraphy, the brainchild of William Thomson, who studied the practical use of transient currents as far back as the 1850s.

In 1874 the Telegraph Construction & Maintenance Company launched a custom-built cable ship and named her *Faraday*. She replaced *Great Eastern*, and Daniel Gooch took his ship to Sheerness. Riding in his familiar cabin, he wrote, "It may be a long time before I have a sail in the old ship again, as I do not know how we are going to employ her in the future." Robert Halpin, the ship's captain, moored the ship off Milford and went down the ladder for the last time. Located where she was, the ship soon became a hazard to maritime traffic.[17]

In 1876 a Manchester engineer named Frederick Appleby obtained a contract to build two large dry docks and found *Great Eastern* moored on the site selected for his largest dock. Old sea dogs frequenting local pubs growled, "Somebody ought to blow her up with gunpowder." But Appleby had a splendid idea. Why not cut her down and *use her as the dry dock?* Once again the clatter of men and machines, just like the old cable days, tore away *Great Eastern's* main deck. When Appleby finished his dock, he opened the locks to move the ship inside, but she would not fit. The surveyors who remeasured the ship said they would have to remove the paddle boxes. After much expense, the big ship squeezed through, but her new owners demanded that her paddle boxes be restored.[18]

She worked no better as a dry dock than she had as a luxury liner. In 1887 Henry Bath & Sons bought her for £16,000, and the stockholders received fourteen cents on the dollar. The new company took her around to Liverpool where she became another obstruction. On November 21 Bath & Sons announced they would break her up, but first they would auction her parts. Everything from her copper fittings to her iron plates and rivets brought $290,000. Miss Hockley's Boarding School at West Kirby bought the captain's deckhouse and set it back up as a clubhouse. A year later Gooch, in failing health, wrote her final epitaph: "It looks like the last of the grand old ship. . . . I would much rather that the ship was broken up than turned to base uses. . . . Poor old ship, you deserved a better fate."[19]

The breaking up began in May 1889, thirty-one years and three months after her launching. One day when workmen breached a compartment in the inner port shell, there came a shriek that stopped all work. A chap by the name of David Duff wrote James Dugan:

> They found a skeleton inside the ship's shell and the tank tops. It was the skeleton of the basher who was missing. Also the frame of the bash boy was found with him. And so there you are, sir, that is all I can tell you of the *Great Eastern.*

Oddly enough, the British press never mentioned it, and Duff's claims went into the records as a hoax.[20]

Daniel Gooch died in October 1889. He lived just long enough to think that his ship might have had ghosts after all, but then again, probably not.

The old Atlantic cablemen were all beginning to fall by the wayside. David Dudley Field, who served as his brother's counsel during the cable years, eventually became the attorney for such New York swindlers as Jay Gould, Jim Fisk, and William Marcy "Boss" Tweed. Cyrus Field became entangled with Gould, who snatched control of Western Union, and the old promoter eventually lost most of his fortune to Gould's manipulations of the stock market. After financially struggling for more than two years, Field's health failed during the spring of 1892. He lost weight, by July 6 dropping to eighty pounds. He would lapse into unconsciousness, and thinking himself deserted on the shores of Valentia, holler: "Hold those ships!" He no longer recognized his family, but the ghostly images of Frederick Gisborne and his Newfoundlanders, Samuel Morse with his tapping machines, Daniel Gooch with his great iron ship, and Wildman Whitehouse with his cable-killing 2,000-volt batteries probably haunted his reveries. On the morning of July 12 the lingering specters slipped away, giving him permanent peace.[21]

The family took his body to the old Congregational Church in Stockbridge, Massachusetts, where his father had preached, and to the church cemetery where his wife, Mary, had been buried a few weeks before. "There, in the sweet summer afternoon," wrote David Dudley Field,

> we laid him to rest in a bed of pine boughs and covered with flowers. Peacefully now he sleeps where he so often wished to sleep, by the side of his wife and close

to his father and mother, his sister and his oldest son. Long as any of us survive, shall we cherish the memory of our beloved brother.[22]

At the time of Field's death, ten cables spanned the Atlantic, carrying an ever increasing load of messages to points around the world. Like aquatic spiders, the men of the Wire Squadron spun their webs under the sea.

"Columbus found one world and left it two. Cyrus W. Field found two continents and left them one." He did it with the help of many, and with his pioneering friends in Great Britain, he gave the world circuits in the sea.[23]

Appendix

Descriptions of Atlantic Cables of 1858 and 1865

Distance from Valentia, Ireland to Trinity Bay, Newfoundland, 1670 nautical miles.

Atlantic Cable of 1858

Conductor: Seven stranded copper wires (six laid around one), weighing 107 pounds per nautical mile.

Insulator: Gutta-percha laid on in three coverings, and weighing 261 pounds per nautical mile.

External Protection: Eighteen strands of charcoal iron wire, each strand composed of seven wires (six laid round one), laid spirally round the core, which latter was previously padded with a serving of hemp saturated with a tar mixture. The separate wires were each .028"; the completed strand, .083".

Circumference of Finished Cable: Two inches.

Weight in Air: 2,000 pounds per nautical mile.

Weight in Water: 1,340 pounds per nautical mile.

Breaking Strain: 6,500 pounds, or equal to 4.85 times the cable's weight in water per nautical mile.

Deepest Water on North Atlantic Route: 2,400 fathoms, or 14,400 feet.

Length of Cable Shipped: 2,174 nautical miles.

Atlantic Cable of 1865

Conductor: Copper strand consisting of seven wires (six laid around one), and weighing 300 pounds per nautical mile, embedded for solidarity in Chatterton's Compound. Diameter of single wire, .048"; diameter of strand, .144".

Insulation: Gutta-percha, four layers, each separated by four thin layers of Chatterton's Compound. The weight of the insulation, 400 pounds per nautical mile. Diameter of core; .464"; circumference of core, 1.46".

External Protection: Ten solid wires .095" in diameter, each wire surrounded separately with five strands of Manila yarn, saturated with a preservative compound, the whole laid spirally round the core, which is padded with ordinary hemp saturated with a preservative mixture.

Circumference of Finished Cable: 3.534".

Weight in Air: 3,575 pounds per nautical mile.

Weight in Water: 1,400 pounds per nautical mile.

Breaking Strain: 15,500 pounds, or equal to eleven times the cable's weight in water per nautical mile.

Deepest Water on North Atlantic Route: 2,400 fathoms, or 14,400 feet.

Length of Cable Shipped: 2,300 nautical miles.

Source: Sir William Thomson Kelvin, "On the Forces Concerned in the Laying and Lifting of Deep-Sea Cables," in Finn, *Development of Submarine Cable Communications*, 164–65.

Notes

Abbreviations for Notes

CUC	Cooper Union Collection
LC	Library of Congress
NA	National Archives
NMM	National Maritime Museum
NOLS	Naval Observatory Letters Sent
NYPL	New York Public Library
RG	Record Group
SIA	Smithsonian Institution Archives

Chapter 1

1. *Hawkins Electrical Guide*, 10 vols. (New York: Theo Audel & Company, 1917), Introduction (no page number).

2. Ibid., 1:3; 8:2,411; James D. Reid, *The Telegraph in America: Its Founders, Promoters, and Noted Men* (New York: Arno Press, 1974), 9–16.

3. Sir William H. Russell, *The Atlantic Telegraph, 1865* (London: Dawson, 1866), 2. Vespucci was an Italian navigator who discovered and explored the mounds of the Amazon in 1499 and declared South America a new continent. He evolved a system for computing nearly exact longitude. His name has been fallaciously connected with Columbus' discoveries, which occurred seven years before the Spanish crown honored Vespucci by naming the New World America.

4. *The Atlantic Telegraph: Its History from the Commencement of the Undertaking in 1854 to the Sail of the* Great Eastern *in 1866* (London: Bacon & Company, 1866), 5–6.

5. Reid, *Telegraph in America*, 17, 69, 70–71.
6. Ibid., 71.
7. Ibid., 71–72.
8. Ibid., 75–77; *Hawkins Electrical Guide*, 1:53–59.
9. Reid, *Telegraph in America*, 73–86.
10. *Joseph Henry, A Memorial*, Smithsonian Institution Archives, printed by order of Congress, 1880.
11. Quoted in Reid, *Telegraph in America*, 79–80.
12. Ibid., 93.
13. J. J. Fahie, *A History of Electric Telegraphy, to the Year 1837* (London: E. and F. N. Spon, 1884), 431.
14. Quotes in Samuel I. Prime, *The Life of Samuel F. B. Morse* (New York: Arno Press, 1974), 616; Miriam Gurko, *The Lives and Times of Peter Cooper* (New York: Thomas Y. Crowell, 1959), 151; Reid, *Telegraph in America*, 101.
15. Quoted in Arthur C. Clarke, *Voice Across the Sea* (New York: Harper & Row, 1974), 22.
16. Samuel Morse to Sidney Morse, May 31, 1844, Samuel F. B. Morse Papers, vol. 18, LC. See also entry on May 25, 1844, in "Journal of the Magnetic Telegraph between Washington and Baltimore" in Alfred Vail Papers, SIA.
17. Quotes in Reid, *Telegraph in America*, 107–108, 112.
18. Robert Luther Thompson, *Wiring a Continent: The History of the Telegraph Industry in the United States 1832–1866* (Princeton, N.J.: Princeton University Press, 1947), 31–34.
19. Clarke, *Voice Across the Sea*, 24; *The Atlantic Telegraph: Its History*, 7.
20. Charles Bright, *Submarine Telegraphs: Their History, Construction, and Working* (London: Crosby, Lockwood & Son, 1898), 5–13l; R. S. Newell, "Facts and Observations Relating to the Invention of the Submarine Cable," in Bernard S. Finn, ed., *Development of Submarine Cable Communications*, 2 vols. (New York: Arno Press, 1980), 1:3–4.
21. Quote in S. A. Garnham and Robert L. Hadfield, *The Submarine Cable* (London: Sampson, Low, Marsten & Company, 1962), 1; Bright, *Submarine Telegraphs*, 248.
22. Reid, *Telegraph in America*, 398; Henry M. Field, *History of the Atlantic Telegraph* (Freeport, N.Y.: Books for Libraries, 1972), 15–16.
23. Reid, *Telegraph in America*, 399; Talafierro P. Shaffner, *The Telegraph Manual* (New York: Pudney & Russell, 1859), 616.
24. Henry M. Field, *The Story of the Atlantic Telegraph* (New York: Scribner's 1892), 11–12.
25. Morse to editor of *Scientific American*, April 23, 1864, draft of letter in Morse Papers.
26. Field, *Story of the Atlantic Telegraph*, 15.

CHAPTER 2

1. Quoted in Isabella Field Judson, *Cyrus W. Field: His Life and Work* (New York: Harper & Brothers, 1896), 58.
2. Quoted in Samuel Carter, III, *Cyrus Field: Man of Two Worlds* (New York: G. P. Putnam's Sons, 1968), 94.

3. Judson, *Cyrus Field*, 56.
4. Field, *Story of the Atlantic Telegraph*, 16–17.
5. Quoted in Carter, *Cyrus Field*, 97.
6. Matthew F. Maury, *Physical Geography of the Sea*, 1st ed. (New York: Harper and Brothers, 1855), 200–201.
7. Ibid., 206.
8. Quoted in Frances Leigh Williams, *Matthew Fontaine Maury: Scientist of the Sea* (New Brunswick, N.J.: Rutgers University Press, 1963), 229.
9. George M. Brooke, Jr., *John M. Brooke: Naval Scientist and Educator* (Charlottesville: University Press of Virginia, 1980), 55–58.
10. Maury to Dobbin, February 22, 1854, NOLS, vol. 10, RG 78, NA.
11. Maury to Morse, February 23, 1854, and Maury to Field, February 24, 1854, NOLS, vol. 10, RG 78, NA.
12. Bright, *Submarine Telegraphs*, 29.
13. Maury to Field, February 24, 1854, NOLS.
14. Morse to Kendall, January 8, 1855, in Edward Lind Morse, ed., *Samuel F. B. Morse: His Letters and Journals*, 2 vols. (Boston: Houghton Mifflin, 1914), 2:336.
15. Field, *Story of the Atlantic Telegraph*, 22, 25.
16. Cooper Union is still the only major tuition-free technical college in the United States.
17. Gurko, *Peter Cooper*, 152.
18. Peter Cooper, "Reminiscences," CUC.
19. Field, *History of the Atlantic Telegraph*, 39.
20. Field, *Story of the Atlantic Telegraph*, 28–29.
21. Ibid., 28–30.
22. Field, *History of the Atlantic Telegraph*, 41–42; Edward C. Mack, *Peter Cooper: Citizen of New York* (New York: Duell, Sloan & Pearce, 1949), 219.
23. Mack, *Peter Cooper*, 222–23.
24. Judson, *Cyrus Field*, 62.
25. David Dudley Field, Jr. Speech, September 1, 1858, Field Papers, NYPL.
26. Ibid.
27. Copy of "An Act to Incorporate a Company under the style and title of The New York, Newfoundland, and London Telegraph Company," passed by the Newfoundland legislature on April 15, 1854, in Morse Papers, vol. 33.
28. Field, *Story of the Atlantic Telegraph*, 34–36.
29. Maury to Field, April 21, 1854, NOLS, vol. 10.
30. Copy of agreement incorporating the New York, Newfoundland, and London Telegraph Company, May 8, 1854, in Morse Papers, vol. 33.
31. Field, *Story of the Atlantic Telegraph*, 38.

CHAPTER 3

1. Cyrus Field to Morse, July 13, 1854, Morse Papers, vol. 33; Morse to Field, July 16, 1856, Letter Book A, Morse Papers; Carlton Mabee, *The American Leonardo: The Life of Samuel F. B. Morse* (New York: Alfred P. Knopf, 1943), 323.
2. Kendall to Morse, June 5 and June 10, 1854, Morse Papers, vol. 33; Morse to Kendall, June 13, 1854, Letter Book A, Morse Papers.

3. Morse to Kendall, June 20 and July 2, 1855, Letter Book A, Morse Papers.
4. Field, *History of the Atlantic Telegraph*, 53–54.
5. Field, *Story of the Atlantic Telegraph*, 42–44.
6. Quoted in Carter, *Cyrus Field*, 110.
7. Maury to Lucian Minor, August 9, 1955, Maury Papers, vol. 4, LC.
8. Peter Cooper, "Reminiscences," CUC.
9. Ibid.
10. Ibid.
11. Ibid.
12. Reid, *Telegraph in America*, 407, 413.
13. Peter Cooper, "Reminiscences," CUC.
14. Taliaferro P. Shaffner to Morse, January 9, 1848, Morse to Shaffner, January 21, 1848, and Shaffner to Morse, January 27, 1848, vol. 23, Morse Papers.
15. Thompson, *Wiring a Continent*, 303, 305.
16. Kendall to Morse, October 1, 1855, vol. 35, Morse Papers.
17. Kendall to Morse, December 7, 1855, vol. 35, Morse Papers.
18. Thomas R. Walker to Morse, March 6, 1856, Vol. 36, Morse Papers. See also Morse to Walker, December 15, 1855, Letter Book B, Morse Papers.
19. Field to Maury, June 22, 1855, with Resolutions signed by Peter Cooper, Maury Papers, vol. 4.
20. Maury to Field, May 1856, reiterated July 21, 1858, in Naval Records, NOLS, vol. 15.
21. Maury to Field, June 13, 1856, Navy Records, NOLS, vol. 13.
22. Maury to Dobbin, May 5, 1856, Navy Records, NOLS, vol. 13.
23. Maury to Field, May 7, 1857, Navy Records, NOLS, vol. 14.
24. Maury to Toucey, May 11, 1857, NOLS, vol. 14.
25. Maury, *Explanations and Sailing Directions to Accompany the Wind and Current Charts*, 8th ed. (Washington, D.C.: William A. Harris, 1858), 1: 183.
26. Maury to Dobbin, February 22, 1854, Navy Records, NOLS, vol. 10. The tiny crustaceans live short lives near the surface of the ocean, sinking to the bottom as they die. Through the ages the shells collected, piling upwards, and where they break through the surface, create formations like the chalk cliffs of England, which eons ago were once under water. See Charles Bright, *The Story of the Atlantic Cable* (New York: D. Appleton and Company, 1903), 33–34.
27. Dayman's report in Field, *Story of the Atlantic Telegraph*, 73. A fathom is six feet, and 2,400 fathoms translate into 14,400 feet, or 2.38 nautical miles.
28. Ibid., 61–64.

CHAPTER 4

1. Field Speech, November 15, 1866, Field Papers, NYPL.
2. Bright, *Story of the Atlantic Cable*, 28.
3. Ibid., 37.
4. Ibid., 43.
5. Russell, *The Atlantic Telegraph*, 10–11.
6. Prime, *Life of Morse*, 2:645.
7. Field, *Story of the Atlantic Telegraph*, 80.

8. Bright, *Story of the Atlantic Cable*, 43–44.

9. Ibid., 44–45.

10. C. Bright, *Submarine Telegraphs*, 30.

11. Quoted in Patrick Beaver, *The Big Ship: Brunel's* Great Eastern (London: Bibliophile Books, 1969), 89.

12. C. Bright, *Submarine Telegraphs*, 31–32; Judson, *Cyrus Field*, 70. Today, the capitalization of the Atlantic Telegraph Company would equal about one billion dollars.

13. Quotes in Judson, *Cyrus Field*, 69.

14. Wilson to Field, November 20, 1856, Field Papers.

15. Morse to Field, October 10, 1856, Field Papers.

16. Quoted in Field, *History of the Atlantic Telegraph*, 92.

17. Quoted in Clarke, *Voice Across the Sea*, 40. Thomson became the first scientist to attain peerage as Lord Kelvin of Kargs. His many accomplishments included 300 books and papers, the design of the gyroscopic compass in 1883, and the absolute scale for determining temperature (degrees Kelvin). His long and eventful life (1824–1907) spanned the technological gap between the first steam locomotive and the first airplane.

18. Bright, *Story of the Atlantic Cable*, 47; Bright, *Submarine Telegraphs*, 54; John Merrett, *Three Miles Deep: The Story of Transatlantic Cables* (London: Hamish Hamilton, 1958), 51–52; Reid, *Telegraph in America*, 19, 74–75.

19. Merrett, *Three Miles Deep*, 52.

20. Russell, *The Atlantic Telegraph*, 12.

21. Seward quoted in Bern Dibner, *The Atlantic Cable* (Norwalk, Conn.: Burdy Library, 1959), 18.

22. Maury to Field, January 22, 1857, Navy Records, NOLS, vol. 14.

23. Cooper to Morse, March 10, 1857, vol. 36, Morse Papers.

24. Field, *History of the Atlantic Telegraph*, 118.

25. Ibid; Judson, *Cyrus Field*, 76.

26. Judson, *Cyrus Field*, 77.

27. Field, *Story of the Atlantic Telegraph*, 102.

28. Bright, *Story of the Atlantic Cable*, 48.

29. Ibid., 46–50.

CHAPTER 5

1. Maury to Field, December 27, 1856, Navy Records, NOLS, vol. 14.

2. Field, *History of the Atlantic Telegraph*, 118.

3. Ibid., 119–21.

4. Debates over the Atlantic cable are abridged in H. Field, *Story of the Atlantic Telegraph*, 97–111.

5. Field, *History of the Atlantic Telegraph*, 123–24.

6. John Mullaly, *The Laying of the Cable or The Ocean Telegraph, Being a Complete and Authentic Narrative of the Attempt to Lay Cable* (New York: D. Appleton, 1858), 78.

7. Field, *Story of the Atlantic Telegraph*, 112–14.

8. *The Atlantic Telegraph. A History of Preliminary Experimental Proceedings*

and a Descriptive Account of the Present State and Prospects of the Undertaking (London, July 1857), 49–50.

9. Mullaly, *Laying of the Cable*, 79.

10. Field, *Story of the Atlantic Telegraph*, 113–15. Lady Franklin referred to the two Grinnell expeditions; the latter led by Elisha Kent Kane. Kane searched to the Lincoln Sea and never found the Franklin expedition but in 1855 established the record for having reached the farthest northern latitude.

11. Ibid., 117–18.

12. London *Times*, July 24, 1857; James Buchanan to Cyrus Field, July 3, 1857, Field Papers.

13. London *Times*, August 3, 1857.

14. Ibid.

15. Ibid.; Russell, *The Atlantic Telegraph*, 20.

16. London *Times*, August 5, 1857.

17. Field, *History of the Atlantic Telegraph*, 153.

18. Morse, *Samuel F. B. Morse*, 2:376–77; Prime, *Life of Morse*, 655–56.

19. Morse to Mrs. Morse, August 4, 1857, vol. 37, Morse Papers.

20. Mullaly, *Laying of the Cable*, 139–40; Morse to Mrs. Morse, August 4, 1857, vol. 37, Morse Papers; E. Morse, *Samuel F. B. Morse*, 2:379.

21. Mullaly, *Laying of the Cable*, 141.

22. Field, *History of the Atlantic Telegraph*, 154–55.

23. Morse, *Samuel F. B. Morse*, 2:240; Bright, *Story of the Atlantic Cable*, 66; Mullaly, *Laying of the Cable*, 144.

24. Mullaly, *Laying of the Cable*. 144, 146.

25. Morse to Mrs. Morse, August 10, 1857, vol. 37, Morse Papers; Bright, *Story of the Atlantic Cable*, 67.

26. Morse to Mrs. Morse, August 10, 1857, vol. 37, Morse Papers; Prime, *Life of Morse*, 659.

27. Mullaly, *Laying of the Cable*, 149.

28. Morse to Mrs. Morse, August 10, 1857, vol. 37, Morse Papers; Prime, *Life of Morse*, 659.

29. Bright, *Story of the Atlantic Cable*, 70–71.

30. Judson, *Cyrus Field*, 83.

31. Ibid.

32. Morse to Mrs. Morse, August 12, 1857, vol. 37, Morse Papers.

33. Quoted in Dibner, *The Atlantic Cable*, 24.

34. Morse to Mrs. Morse, August 13, 1857, vol. 37, Morse Papers.

35. Field to Mary Field, August 13, 1857, Field papers.

CHAPTER 6

1. Field, *Story of the Atlantic Telegraph*, 138–40.
2. Bright, *Story of the Atlantic Cable*, 74–75.
3. Shaffner, *Telegraph Manual*, 629–30.
4. Ibid., 631–34.
5. Thompson, *Wiring a Continent*, 310.
6. Field, *History of the Atlantic Telegraph*, 167.

7. Morse to Richard Morse, October 15, 1857, Letter Book C, Morse Papers.
8. Kendall to Morse, March 15, 1858, vol. 38, Morse Papers.
9. Minutes of the Atlantic Telegraph Company, January 27 and March 26, 1858, Field Papers.
10. Morse to Cyrus Field, Letter Book C, March 12, 1858, Morse Papers.
11. Field, *History of the Atlantic Telegraph*, 173–74.
12. Ibid., 177.
13. C. Bright, *Story of the Atlantic Cable*, 89.
14. Field, *History of the Atlantic Telegraph*, 178.
15. Bright, *Story of the Atlantic Cable*, 91; Mullaly, *Laying of the Cable*, 228.
16. Mullaly, *Laying of the Cable*, 226.
17. Ibid., 230.
18. Ibid., 231.
19. London *Times*, July 13, 1858.
20. Mullaly, *Laying of the Cable*, 231.
21. Ibid., 233.
22. Nicholas Wood, London *Times*, July 13, 1858.
23. Field, *History of the Atlantic Telegraph*, 181.

CHAPTER 7

1. Log of *Niagara*, June 26, 1858, Navy Records, NA.
2. Bright, *Story of the Atlantic Cable*, 108.
3. Quoted in Carter, *Cyrus Field*, 153.
4. Field, *History of the Atlantic Telegraph*, 184–85.
5. Log of *Niagara*, June 29, 1858, Navy Records, NA.
6. Bright, *Story of the Atlantic Cable*, 112.
7. Ibid., 113.
8. Ibid.
9. William Brown to Field, July 12, 1858, Field Papers.
10. Bright, *Story of the Atlantic Cable*, 186; Field, *History of the Atlantic Telegraph*, 188.
11. Field, *Story of the Atlantic Telegraph*, 165.

CHAPTER 8

1. Bright, *Story of the Atlantic Cable*, 116.
2. Nicholas Wood, London *Times*, August 11, 1858.
3. Field, *History of the Atlantic Telegraph*, 190. Salt horse is not horse meat but salted beef.
4. Field Diary, July 26, 27, 1858, quoted in Mullaly, *Laying of the Cable*, 304.
5. Ibid., July 28, 1858.
6. London *Times*, August 11, 1858.
7. Field Diary, July 29, 1858, quoted in Mullaly, *Laying of the Cable*, 284.
8. Ibid.
9. London *Times*, August 11, 1858.
10. Mullaly, *Laying of the Cable*, 248.

11. London *Times*, August 11, 1858.

12. From the *Sydney Morning Herald*, quoted in Clarke, *Voice Across the Sea*, 57.

13. Field Diary, July 29, 1858, in Mullaly, *Laying of the Cable*, 305.

14. London *Times*, August 11, 1858.

15. Mullaly, *Laying of the Cable*, 306.

16. Field Journal, August 4, 1858, in Mullaly, *Laying of the Cable*, 306–7.

17. London *Times*, August 11, 1858.

18. Judson, *Cyrus Field*, 94.

19. Mullaly, *Laying of the Cable*, 287–88, 307.

20. Field to Mary Field, and Field to Associated Press, August 5, 1858, Field Papers; Mullaly, *Laying of the Cable*, 308–9.

21. Field to President Buchanan, August 5, 1858, Field Papers.

22. Field to Peter Cooper, August 5, 1858, ibid.

23. Engineer's Log of the *Niagara*, August 5, 1858, Navy Records.

24. London *Times*, 2nd ed., August 5, 1858.

25. London *Times*, August 7, 1858.

CHAPTER 9

1. Hewitt to Eleanor Cooper, August 12, 1858, Hewitt Papers, CUC.

2. Morse, *Samuel F. B. Morse*, 2:386–87.

3. London *Times*, August 6, 1858.

4. Ibid.

5. Ibid.

6. Field, *History of the Atlantic Telegraph*, 219–20.

7. Ibid., 221.

8. James Buchanan to Cyrus Field, August 5, 1858, Field Papers.

9. Quotes in Philip B. McDonald, *A Saga of the Seas: The Story of Cyrus W. Field and the Laying of the First Atlantic Cable*, (New York: Wilson-Erickson, 1937) 1.

10. Russell, *The Atlantic Telegraph*, 26.

11. Ibid.

12. Queen Victoria to President Buchanan, August 16, 1858, Buchanan Papers, LC.

13. President Buchanan to Queen Victoria, August 16, 1858, Buchanan Papers.

14. Field, *History of the Atlantic Telegraph*, 235.

15. Field to Directors, August 18, 1858, Field Papers.

16. Saward to Field, August 6, 1858, Field Papers.

17. Field, *History of the Atlantic Telegraph*, 255, 256.

18. Ibid. 255.

19. Bright, *Story of the Atlantic Cable*, 149.

20. New York *Times*, August 27, 1858. Daniel F. Tiemann was New York's mayor from 1858 to 1860. He married Martha Clowes, a niece of Peter Cooper.

21. Henry to Bache, August 31, 1858, Joseph Henry Papers, SIA.

22. Edward Brailsford Bright, *The Life Story of the Late Sir Charles Tilston Bright*. 2 vols. (Westminster, U.K.: Archibald Constable & Company 1898), 1:343.

23. London *Daily News*, August 20, 1858.

24. Bright, *Life of Bright*, 1:325.

25. Quoted from the *Morning Post* by E. Bright, in *Life of Bright*, 1: 324–25, 326 n1.

26. David Dudley Field, Jr.'s speech appeared in the New York *Times*, September 2, 1858. See also Field Papers.

27. Judson, *Cyrus Field*, 243–44; New York *Times*, September 2, 1858.

28. Field's speech, New York *Times*, September 3, 1858.

29. Telegram to Field, September 2, 1858, Field Papers; New York *Times*, September 3, 1858.

30. Peabody to Field, August 15, 1858, Field Papers.

31. London *Times*, September 6, 1858; Russell, *The Atlantic Telegraph*, 27–28.

32. De Sauty to Field, September 25, 1858, Field Papers.

33. Maury to Field, September 28, 1858, Navy Records, NOLS, vol. 16, NA; Joseph Henry to Bache, September 28, 1858, Joseph Henry Papers, SIA.

34. Bright, *Life of Bright*, 1:98–99; Field, *History of the Atlantic Telegraph*, 247.

35. Field, *History of the Atlantic Telegraph*, 245.

CHAPTER 10

1. Field, *History of the Atlantic Telegraph*, 246–48.

2. T. A. Masey, "The Submarine Telegraph," *The Electrician* February 6, 1863, 160. Bright counted 732 messages, but some were unintelligible. See Bright, *Submarine Telegraphs*, 50.

3. Mabee, *The American Leonardo*, 337.

4. Morse to John Brett, December 27, 1858, Letter Book C, Morse Papers.

5. Bright, *Life of Bright*, 1:333–34.

6. Bright, *Submarine Telegraphs*, 52.

7. George Saward, *The Transatlantic Submarine Telegraph* (London, 1878), 33.

8. Morse to the Provisional Committee of the Atlantic Telegraph Company, no date, Letter Book D, Morse Papers.

9. Bright, *Life of Bright*, 1:348–49.

10. Arthur Dearlove, "Lord Kelvin and Submarine Telegraphy," *The Electrician* June 19, 1896, 236.

11. Bright, *Life of Bright*, 1:353.

12. Ibid., 354.

13. Bright, *Story of the Atlantic Cable*, 157.

14. Ibid.; E. Bright, *Life of Bright*, 1:357–58.

15. William Thomson, "The Electric Telegraph," *The Encyclopedia Britannica*, 8th edition, 1860, quoted in Bright, *Life of Bright*, 1:358–59.

16. Field, *History of the Atlantic Telegraph*, 252.

17. Quoted in John A. Stevens, Jr., *Report of Proceedings of a Meeting Called to Further the Enterprise of the Atlantic Cable* (New York, 1863), 8.

18. Shaffner, *Telegraph Manual*, 648.

19. Carter, *Cyrus Field*, 179.

20. Edward O. W. Whitehouse, *Reply to the Statement of the Directors of the Atlantic Telegraph Company* (London, 1858), 10.
21. Ibid., 1–27 *passim.*

CHAPTER 11

1. Bright, *Life of Bright*, 1:364.
2. Shaffner, *Telegraph Manual*, 843.
3. Financial records of the New York, Newfoundland, and London Telegraph Company are in the Field Papers.
4. Shaffner, *Telegraph Manual*, 840–44.
5. Ibid., 843.
6. Masey, "The Submarine Telegraph," 161.
7. Bright, *Life of Bright*, 1:488.
8. Ibid., 1:490.
9. Ibid., 1:482, 491–92.
10. McClintock's Report, December 6, 1860, in E. Bright, *Life of Bright*, 1:482.
11. Bright, *Life of Bright*, 1:492–93.
12. Ibid., 1:362.
13. Quoted in Bright, *Story of the Atlantic Cable*, 166.
14. Masey, "The Submarine Telegraph," 161.

CHAPTER 12

1. Field, *History of the Atlantic Telegraph*, 263.
2. Masey, "The Submarine Telegraph," 160.
3. Russell, *The Atlantic Telegraph*, 112, 114.
4. Judson, *Cyrus Field*, 125–26.
5. Quoted in Field, *History of the Atlantic Telegraph*, 266.
6. Ibid., 269.
7. Judson, *Cyrus Field*, 136.
8. McClellan to Field, December 12, 1861, Field Papers.
9. Judson, *Cyrus Field*, 137–38.
10. Seward to Field, January 9, 1862, Field Papers.
11. Judson, *Cyrus Field*, 139.
12. Quoted in Carter, *Cyrus Field*, 194.
13. Quoted in David Homer Bates, *Lincoln in the Telegraph Office* (New York: D. Appleton-Century, 1939), 257–58.
14. James D. Richardson, *A Compilation of the Messages and Papers of the Presidents, 1789–1902*, 11 vols. (Washington, D.C.: Bureau of National Literature and Art, 1907), 6:181.
15. Albert A. Woldman, *Lincoln and the Russians* (Cleveland: World Publishing Company, 1952), 279.
16. Bates, *Lincoln in the Telegraph Office*, 257.
17. Judson, *Cyrus Field*, 139–40, 143–44.
18. Quotes in Carter, *Cyrus Field*, 195–96.
19. Reuter to Field, November 19, 1862, Field Papers.

20. Judson, *Cyrus Field*, 141.
21. Ibid., 141–42.
22. Ibid., 144.
23. *The Atlantic Telegraph: A History*, 95.
24. Mabee, *The American Leonardo*, 337–38; Thompson, *Wiring a Continent*, 329, 331–35, 342.
25. Judson, *Cyrus Field*, 145.
26. Glass, Elliot & Company to Field, February 17 and October 20, 1862, Field Papers.

CHAPTER 13

1. Field to Saward, January 27, 1863, Field Papers.
2. Minutes from Chamber of Commerce meeting, March 4, 1863, Field Papers.
3. Resolution of the New York Chamber of Commerce, March 4, 1863, Field Papers.
4. Field, *History of the Atlantic Telegraph*, 272.
5. Field to Saward, March 24, 27, and May 8, 1863, Field Papers.
6. Field & Company financial report, July 18, 1863, Field Papers.
7. Saward to Field, June 16, 1863, Field Papers.
8. Field & Company to Field, July 1, 1863, Field Papers.
9. Judson, *Cyrus Field*, 160–61.
10. Field & Company to Field, July 15, 1863, Field Papers.
11. Judson, *Cyrus Field*, 159.
12. Chase to Field, August 18, 1863, Field Papers.
13. Chase to Field, October 7, 1863, Field Papers. Field to Chase, October 9, 1863, Chase Papers, LC.
14. Judson, *Cyrus Field*, 171.
15. *Telegraphic Journal*, February 6, 1864, NMM.
16. Sir Arthur Helps, *Life and Labours of Mr. Brassey* (New York: Augustus M. Kelley, 1969), 161–68, 308. In Helps' 386-page biography of Thomas Brassey, he never mentioned his subject's involvement in the Atlantic cable. Brassey later received a peerage, becoming Civil Lord and Secretary of the Admiralty.
17. Judson, *Cyrus Field*, 172.
18. Ibid., 172–73; Willoughby Smith, *The Rise and Extension of Submarine Telegraphy* (London: J. S. Virtue & Company, 1891), 117–18.
19. James Dugan, *The Great Iron Ship* (New York: Harper and Bros., 1953), 20–21.
20. Ibid., 73.

CHAPTER 14

1. Quoted in Dugan, *Great Iron Ship*, 2.
2. Ibid., 9; London *Times*, November 2, 1857.
3. Dugan, *Great Iron Ship*, 12.
4. Ibid., 13.
5. Beaver, *The Big Ship*, 55, 57; Clarke, *Voice Across the Sea*, 124.

6. Roger Burdett Wilson, ed., *Sir Daniel Gooch: Memoirs & Diary* (Newton Abbot, U.K.: David & Charles, 1972), 76–77.
7. Ibid., 78.
8. Ibid.
9. Ibid., 81.
10. Ibid., 90.
11. Ibid., 92; Dugan, *Great Iron Ship*, 160–61.
12. Wilson, *Gooch Memoirs & Diary*, 92; Quote in Helps, *Life and Labours of Mr. Brassey*, 280–81.
13. Anderson to Field, October 25, 1864, Field Papers.
14. Bright, *Submarine Telegraphs*, 86; K. R. Haigh, *Cableships and Submarine Cables* (London: A. Giles, 1968), 58.
15. Haigh, *Cableships*, 58–59; C. Bright, *Submarine Telegraphs*, 87.
16. Judson, *Cyrus Field*, 179.
17. Ibid., 180–81. General Dix, in his autobiography, sets the time of the incident in December. The St. Albans raid occurred on October 19, 1864. See *War of the Rebellion, A Compilation of the Official Records of the Union and Confederate Armies* (Washington D.C.: Government Printing Office, 1893), vol. 43, part 2, 420–21.
18. The two Confederate commerce raiders built by the British were *Florida* and *Alabama*. Two others, *Georgia* and *Shenandoah*, were converted from British merchant vessels.
19. Anderson to Field, March 19, 1865, Field Papers.
20. Judson, *Cyrus Field*, 186.
21. Russell, *The Atlantic Telegraph*, 41.
22. London *Star*, May 4, 1865.
23. Field, *History of the Atlantic Telegraph*, 296, 297–98.
24. Ibid., 298.

Chapter 15

1. Wilson, *Gooch Memoirs and Diary*, 97; London *Times*, June 19, 1865.
2. Field, *History of the Atlantic Telegraph*, 300.
3. Ibid., 302–303.
4. Ibid., 303, 305.
5. Ibid., 305; Smith, *Submarine Telegraphy*, 133.
6. Smith, *Submarine Telegraphy*, 133.
7. Ibid., 134.
8. Wilson, *Gooch Memoirs and Diary*, 98.
9. Ibid.
10. Werner von Siemens of Germany created the great electronics conglomerate that still bears his name.
11. Russell, *The Atlantic Telegraph*, 46–50; R. Routledge, "Making and Laying Submarine Cables," in Finn, *Development of Submarine Cable Communications*, 1:168.
12. Field to Mary Field, July 22, 1865, Field Papers.
13. Russell, *The Atlantic Telegraph*, 51; Field, *Story of the Atlantic Telegraph*, 309.

14. Russell, *The Atlantic Telegraph*, 51.
15. Field, *History of the Atlantic Telegraph*, 310.
16. Smith, *Submarine Telegraphy*, 137, 335–54.
17. Field, *History of the Atlantic Telegraph*, 311.
18. Ibid., 313.
19. Russell, *The Atlantic Telegraph*, 60; Daniel Gooch Diary, July 25, 1865, Birmingham City Archives.
20. Russell, *The Atlantic Telegraph*, 63.
21. Ibid., 64.
22. Ibid., 69.
23. Ibid., 71.
24. Field, *History of the Atlantic Telegraph*, 316.
25. Ibid., 317.
26. Russell, *The Atlantic Telegraph*, 77–78.
27. From "The Atlantic Telegraph," in Judson, *Cyrus Field*, 194.
28. Wilson, *Gooch Memoirs and Diary*, 100–101.

CHAPTER 16

1. Russell, *The Atlantic Telegraph*, 81.
2. Log of *Great Eastern*, August 4, 1865, NMM.
3. Wilson, *Gooch Memoirs and Diary*, 101.
4. Russell, *The Atlantic Telegraph*, 94.
5. Ibid., 94–95; Log of *Great Eastern*, August 11, 1865.
6. Judson, *Cyrus Field*, 195; Russell, *The Atlantic Telegraph*, 95.
7. Field, *History of the Atlantic Telegraph*, 322.
8. Ibid., 286.

CHAPTER 17

1. Dugan, *Great Iron Ship*, 185.
2. Russell, *The Atlantic Telegraph*, 97.
3. Dugan, *Great Iron Ship*, 185.
4. Russell, *The Atlantic Telegraph*, 99.
5. Wilson, *Gooch Memoirs and Diary*, 110; Carter, *Cyrus Field*, 334–35.
6. Judson, *Cyrus Field*, 197.
7. Anderson to Field, November 3, 1865, Field Papers.
8. Field to Saward, December 13, 1865, Field Papers.
9. Judson, *Cyrus Field*, 197.
10. Wilson, *Gooch Memoirs and Diary*, 110.
11. Judson, *Cyrus Field*, 199; Helps, *Life and Labours of Mr. Brassey*, 143–52.
12. Bright, *Story of the Atlantic Cable*, 189.
13. Quoted in Thompson, *Wiring a Continent*, 433.
14. John Bright to Field, March 26, 1866, Field Papers.
15. Richardson, *Messages and Papers of the Presidents*, 6:128, 181, 244, 455.
16. Field, *History of the Atlantic Telegraph*, 346; *The Atlantic Telegraph: Its*

History, 89; Haigh, *Cableships*, 59; Routledge, "Making and Laying Submarine Cables," 160–65.

17. Smith, *Submarine Telegraphy*, 142–43.
18. Haigh, *Cableships*, 30, 59–61.
19. Bright, *Life of Bright*, 1:392.
20. Gooch Diary, June 30, 1866, Birmingham City Archives.
21. Smith, *Submarine Telegraphy*, 148–61.
22. Wilson, *Gooch Memoirs and Diary*, 113; Smith, *Submarine Telegraphy*, 163–64.
23. Field, *History of the Atlantic Telegraph*, 349.
24. Ibid., 351; London *Daily News*, July 8, 1866.
25. Field, *Story of the Atlantic Telegraph*, 319.
26. Smith, *Submarine Telegraphy*, 168.
27. Wilson, *Gooch Memoirs and Diary*, 115.
28. Smith, *Submarine Telegraphy*, 170.
29. Gooch Diary, July 20, 1866.
30. Judson, *Cyrus Field*, 203.
31. Ibid.
32. Ibid.
33. Ibid.
34. Ibid., 205.
35. Ibid., 206.
36. Ibid.
37. Gooch Diary, July 27, 1866.
38. Field to the Associated Press, August 27, 1866, Field Papers.
39. Merrett, *Three Miles Deep*, 150.
40. Gooch Diary, July 28, 1866; Field to Mary Field, July 27, 1866, Field Papers.
41. Anderson to Mary Field, August 7, 1866, Field Papers.
42. Quoted in Carter, *Cyrus Field*, 255.
43. Routledge, "Making and Laying of Submarine Cables," 192–93.
44. Field's speech, made in London on March 10, 1868, in Field Papers.
45. Bright, *Story of the Atlantic Cable*, 201.
46. Deane's quotes in C. Bright, *Story of the Atlantic Cable*, 203; Dibner, *The Atlantic Cable*, 82; London *Times*, September 5, 1866.
47. Field to Mary Field, September 2, 1866, Field Papers.
48. Bright, *Story of the Atlantic Cable*, 206; Reid, *Telegraph in America*, 404.
49. Field's speech, March 10, 1868, Field Papers.
50. Anderson to Mary Field, September 9, 1866, Field Papers.

CHAPTER 18

1. Field, *Story of the Atlantic Telegraph*, 371.
2. Reid, *Telegraph in America*, 513; Masey, "The Submarine Telegraph," 162.
3. Reid, *Telegraph in America*, 508–10.
4. *The Atlantic Telegraph: Its History*, 97–102; Thompson, *Wiring a Continent*, 371–72, 410.
5. Morse to Collins, November 29, 1861, Letter Book E, Morse Papers.

6. George Kennan, *Tent Life in Siberia* (New York: G. P. Putnam's Sons, 1910), 411–18.

7. Ibid., 428–29; E. Morse, *Samuel F. B. Morse*, 2:444–46. For a recent history of the Russian cable, see Rosemary Neering, *Continental Dash* (Ganges, British Columbia: Horsdale & Schubert Publishers 1989).

8. Lord Derby to Sir Stafford Northcote, September 29, 1866, in Garnham and Hadfield, *Submarine Cable*, 158–59; Seward to Cyrus Field, January 7, 1869, Field Papers.

9. Quoted in Carter, *Cyrus Field*, 263.

10. Quoted in Merrett, *Three Miles Deep*, 150.

11. Quoted in Garnham and Hadfield, *Submarine Cable*, 153–54.

12. Mack, *Peter Cooper*, 227–28, 408 n.18.

13. Haigh, *Cableships*, 59.

14. Quoted in Clarke, *Voice Across the Sea*, 102.

15. Bill Scanlon, "20,000 Cables Under the Sea," *eWeek*, April 23, 2002.

16. Quotes from Andy Kessler, *Wall Street Journal*, March 21, 2002.

17. Quoted in Dugan, *Great Iron Ship*, 240.

18. Ibid., 241.

19. Wilson, *Gooch Memoirs and Diary*, August 26 and November (n.d.), 1888, 351–52.

20. Quoted in Dugan, *Great Iron Ship*, 267.

21. Mack, *Peter Cooper*, 180; Carter, *Cyrus Field*, 359.

22. Quoted in Carter, *Cyrus Field*, 361.

23. William Maxwell Evarts, October 6, 1892, in Judson, *Cyrus Field*, 330.

Bibliography

Documents

Birmingham City Archives, Birmingham, England
  Daniel Gooch Diary, 1865–1869
Cable and Wireless Archive, Porthcurno and Collections Trust, Porthcurno, Cornwall, U.K.
  Charles Bright Letter Book
  Charles Bright—Out Letter Book, Engineer's Office
Cooper Union, Cooper Union Collection, New York City
  Peter Cooper Autobiography
  Peter Cooper "Reminiscences"
  Peter Cooper—Abram Hewitt Papers
Library of Congress
  Papers of James Buchanan
  Papers of Salmon P. Chase
  Papers of Peter Cooper and Abram Hewitt
  Papers of Cyrus Field
  Papers of Matthew F. Maury
  Papers of Samuel F. B. Morse
National Archives and Records Administration
  Navy Records (NR)
    Naval Observatory Letters Sent (NOLS) Record Group 78
National Maritime Museum, Greenwich, London, U.K.
  Logbook of *Agamemnon*, 1857–1858, Record NVP/16
  Logbook of *Great Eastern*, 1865–1866, Record NVP/16
  Papers of the Telegraph and Maintenance Company, Record TCM/16
  Papers of *Great Eastern*, 1866, Record TCM/16
  Telegraphic Journal, Record THP/5

Log of the USS *Niagara*
New York Public Library, Manuscript Division
Papers of Cyrus Field
Smithsonian Institution Archives
Joseph Henry Papers
Joseph Henry, A Memorial, printed by order of Congress, 1880
Alfred Vail Papers
U.S. Department of State, "Communication of Hon. William H. Seward, Secretary of State, upon the subject of an intercontinental telegraph" (Washington, D.C.: Government Printing Office, 1864)
Yale University, Sterling Memorial Library
Field Family Collection (Group Number 630)

Newspapers

London *Daily News*
London Illustrated Times
London Illustrated News
London *Star*
London *Telegraphic Journal*
London *Times*
Wall Street Journal

Books and Articles

The Atlantic Telegraph. A History of Preliminary Experimental Proceedings and a Descriptive Account of the Present State and Prospects of the Undertaking. London: Atlantic Telegraph Company, Ltd., July 1857.

The Atlantic Telegraph: Its History from the Commencement of the Undertaking in 1854 to the Sail of the Great Eastern *in 1866*. London: Bacon & Company, 1866.

The Atlantic Telegraph: Report of the Proceedings at a Banquet, Given to Cyrus W. Field, By the Chamber of Commerce of New-York, at the Metropolitan Hotel, November 15th, 1866. New York: New York Chamber of Commerce, 1866.

Babcock, F. Lawrence. *Spanning the Atlantic*. New York: Alfred P. Knopf, 1931.

Bates, David Homer. *Lincoln in the Telegraph Office*. New York: D. Appleton-Century, 1907.

Beaver, Patrick. *The Big Ship: Brunel's* Great Eastern. London: Bibliophile Books, 1969.

Briggs, Charles F. and Augustus Maverick. *The Story of the Telegraph and a History of the Great Atlantic Cable*. New York: Rudd & Carleton, 1858.

Bright, Charles. "The Electric Telegraph." *The Encyclopedia Britannica*, 8th ed., 1860.

———. *The Story of the Atlantic Cable*. New York: D. Appleton and Company, 1903.

———. *Submarine Telegraphs: Their History, Construction, and Working*. London: Crosby Lockwood & Son, 1898.
Bright, Edward Brailsford. *The Life Story of the Late Sir Charles Tilston Bright*. 2 vols. Westminster, U.K.: Archibald Constable & Company, 1898.
Brooke, George M., Jr. *John M. Brooke: Naval Scientist and Educator*. Charlottesville: University Press of Virginia, 1980.
Brunel, Isambard. *The Life of Isambard Kingdom Brunel*. London: Longmans, Green, 1870.
Carter, Samuel, III. *Cyrus Field: Man of Two Worlds*. New York: G. P. Putnam's Sons, 1968.
Clarke, Arthur C. *Voice across the Sea*. New York: Harper & Row, 1974.
Collins, Perry McD. *Overland Explorations in Siberia, Northern Asia, and the Great Amoor River Country*. New York: D. Appleton, 1864.
Coon, Horace. *American Tel. & Tel., The Story of a Great Monopoly*. New York: Longmans, Green, 1939.
Dearlove, Arthur. "Lord Kelvin and Submarine Telegraphy." *The Electrician*, June 19, 1896, 236–38.
Dibner, Bern. *The Atlantic Cable*. Norwalk, Conn.: Burndy Library, 1959.
Dugan, James. *The Great Iron Ship*. New York: Harper and Bros., 1953.
Dwyer, John B. *To Wire the World: Perry M. Collins and the North Pacific Telegraph Expedition*. Westport, Conn.: Praeger, 2000.
Fahie, J. J. *A History of Electric Telegraphy to the Year 1837*. London: E. and F. N. Spon, 1884.
"Failure to Lay the Atlantic Cable." *U.S. Nautical Magazine and Naval Journal* 6 (September 1857): 464–71.
Field, Henry. *History of the Atlantic Telegraph*. Freeport, N.Y.: Books for Libraries, 1972.
———. *The Story of the Atlantic Telegraph*. New York: Scribner's, 1892.
Finn, Bernard S., ed. *Development of Submarine Cable Communications*. 2 vols. New York: Arno Press, 1980.
Garnham, S. A., and Robert L. Hadfield. *The Submarine Cable*. London: Sampson, Low, Marston & Company, 1962.
Gooch, Sir Daniel. *Diaries of Sir Daniel Gooch, Baronet*. London: Kegan Paul, Trench, Trubner & Co. Ltd., 1892.
Gurko, Miriam. *The Lives and Times of Peter Cooper*. New York: Thomas Y. Crowell, 1959.
Haigh, K. R. *Cableships and Submarine Cables*. London: A. Giles, 1968.
Hawkins Electrical Guide. 10 vols. New York: Theo Audel & Company, 1917.
Hearn, Chester G. *Tracks in the Sea: Matthew Fontaine Maury and the Mapping of the Oceans*. Camden, Maine: International Marine/McGraw-Hill, 2002.
Helps, Sir Arthur. *Life and Labours of Mr. Brassey*. New York: Augustus M. Kelley, 1969.
Judson, Isabella Field. *Cyrus W. Field, His Life and Work*. New York: Harper & Brothers, 1896.
Kennan, George. *Tent Life in Siberia*. New York: G. P. Putnam's Sons, 1910.
Latham, Jean Lee. *Young Man in a Hurry: The Story of Cyrus Field*. New York: Harper & Bros., 1958.

Mabee, Carlton. *The American Leonardo: the Life of Samuel F. B. Morse*. New York: Alfred P. Knopf, 1943.

Mack, Edward C. *Peter Cooper, Citizen of New York*. New York: Duell, Sloan & Pearce, 1949.

Masey, T. A. "The Submarine Telegraph." *The Electrician*, February 6, 1863, 157–63.

Maury, Matthew F. *Explanations and Sailing Directions to Accompany the Wind and Current Charts*. 8th ed. 2 vols. Washington, D.C.: William A. Harris (vol. 1), 1858; Cornelius Wendell (vol. 2), 1859.

———. *Physical Geography of the Sea*. 1st ed. New York: Harper and Brothers, 1855.

McDonald, Philip B. *A Saga of the Seas: The Story of Cyrus W. Field and the Laying of the First Atlantic Cable*. New York: Wilson-Erickson, 1937.

Merrett, John. *Three Miles Deep: The Story of the Transatlantic Cables*. London: Hamish Hamilton, 1958.

Morse, Edward Lind, ed. *Samuel F. B. Morse: His Letters and Journals*. 2 vols. Boston: Houghton Mifflin, 1914.

Mullaly, John. *The Laying of the Cable or The Ocean Telegraph, Being a Complete and Authentic Narrative of the Attempt to Lay the Cable*. New York: D. Appleton, 1858.

Neering, Rosemary. *Continental Dash: The Russian-American Telegraph*. Ganges, British Columbia: Horsdal & Schubert Publishers Ltd., 1989.

Prescott, George B. *History, Theory, and Practice of the Electric Telegraph*. Boston: Ticknor and Fields, 1860.

Prime, Samuel I. *The Life of Samuel F. B. Morse*. New York: Arno Press, 1974.

Reid, James D. *The Telegraph in America: Its Founders, Promoters, and Noted Men*. New York: Arno Press, 1974.

Richardson, James D. *A Compilation of the Messages and Papers of the Presidents, 1789–1902*. 11 vols. Washington, D.C.: Bureau of National Literature and Art, 1907.

Rolt, L.T.C. *Isambard Kingdom Brunel*. New York: St. Martin's Press, 1959.

Russell, Sir William H. *The Atlantic Telegraph, 1865*. London: Dawson, 1866.

Saward, George. *The Transatlantic Submarine Telegraph*. London: privately printed, 1878.

Scanlon, Bill. "20,000 Cables Under the Sea." *eWeek*, April 23, 2002.

Shaffner, Taliaferro P. *The Telegraph Manual*. New York: Pudney & Russell, 1859.

Smith, Willoughby. *The Rise and Extension of Submarine Telegraphy*. London: J. S. Virtue & Company, 1891.

Stevens, John A., Jr. *Report of Proceedings of a Meeting Called to Further the Enterprise of the Atlantic Cable*. New York: privately printed, 1863.

Stewart, Doug. "There Was Too Much Jonah in Brunel's Hapless Leviathan." *Smithsonian* 25:8 (November 1994): 62–73.

Taylor, William B. *An Historical Sketch of Henry's Contribution of the Electro-magnetic Telegraph; with an Account of the Origins and Development of Prof. Morse's Invention*. Washington, D.C.: Government Printing Office, 1879.

Thompson, Robert Luther. *Wiring a Continent: The History of the Telegraph In-*

dustry in the United States 1832–1866. Princeton, N.J.: Princeton University Press, 1947.

War of the Rebellion, A Compilation of the Official Records of the Union and Confederate Armies. 120 vols. Washington, D.C.: Government Printing Office, 1880–1901.

Whitehouse, Edward O. W. *Reply to the Statement of the Directors of the Atlantic Telegraph Company*. London: privately printed, 1858.

Williams, Frances Leigh. *Matthew Fontaine Maury: Scientist of the Sea*. New Brunswick, N.J.: Rutgers University Press, 1963.

Wilson, Roger Burdett, ed. *Sir Daniel Gooch: Memoirs & Diary*. Newton Abbot, U.K.: David & Charles, 1972.

Woldman, Albert A. *Lincoln and the Russians*. Cleveland: World Publishing Company, 1952.

INDEX

About the Author

CHESTER G. HEARN retired from industry as a vice president in 1990 and has since written and published 18 books.